MEXICAN MARXIST—VICENTE
LOMBARDO TOLEDANO

Fotografías de Guillermo Zamora
Mexico, D.F.

Vicente Lombardo Toledano
Secretary General of the Partido Popular Socialista

MEXICAN MARXIST

Vicente Lombardo Toledano

by
Robert Paul Millon

THE UNIVERSITY OF NORTH CAROLINA PRESS · CHAPEL HILL

Copyright © 1966
The University of North Carolina Press
Library of Congress Catalogue Card Number 66-19276
Printed by the Seeman Printery, Durham, N. C.
Manufactured in the United States of America

Preface

Vicente Lombardo Toledano has spent his life in study and in struggle to promote the progress of the Mexican Revolution. He has served during his career as an educator and administrator, as a leader in the national and international labor movements, and as the director of a socialist political party. He is the author of numerous books and pamphlets and has contributed articles to a number of Mexican and foreign periodicals. He has founded—and in many cases also directed—more than a dozen journals.

The present study stresses Lombardo's intellectual development and the content of his mature thought. Chapters are included on Lombardo's career as a labor leader and on the program, structure, and development of the Partido Popular Socialista (in which Lombardo serves as secretary-general) only to indicate some of the practical consequences of Lombardo's intellectual evolution. Biographical information is included in the first chapter the better to indicate interconnections between Lombardo's practical experiences and his intellectual evolution.

The briefing of Lombardo's career as a labor leader and as head of a socialist political party is not definitive and will serve merely to orient the reader. The task of writing such a biography at this time would be herculean. This fact is true not only because Lombardo has had an extremely multifaceted and active career which has been intimately associated with a half-century of Mexican history, but also because there does not yet exist a basic collection of Lombardiana which can be used as a point of origin. The Universidad Obrera presently is collecting data on Lombardo's life which can serve as the basis for a biography.

Marxists such as Lombardo both think and act. There is no better test of their ideas, then, than their effectiveness as guides for human conduct. In the conclusions, therefore, I make a purely tentative effort to evaluate Lombardo's ideas by comparing the practical implications of his thinking with objective reality. As with all thinkers, Lombardo's historical prestige will depend upon the practical consequences of his ideas for humanity.

Mexico, D.F.
March, 1966

R.P.M.

Acknowledgments

I would like to express my appreciation to the Waddell Memorial Fellowships committee of The University of North Carolina at Chapel Hill and to the Grace and Henry Doherty Fellowship Foundation for financial assistance granted to me in support of my research in Chapel Hill, North Carolina, in Washington, D.C., and in Mexico, D.F. I am grateful to Vicente Lombardo Toledano and to other members of the Partido Popular Socialista for their time and for the assistance which they lent me in locating some materials used in this study. Finally, I especially want to express my gratitude to Dr. Harold H. Bierck, professor of history at The University of North Carolina at Chapel Hill, for his assistance in directing the dissertation that served as a basis for this book.

Table of Contents

Preface — v

Acknowledgments — vii

I EARLY CAREER AND FORMATIVE INTELLECTUAL DEVELOPMENT — 3

II NEW ORIENTATION: MARXIST PHILOSOPHY — 29

III IMPERIALISM AND THE MEXICAN ECONOMY — 42

IV THE SOCIAL AND POLITICAL STRUCTURE OF MEXICO — 59

V A PEOPLE'S DEMOCRACY AND SOCIALISM: THE NEW HUMANISM — 81

VI INTERNATIONAL AFFAIRS — 93

VII CAREER AS A LABOR LEADER, 1933-1962 — 117

VIII THE PARTIDO POPULAR SOCIALISTA — 155

IX SUMMARY AND CONCLUSIONS — 182

Appendixes

   A. Vicente Lombardo Toledano: Biographical Data — 199

   B. List of Abbreviations — 202

List of Works Cited — 205

Index — 215

MEXICAN MARXIST—VICENTE LOMBARDO TOLEDANO

I. Early Career and Formative Intellectual Development

Born and reared in a familial and social-class environment in which Marxist concepts were unknown, unexpressed, or distorted, Vicente Lombardo Toledano rather naturally accepted the philosophically idealistic precepts of his mentors. His intellectual orientation changed, however, as a consequence of his experience in the 1920's as a member of the Mexican labor movement and as an observer of the slow and contradictory manner in which the ideals of the Mexican Revolution of 1910 were being realized in practice. In the late 1920's, he undertook a thorough study of the writings of Marx, Engels, Lenin, and others and, by 1930, he considered himself a dialectical materialist.

The son of middle-class parents, Lombardo was born in Teziutlán, Puebla, on July 16, 1894.[1] His grandfather, a staunch supporter of Garibaldi, had come to Mexico from Italy in response to an appeal by the Mexican government for agricultural experts. The turmoil of the Three Years' War (1857-1860) prevented the Juárez government from fulfilling its obligations to the immigrant. The *garibaldista*, nevertheless, determined to remain; he soon prospered in the village of Gutiérrez Zamora which he founded in the State of Veracruz. Later, the Lombardo family moved to the

1. The biographical information presented in this chapter is taken from the following sources: information supplied personally to the author by Vicente Lombardo Toledano; Alfredo Kawage Ramia, *Con Lombardo Toledano; Un Hombre, una Nación, un Continente* (Mexico, 1943), pp. 16-24, *passim*; Enrique Ramírez y Ramírez, *La Obra y La Lucha de Vicente Lombardo Toledano* (Mexico, 1952), pp. 3-10; "Vicente Lombardo Toledano, Un Militante de la Clase Obrera de México," *Futuro*, LXI (March, 1941), 35-42; Universidad Obrera de México, *Vicente Lombardo Toledano; Curriculum Vitae* (Mexico, 1961), pp. 1-6 (see Appendix A); Verna Carleton Millan, *Mexico Reborn* (Boston, 1939), pp. 80-83; "Lombardo Toledano, Líder de los Trabajadores de México, es Entrevistado por la 'Revista del Trabajo,'" *Revista del Trabajo*, XI (Jan., 1941), 8-9; *Current Biography, 1940* (New York, 1940), pp. 516-517; *Who's Who in Latin America* (2nd ed.; Stanford, 1940), pp. 286-287; Michael Rheta Martin and Gabriel H. Lovett, *An Encyclopedia of Latin American History* (New York, 1956), p. 225; *World Biography* (New York, 1948), II, 2852; Miguel Angel Peral, *Diccionario Biográfico Mexicano* (Mexico, [1944]), II, 453; *The International Who's Who* (London, 1952), pp. 581-582.

more pleasant and healthful Teziutlán where Vicente spent his youth. His father built a small fortune as a traveling merchant, vending various types of insurance as well as petroleum products and other commodities in a large region of east central Mexico. Meanwhile, his grandfather likewise accumulated wealth as he took advantage of his training in mining engineering received in Turin to discover and develop a copper mine.

Along with the Ávila Camacho brothers (one of whom was to become a future president of Mexico), the young Lombardo attended a non-sectarian primary school in Teziutlán. In 1909, his parents sent him to Mexico City to study in the national business school; instead, Lombardo elected to take the five-year course of the National Preparatory School. At that time, this school offered a well-rounded education with strong emphasis on the sciences. Lombardo's first interests were in engineering and mathematics, later in the biological sciences, and finally in philosophy. Upon graduation, he enrolled simultaneously in the programs offered in the law school and in the School of Higher Studies (philosophy and letters) of the National University of Mexico.

In the meantime, the vicissitudes of the Revolution of 1910 had caused grandfather Lombardo to lose part of his fortune and had interfered with Vicente's father's business to such an extent that the family was obliged to move to Mexico City to seek a livelihood. Vicente's father became treasurer of Mexico City. The son was forced to numerous expedients to provide for his own expenses; he tutored students, taught classes, worked for the newspaper *El Universal,* and worked for the Universidad Popular.

At the time of Lombardo's attendance, the University of Mexico was under the influence of intellectuals known as the Generation of 1910. These intellectuals, of whom Antonio Caso was the most prominent, reacted against the positivism of the preceding epoch of Porfirio Díaz. The essential postulate of positivism, of course, is that the real can be reduced to the properties of knowable things. In other terms, only that which appears to consciousness, which can be perceived, has existence. On the basis of empirical observations science can develop generalizations or laws which explain how phenomena behave, but which cannot explain why they behave as they do. The positivists thought that order could be brought permanently to Mexican society by educating all Mexicans in the basic truths demonstrated by positive science.

Social order would pave the way for permanent material progress. Science was the god who would lead the Mexican people to their heaven of order and progress.

Positivist philosophy served as the ideological arm of the oligarchy which dominated Mexico during the Díaz era. In practice, "order" meant the preservation of the economic, social, and political privileges of the oligarchy and "progress" meant the accumulation of wealth by the oligarchy.[2]

Positivist thought influenced the several generations of Mexicans who passed through the National Preparatory School from the 1870's to the 1900's. In the political sphere, positivism became the official creed of a small but influential group of lawyers, financiers, and politicians who surrounded Porfirio Díaz. These individuals—in general despised by most of the Mexican people—were known as the *científicos*. They used the doctrines of positivism to justify their self-enrichment and their monopolization of political power and elevated social position. According to the *científicos*, their tutelage of Mexican national life was essential in order to insure Mexico the material progress of capitalist enterprise. The temper of their thought was well reflected in the writings of the *científico*, Francisco Bulnes. Writing in a pseudo-scientific manner which included the amassing of statistical data, Bulnes ridiculed Mexico's national heroes, belittled both her Indian and her Spanish heritage, and criticized the Mexican (and Latin-American) emphasis upon art and the universal. Mexico, according to Bulnes, needed to emphasize the particular, hard work, and material progress.[3]

The Ateneo de la Juventud, organized in 1908, rejected the influence of positivism in Mexican life. Members of the Ateneo, or the Generation of 1910, included the philosophers Antonio Caso and José Vasconcelos; the humanist Pedro Henríquez Ureña; the essayists Alfonso Reyes, Julio Torris, and Jesús T. Acevedo; the critic Eduardo Colín; and the poet Enrique González Martínez. The common objectives of this group were to promote the moral enlightenment and to develop the spiritual quality of the Mexican

2. See the two-volume study on positivism in Mexico by Leopoldo Zea, *El Positivismo en México* (Mexico, 1943) and *Apogeo y Decadencia del Positivismo en México* (Mexico, 1944).

3. See Francisco Bulnes, *El Porvenir de las Naciones Hispano-Americanas ante las Conquistas Recientes de Europa y los Estados Unidos* (Mexico, 1899), and *Las Grandes Mentiras de Nuestra Historia* (Mexico, 1904).

people. Positivistic utilitarianism was criticized and rejected in favor of the cultivation in Mexican youth of a sense of spiritual values. The essence of life, according to these thinkers, lay not in material gain but in the realization of the moral and spiritual capabilities of mankind. Hence, this brand of philosophic idealism was known frequently as "spiritualism."

The Ateneo youth were attracted forcefully by the expressions of idealism or spiritualism in contemporary European philosophy. Especially attractive to them was Henri Bergson's intuitionism. Bergson shook the philosophical bases of positivism with his proposition that reason (and scientific method) were inadequate to attain a complete, unfalsified understanding of the whole of experience. The true, inner reality of experience can be gained only by means of intuition; through intuition the human mind can grasp the surging, spontaneous, and creative essence of experience. This essence, which Bergson termed *élan vital*, emanates from a central point—from God.[4]

The Ateneo youth were especially critical of Mexico's educational system as reformed in the late 1860's under the influence of Gabino Barreda. Reflecting the positivistic concepts of its mentor, that system emphasized instruction in the exact sciences.[5] The reorganization by Gabino Barreda—who presently is regarded by most Mexicans as an outstanding personage of Mexican educational history—brought with it many beneficial consequences, especially insofar as it eliminated much of the traditional scholastic influences in Mexican education. To the Generation of 1910, however, positivistic education was thought to lack cultural breadth and depth. University and preparatory education fell under their influence. The School of Higher Studies which Lombardo attended was established in 1910 precisely to remedy the deficiency in humanistic education. As indicated earlier, however, Lombardo also benefited (in his preparatory training) from the positivistic emphasis upon science.[6]

4. See Henri Bergson, *Creative Evolution* (New York, 1944), pp. 194-196, 294-295, *passim*.
5. See Zea, *El Positivismo*, pp. 55-73, 109-152.
6. For a brief discussion of the Ateneo, including its influence upon Mexican thought and its opposition to positivism, see Samuel Ramos, *Profile of Man and Culture in Mexico* (Austin, Tex., 1962), pp. 85-93. Zea, *Apogeo y Decadencia*, pp. 254-286, contrasts the thought of the new generation with that of the positivists.

Lombardo fell under the sway of the idealist, spiritualist, antirationalist, and antipositivist thought of the Generation of 1910. Always a brilliant and avid student, he became one of the prize pupils of the master, Antonio Caso, who was, perhaps, Mexico's most able exponent of idealist and intuitionalist philosophy. Although the concepts of dialectical materialism which Lombardo was to accept later are at variance with the basic propositions of Caso's philosophy, nevertheless Caso's influence upon his student was important and, in some respects, permanent. Lombardo especially was influenced by Caso's humanism, which stressed that the objective of life was the attainment of human happiness through the fullest realization of human potential. According to Caso, every man, in order to make his life worth living, must strive with courage, enthusiasm, and artistry for the realization of attainable ideals. Further, Lombardo almost certainly was affected by Caso's strong sense of nationalism, by his desire to help forge and uplift the national culture. Finally, his social consciousness must have been stirred additionally by Caso in that he, although a proponent of the system of private property, was nevertheless a critic of unrestrained bourgeois individualism. Caso spoke of the indissoluble union of the individual and the social and warned against excessive emphasis upon either. Similarly, Caso spoke of the social origin of human values—although he also declared such values to be absolute and eternal. Caso never resolved or apparently never attempted to resolve this contradiction in his thought.[7]

The influence which Caso had upon Lombardo is apparent when one notes that throughout his life Lombardo has expressed forcefully that the motivation and objective of his activities has been the practical realization of human ideals and human potentials. It is impossible, of course, to know precisely to what degree Lombardo's development was the result of the influence of Caso and others of the Generation of 1910 and to what degree it was the result of his own personal qualities of intelligence, courage, and

7. See Antonio Caso, *Filósofos y Doctrinas Morales* (Mexico, 1915); *Problemas Filosóficos* (Mexico, 1915); *Discursos a la Nación Mexicana* (Mexico, 1922); *Doctrinas e Ideas* (Mexico, 1924); *El Acto Ideatorio: las Esencias y los Valores* (Mexico, 1934). Summaries of Caso's thought can be found in William Rex Crawford, *A Century of Latin-American Thought* (rev. ed.; Cambridge, Mass., 1961), pp. 276-293 and Patrick Romanell, *Making of the Mexican Mind; A Study in Recent Mexican Thought* (Lincoln, Neb., 1952), pp. 69-92.

a questing mind—characteristics which seem to exert an influence on their own account in the development of idealistic and altruistic sentiments in young people. Certainly Caso's influence helped to develop these sentiments.

At the time Lombardo was a student, Marxism was ignored by Caso and the other professors and, owing in part to the unavailability of first-class Spanish translations of Marxist works and in part to the idealist orientation of his thinking which did little to stimulate him to investigate the roots of Marxism, Lombardo learned little of Marxist socialism on his own. Lombardo mentions that in 1918 he came across a Spanish version of Lenin's *Materialism and Empirio-Criticism*, but the translation was so poor that the work was unintelligible to him.

Lombardo's early writings reflect the influence of his spiritualistic philosophical training. A speech Lombardo delivered under the auspices of the Universidad Popular to the Alliance of Railroad Workers on May 5, 1918, was printed under the title *La Influencia de los Héroes en el Progreso Social*.[8] The speech reveals the strong influence upon Lombardo of Bergson's intuitionism; it also palpitates with the (non-philosophic) idealism, humanism, and nationalism which he was to express throughout his life. In discussing the relationship between genius and society Lombardo took a middle position between the belief of Thomas Carlyle that society is the fruit of genius and that of Hippolyte Taine that genius is the fruit of society. In so doing, he placed strong emphasis upon the positive force of ideals and illusions firmly held through intuitive conviction and acted upon in spite of reasoned doubts. At one point Lombardo stated that he almost could agree with skeptics who argue: "It is intelligence which makes us doubt everything; never meditate; if you wish to be happy, restrain your intelligence."[9]

The speech is replete with allusions to classical Greece and to idealist philosophers, including Henri Bergson. These allusions together with the highly literary form of the address contrast with the greater simplicity of presentation Lombardo employed in subsequent speeches.

Lombardo's second publication—his law degree thesis entitled *El Derecho Público y Las Nuevas Corrientes Filosóficas*[10]—is in-

8. Mexico, 1919.
9. *Ibid.*, p. 5.
10. Mexico, 1919.

teresting for the contrasts it presents to his future thought. Lombardo attempted to emphasize what he considered to be a new current in philosophical thought and in international law which replaced the old conception of the absolute autonomy of the individual and of the nation. This new current emphasized not only individual and national rights but also corresponding duties to other individuals and to social entities. These new concepts he said were laying the basis for a genuine international reign of law based upon both individual and social rights and duties.

Lombardo's thinking along these lines led him to accept Woodrow Wilson's thesis that only popular, democratically elected governments should be recognized diplomatically and, further, to accept a doctrine of the right of foreign intervention into a nation's affairs if such intervention were intended to secure a popularly based regime.

Furthermore, Lombardo examined briefly the Mexican Constitution of 1917 to discover there any precepts which might be contrary to the new currents in legal and philosophical thought. He reviewed in detail the provision for profit-sharing contained in Article 123. This provision, he claimed, was based upon the false Marxist thesis of surplus value. He warned that "Mexico needs foreign capital which will not be completely disposed to invest on our soil if it does not have full guarantees of liberty."[11] Without delving further Lombardo concluded that Articles 27, 3, "and others" presented obstacles "to the free play of the material and moral activities of man" and therefore also are obstacles "to the internal development of the Republic and sources of future international controversies which we are already witnessing and, fortunately, seeing resolved."[12]

Articles 123, 27, and 3 which Lombardo here criticizes are those which provide, among other things, for labor and land reform, for the national ownership of all subsoil resources, and for limitations upon the church's power—some of the features which he was later to consider the very essence of the progressive aspects of the constitution.

Considering that Lombardo was later to be recognized as Mexico's foremost Marxist theoretician, we note with interest his early anti-Marxist attitude. He completely and scornfully re-

11. *Ibid.*, p. 69.
12. *Ibid.*

jected Karl Marx in this thesis, even though he referred to the *Communist Manifesto* as "the most important document of the nineteenth century" and to Marx as "the most important figure of the century in the history of moral and political doctrines."[13] He did not elaborate upon these statements.

Lombardo readily confesses today that he was ignorant of Marx's writings in his early life. This lack of knowledge is most apparent in his law thesis. Thus, Lombardo did not list a single work by Marx in his bibliography; in the footnotes to his discussion of Marx he listed only two rather obscure secondary works. Obvious errors are numerous. Not only did Lombardo make the minor error of listing the date of Marx's death as 1863 instead of 1883 (which might have been a typographical error, although it was not corrected in the table of errors), but he made the major mistake of citing Pierre Joseph Proudhon instead of Ludwig Feuerbach as the author of the work *The Philosophy of Misery* to which Marx replied in his book, *The Misery of Philosophy*. Furthermore, he claimed that the *Critique of Classical Political Economy* [sic] was more important than *Das Kapital* or other writings because it was in the preface to the former work that Marx formulated his materialist conception of history. The preface does indeed contain the most famous statement of the theory of historical materialism by Marx, but the theory was actually formulated much earlier and appears in developed form in the *Communist Manifesto*. Finally, in briefly presenting Marx's materialist conception of history, Lombardo overemphasized the role Marx gave to economic forces in social development and made no mention of Marx's emphasis upon the interaction between economic and other forces.

Toward the end of the thesis Lombardo praised the "pure socialism" of Proudhon which arose as a just reaction "against an economic individualism impotent to resolve the grave questions of the epoch"[14] and contrasted it with what he considered the vulgar and unscientific socialism of Marx.

Lombardo criticized Marx's theory of surplus value as "false" and "fantastic."[15] Lombardo repeated two age-old arguments concerning the nature of profits—that profits are necessary in-

13. *Ibid.*, p. 9.
14. *Ibid.*
15. *Ibid.*, p. 66.

centives to production and that profits are the "wages of capital" or, in Lombardo's terms, the payment for the intellectual contribution to production made by the entrepreneur.

Lombardo's argument throughout the thesis was philosophically idealistic, with emphasis upon free will and moral duty. He took his departure from, among others, Kant, Schopenhauer, James, and Bergson who, he said, had brought about "a revindication of the spirit, of the personal value of man, of the substantive reality of things, of the perennity of religious sentiment, of the value of metaphysical speculations and of the just autonomy of Ethics."[16] The concepts of these individuals were upheld in contrast to what he considered the "false intellectualism of the nineteenth century,"[17] to positivism and to the various forms of materialism.[18]

Lombardo was in this early period of life typical of the liberal, middle-class intellectuals who supported the revolution. The seeds of Lombardo's future attachment to Marxism can be found in his broad social consciousness and in his socially rather than individualistically oriented idealism and humanism. Yet Lombardo was not unique in this social consciousness, for it was shared by other liberal intellectuals.

What caused Lombardo to develop into a Marxist socialist while others, such as Luis Cabrera, remained middle-class liberals and still others, such as José Vasconcelos, flirted with fascism? Surely many factors contributed to this development. The depth of Lombardo's (non-philosophic) idealism and humanism and the high level of his personal honesty and courage must have played a part. But certainly not of least importance was his early and continued association with the Mexican labor movement. In his long career Lombardo contributed a great deal to the progress of the labor movement. In turn, the labor movement made important contributions to his own personal development.

Lombardo began his close association with the Mexican working class in 1917 when he was appointed secretary of a school named Universidad Popular, an institution founded in 1912 by members of the Ateneo to spread the seeds of humanistic culture among

16. *Ibid.*, p. 19.
17. *Ibid.*, pp. 18-19.
18. *Ibid.*, pp. 7-20, 59-63, 65-69.

the populace. As secretary, Lombardo was virtually in complete charge of managing the Universidad Popular. In addition, he gave public lectures to audiences composed largely of workers.

As representative of the Universidad Popular, in May 1918, Lombardo attended the labor congress held in Saltillo, Coahuila, which organized the Confederación Regional Obrera Mexicana (CROM). Lombardo's role in the congress was minor but he proposed the organization of cultural centers for the workers.

In the same year Lombardo began teaching a course in ethics in the National Preparatory School. The following year he received degrees both in law and in philosophy from the National University of Mexico. His increasing interest in the labor movement bore fruit in 1920 when he organized Mexico's first teachers' union.

In 1921, Lombardo came into direct contact with the Mexican rural workers and peasants when he was named chief clerk (*oficial mayor*) of the Federal District Government. In this capacity he participated, frequently on his own initiative, in the distribution of lands to the peasant villages of the Federal District. As a representative of the Federal District Government, Lombardo gave a speech at the First Agrarianist Congress held in Ixtapalapa, D. F.,[19] in which he defended the land reform program. As in his earlier statements, the seeds of his future thinking are evident, as he claimed that the genuinely revolutionary principles of the Mexican Revolution were contained in Article 27 (land reform) and Article 123 (labor reform); the rest of the constitution, he felt, merely repeated the antiquated Jacobin precepts of the Constitution of 1857. He did not refer to his previous criticisms of these articles. Further, Lombardo pointed out that legal doctrines and codes have not an absolute but rather a social origin and basis and consequently must change as social prerequisites change. In addition to his social interpretation of law, Lombardo presented the concept that popular organizations of economically equal individuals will gradually come to substitute a genuine popular democracy for the old system of political parties and of political domination of, by, and for the few. Lombardo's concern for the

---

19. *Discurso Pronunciado por el Lic. Vicente Lombardo Toledano en Representación del Gobierno del Distrito Federal, al Clausurarse el Primer Congreso Agrarista Celebrado en Ixtapalapa, D.F.* (Mexico, 1921).

development of the Mexican nation was apparent throughout the speech.[20]

Lombardo published two works in 1922: *Ética*[21] and *Definiciones sobre Derecho Público*.[22] In the former, the continued influence of Antonio Caso upon Lombardo's thinking is evident. *Ética* is a study in the methodology of teaching moral values to students. Lombardo was concerned with promoting the development of the Mexican nation by strengthening the moral fabric of its youth. He claimed that schools must make a formal and systematic effort to increase the moral stature and comprehension of students by employing the intuitive Socratic or pragmatic method of instruction. Ethical concepts must be examined, discussed, and criticized or, in the case of elementary school children, the biographies of great men and didactic tales must be examined and discussed. Thereby, the free will of each student, influenced by his experiences at home and elsewhere, will select and form a system of moral concepts. Ethical concepts are considered to form an absolute ideal category which possesses an independent development.[23]

Lombardo's references to Marxism in *Ética* are worth noting. Although historical materialism was rejected as "false," he displayed none of the hostility toward Marxism that he had in his law thesis. He went so far as to claim that both historical materialism and anarchism "contain something of the truth in their substance as do all profound vindications of humanity against tyranny."[24] Liberalism, however, was rejected outright as "absolutely false" and as an obstacle detaining "the movement for justice for which all humanity clamors."[25] Lombardo did not provide a specific definition of "liberalism" nor did he single out the ideas of specific liberals for criticism. One may assume from his use of the word "liberalism," however, that he referred to that rather loose body of concepts which provided ideological support for the ideal of competitive capitalism.

Without going into details, it can be said that in *Ética* Lombardo revealed the seeds of his future acceptance of dialectical

20. *Ibid.*, pp. 9, 11-13, 15-16.
21. Mexico, 1922.
22. Mexico, 1922.
23. Lombardo Toledano, *Ética*, pp. 9-32, 105-108.
24. *Ibid.*, p. 78.
25. *Ibid.*, pp. 78-79.

materialism in his emphasis on inductive reasoning, on the approximative, pragmatic nature of systematic thought, on the concept that being is becoming, and on the total inadequacy of liberal thought for modern needs. (These concepts, of course, are found in various philosophies—and in Lombardo's case probably were derived from positivism—but Lombardo at this time did not give them the rich and complex interpretation of dialectical materialism.) On the other hand, his emphasis upon free will and the absolute nature of ideas gave his general argument a philosophically idealistic overtone, quite at variance with his future intellectual orientation.

Lombardo's social consciousness shows a broad development in *Definiciones Sobre Derecho Público*. Many advanced concepts were presented. He criticized the liberal conceptions of law and human rights and claimed that there are no natural rights with which one is born; such a conception is an abstraction "which has no reality."[26] Furthermore, all men are not equal but have different capacities and needs. Law actually "is a fruit of social life, the result of the spiritual and material necessities of a given people."[27] Law serves to bind society together, to promote social solidarity, and hence (by implication) to promote social survival. Laws are made by small groups of men in control of public power and are enforced upon the rest of society, but these laws must express the need for collective solidarity and for the construction of collective life or they will be superseded. Early in the book, Lombardo conceived society to be developing toward a stage in which every person freely will contribute according to his capacity and each will be rewarded according to his need; in the conclusions, the reward was to be according to capacity. Thus, Lombardo at one point in the book seemed to uphold the values of a communist society (reward according to need); in the conclusions, however, the values upheld were those of socialism (reward according to capacity).[28]

Lombardo's criticisms of liberalism and his conceptualization of the social origins of law correspond to interpretations that Marxists have made of the same phenomena. Contrary to what might be expected in a Marxist analysis, however, Lombardo did

26. Lombardo Toledano, *Definiciones*, p. 26.
27. *Ibid.*, p. 27.
28. *Ibid.*, pp. 23-28, 87-88.

Early Career and Formative Intellectual Development [15]

not discuss the relationships of law to social classes other than to state that law has been and still is made by ruling groups, nor did he present a conceptualization of the dynamics of social (and hence also legal) change.

In 1923, Lombardo took a broad step toward increased contact with the Mexican working class, effectively launching himself upon his long career as a labor leader, when he became a member of the central committee of the most important labor confederation of the 1920's, the Confederación Regional Obrera Mexicana (CROM). As its secretary of education, his duties were to give legal advice to members in conflicts with employers and to educate the workers in labor law, union rights, labor history, Mexican and world history, science, culture, in a word, in anything that would increase the general knowledge and class consciousness of the workers.

The leaders of the CROM—Luís Morones, the secretary of the labor confederation, and his cohorts—were corrupt. This small group of leaders, originally eighteen in number and known as the Grupo Acción, dominated the union for their own ends. A political party, the Partido Laborista Mexicano (PLM), was organized in order to increase the political influence of the members of the Grupo Acción. Furthermore, the Grupo Acción set out to control every labor union in Mexico and, with the assistance of the national government, almost succeeded in its designs. Members of the Grupo Acción acquired fortunes, partly from their practice of forcing bribes from industrialists in return for freedom from labor troubles. The leaders laid greater stress upon the collaboration of labor and capital for economic progress than upon class struggle. Morones became secretary of industry during the presidency of General Plutarco Elías Calles.[29]

CROM policies yielded some positive results. The CROM's collaboration with the government was an aid to the latter in its attempts to remake the semifeudal aspects of Mexico's economic and social structure by instituting such measures as the partitioning of lands and increasing the recognition of rights of industrial

---

29. Ernest Gruening, *Mexico and Its Heritage* (New York, 1928), pp. 357-360, 376-377, 389-390, *passim*; Henry Bamford Parkes, *A History of Mexico* (2nd ed.; Boston, 1950), pp. 365, 375-376, 382-383; Rosendo Salazar, *Líderes y Sindicatos* (Mexico, 1953), pp. 72-86, 96-103; Nathaniel and Sylvia Weyl, *The Reconquest of Mexico; The Years of Lázaro Cardenas* (London, 1939), p. 235.

workers. Mexican labor was organized and its rights were respected as they never had been previously in Mexican history. The workers made some gains in the form of higher wages and of indemnities for injuries and unwarranted dismissals. This policy of collaboration with the government had negative consequences, however, as the CROM leaders became more concerned with political maneuverings for their personal advantage than with promoting the interests of the working class. The independent action of the working class in pursuit of its own class interests was attenuated.[30]

The members of the Grupo Acción looked upon Lombardo's tasks as mere diversions that would keep the workers emotionally satisfied while the leaders proceeded to use their positions to promote their personal fortunes. Lombardo was aware of the activities of the leaders and of their conception of his role in the labor confederation. Yet he took his tasks as educator and legal advisor quite seriously, making hundreds of speeches throughout Mexico. He realized that by so doing he was increasing class consciousness and the sense of unity among the workers, and he believed that sometime in the future this would help the workers rid themselves of their false leaders and organize an independent and militant confederation. If Lombardo as a neophyte had made a gallant gesture of defiance to the corrupt leaders, he would have been expelled from the confederation and thereby removed from any influence over the hundreds of thousands of members. Lombardo's attitude sprang from a conviction that theory and practice must be unified, that a revolutionary must always work in close contact with the workers if he is to be effective. The Marxist attitude is, of course, the same.[31]

While serving as a labor leader in the CROM, Lombardo continued his academic and public career. In academic affairs during the 1920's and early 1930's, Lombardo served at various times as director of the National Preparatory School of the National University, as founder and director of the National Preparatory

30. Gruening, pp. 389-390, *passim*; Vicente Lombardo Toledano, *Teoría y Práctica del Movimiento Sindical Mexicano* (Mexico, 1961), pp. 60-62; Alfonso López Aparicio, *El Movimiento Obrero en México* (2nd ed.; Mexico, 1958), pp. 186-189.

31. This interpretation is expressed in Ramírez y Ramírez, *La Obra y la Lucha*, pp. 6-10 and is confirmed by Lombardo. It is worth noting that this interpretation is *ex post facto* and attributes a Marxist motivation to Lombardo's behavior before Lombardo indeed was overtly a Marxist.

Night School, as director of the Summer School for Foreigners of the National University, and as director of the Central School of Plastic Arts of the National University. At various times from 1918 to 1933, Lombardo served as professor in the National Preparatory School, in the Faculty of Law, in the Summer School, and in the Faculty of Commerce and Administration of the National University.

During the same period (1918-1933) Lombardo held the following public offices at various times: chief clerk of the Federal District Government, chief of the Department of Libraries of the Secretariat of Public Education, interim governor of the State of Puebla, alderman (*regidor*) of the muncipal government of Mexico City, and deputy to the National Congress for two sessions. He held most of these offices as a result of the political influence of the Grupo Acción.

The positions as governor, alderman, and national deputy were held by Lombardo as a member of the Partido Laborista Mexicano. Lombardo received the interim governorship of Puebla for a few months in 1923-1924 when the regular governor was removed because of his support of the de la Huerta rebellion against the national government headed by General Álvaro Obregón.[32] In contrast to the series of corrupt governors who had preceded (and followed) him, Lombardo's rule was thoroughly honest, a circumstance about which opinion is unanimous.[33]

By 1924, Lombardo was clearly advocating the gradual transition of Mexico into a socialist society. This attitude was not contrary to opinions expressed by many within the CROM and the government. As a rule, however, socialist phraseology was employed merely as a sop to the workers. But Lombardo's evolutionary socialist concepts strike one as being genuine.

In November 1924 Lombardo made a report to the sixth national convention of the CROM held in Ciudad Juárez, Chihuahua, which was published under the title *El Problema de la Educación*

32. U.S. Department of State, Dispatch from W. O. Jenkins, U.S. Consular Agent, Puebla to George T. Summerlin, Chargé d'Affaires, American Consular Service, Mexico City, Dec. 8, 1923; John W. F. Dulles, *Yesterday in Mexico: A Chronicle of the Revolution, 1919-1936* (Austin, Tex., 1961), pp. 223-227.

33. Gruening, pp. 389, 468; Millan, p. 85; Marjorie Clark, *Organized Labor in Mexico* (Chapel Hill, N.C., 1934), p. 110; Mary Margaret Harker, "Organization of Labor in Mexico Since 1910" (unpublished Ph.D. dissertation, University of Southern California, 1937), p. 58.

en México.³⁴ In this report Lombardo claimed that Mexican education had reached a crisis. A variety of educational theories were being discussed in the nation but no definite orientation or unified program had as yet been found. The origin of this crisis lay, Lombardo felt, in the fact that Mexico was half liberal-democratic and half socialistic in its thinking. He did not propose a complete theoretical and practical program that would overcome these difficulties in Mexican education; he did, however, make some interesting suggestions.

Lombardo emphasized that it is impossible for education to be neutral in regard to the vital interests of given social classes. Consequently he felt it should be made to serve the socialist, corporative interests of the working class. Education should be a primary motive force and prerequisite for the gradual socializing of Mexico; education would enable the workers to replace the privileged monopolizers of essential knowledge. It should be noted that Lombardo's position is idealistic in that he does not tie the increase in the general level of the workers' knowledge to the industrialization of the nation, which would need a skilled labor force with a higher general level of knowledge.

As part of this general position, Lombardo stressed the fundamental importance to Mexico of increasing the understanding and unity among the various ethnic groups in the nation. In addition to the general concepts mentioned above, and as a solution to the problem, Lombardo suggested the creation of special schools adapted to the special needs of the various Indian groups in Mexico. These schools would recognize and develop the positive aspects of each native culture as well as impart useful instruction drawn from the progressive features of the national culture. In contrast to his future ideas on the subject, Lombardo did not mention instructing the Indians in their native tongues. Lombardo's comments served to emphasize concepts on Mexico's ethnic problems which had by that time gained general acceptance among Mexico's more progressive elements.

Additional comments by Lombardo included demands that technical schools be created, that the training of artisans should in no way impede the organization of labor unions, that the monopoly of university education by one social class must be broken and the university must devote itself to scientific research

34. Mexico, 1924.

related to Mexican problems, that the deficiencies in the social orientation of the Mexican teacher must be removed by organizing the teachers "in accordance with the corporative principle,"[35] and that special attention must be given to the education of women. Finally, referring to the role of the CROM, Lombardo called for the founding of schools by this labor confederation to meet the needs of its members, for the scientific study of the educational needs of all regions of Mexico, for the convocation of a national teachers' congress to study the problems of the education of the proletariat, and for nationwide propaganda by the CROM in support of this program.

Throughout his report Lombardo continued to express the strong sentiments of nationalism manifested in his earliest writings. In addition to expressing his primary concern with the ethnic unity of Mexico, at several places in the report he spoke against importing foreign ideas on education which did not fit Mexican realities.[36]

As is evident from this presentation of his report, Lombardo continued his interest in and deepened his analysis of the institution which was to be, in one form or another, a lifelong concern to him: education.[37] The increased socialist orientation of his thinking and his deepened interest in the education of the working class are forecast in his creation (in 1936) of a worker's university designed for the Marxist education of working class cadres.

In 1926 Lombardo published his first major book, the well-written and scholarly *La Libertad Sindical en México*.[38] The book was written in response to a specific request for such a work made by the International Labor Office in Geneva. The book was part of a world study on the subject of labor union liberty. The work traced the historical and legal evolution of the Mexican labor movement and discussed the contemporary types of employer and labor associations in Mexico together with their corresponding legal rights and possibilities for action in promoting their respec-

35. *Ibid.*, p. 28.
36. *Ibid.*, pp. 7-11, 17-19, 24-29.
37. In regard to Lombardo's role in education, it is interesting to note that he claims to have suggested to José Vasconcelos the rural education and Indian regeneration programs which the latter instituted. Source: Selden Rodman, *Mexican Journal: The Conquerors Conquered* (New York, 1958), p. 153.
38. Mexico, 1926.

tive interests. Lombardo stated his principal conclusion as follows: "We said at the beginning of this study that, from the literal sense of the laws, labor union freedom is, in Mexico, a new road created by the state for the integral emancipation of the proletariat and, for the capitalists, a right limited to the defense of its [the proletariat's] material interests. As we have seen, this statement corresponds to reality."[39]

In this work Lombardo presented an interesting interpretation of the struggle for labor union rights in Mexico. Many authors consider the role of the Mexican government as overriding in influence.[40] Although recognizing the importance of such influence, Lombardo stressed the significance of the workers' daily struggles in forcing employers and the state to accept in practice rights which had been granted formally by law. He stressed especially that, on the whole, the working class in its struggles received little support from the intellectuals or from the middle class in general.[41] In this connection, it should be noted that whereas Lombardo did discuss government intervention in labor disputes in behalf of labor, he made no mention of the documented favoritism shown the CROM.[42]

Lombardo's socialist concepts were still similar to those expressed in 1924. He presented a lengthy exposition of the guiding concepts of the CROM expressed in resolutions adopted in its assemblies and in public pronouncements made by its leaders. The goal of the CROM, he claimed, was "the socialization of wealth and a change in the organization of the state."[43] For achievements of these objectives it would be necessary ultimately for the working class movement to gain complete control of the government. At the same time, Lombardo completely rejected communistic (as well as anarchistic) ideas and parties as alien to Mexican experiences and realities and as subject to at least partial foreign control and financing. He defended the tactics of the CROM on the basis of the results achieved, whereas he criticized

39. *Ibid.*, p. 203.
40. Moises Poblete Troncoso and Ben G. Burnett, *The Rise of the Latin American Labor Movement* (New York, 1960), pp. 99-102; Frank Tannenbaum, *Mexico: The Struggle for Peace and Bread* (New York, 1950), pp. 64-65, 114; Harker, pp. 46-75, *passim*.
41. Lombardo Toledano, *La Libertad Sindical*, pp. 34-80.
42. Harker, pp. 39-42, 46-47, 59-63, *passim*.
43. Lombardo Toledano, *La Libertad Sindical*, p. 126.

the tactics of these leftist groups—the Mexican Communist party, the General Confederation of Workers (CGT), and others—for their impracticality and consequent meager positive results. In all these discussions, the corruption of the CROM and particularly of its directive Grupo Acción was never mentioned. In fact, the latter group was referred to but once (in a footnote) and then only in a non-derogatory, explanatory manner.[44]

The strong nationalism expressed in his previous writings and again manifested in his criticism of "foreign ideologies" was most clearly evidenced in the following quotation describing what he considered the salient characteristic of the Mexican Revolution: "The Revolution has had a singular characteristic which raised it above its errors: it has been a movement for reconquest by the genuinely Mexican. Since 1915 it has begun to be seen clearly, as we have said already, that Mexico is a conjunction of human groups, not of one alone; that it is necessary at all costs to attain the unification of these groups in order to achieve the existence of a nation...."[45]

As a representative of the municipal government of Mexico City, Lombardo attended a 1925 world conference on urbanism held in New York City. He took advantage of the excellent library facilities and of the numerous bookstores in the city to search for Marxist books in English, because first-class Spanish translations were still scarce. Upon his return to Mexico City, Lombardo spent virtually every evening for six months studying the three volumes of *Das Kapital* which he had purchased in New York. From 1925 to 1930 Lombardo continued his study of Marxism, political economy, and materialist philosophy. "These were very difficult years for me," he says, "because I had to rectify all that I had learned." He did not have any contact with the Mexican Communist party during this period, yet Lombardo was a Marxist by 1930.[46]

44. *Ibid.*, pp. 86, 123-129, 135-139.
45. *Ibid.*, p. 197.
46. Information supplied personally to the author by Vicente Lombardo Toledano in May 1962. Lombardo wished to give the impression that it was the lack of adequate translations which had delayed his investigations into Marxism in the past. Although many of the translations of Marxist works were poor and the Spanish version of *Das Kapital* was incomplete, the existing translations were adequate and would have given Lombardo a basic understanding of Marxism. Also, it seems that Lombardo could have ordered English, French, or Italian translations (he read these languages with ease)

That his studies were having some influence upon him is evident in his book, *La Doctrina Monroe y el Movimiento Obrero*.[47] Lombardo began the work by claiming the value to historical interpretation of Marx's historical materialism and then proceeded to employ concepts both of historical materialism and of geographical determinism in a brief analysis of world history. For the first time in print, Lombardo presented an interpretation of a subject which was to dominate his future thinking: imperialism.

The world, he claimed, was divided into five groups of nations, semicolonies, and colonies with each group headed by one dominant nation which within its area sought raw materials, markets (for products and for capital), virgin territories, and control of trade routes and strategic points. These group were "(1) America, (2) The British Empire, (3) The Far East (China and Japan), (4) Russia, (5) France, 'Mittel-Europa' and North Africa."[48] With the exception of Russia, the governments of these nations were said to be dominated either directly or indirectly by groups of capitalists. No further mention was made of Russia, which he evidently then considered to be an imperialist power.

The Spanish-American War, wrote Lombardo, had marked the entrance of the United States on the world scene as a major industrial, imperialist power. Lombardo traced the increasing hegemony of the United States over Latin-America which followed that event. Included was a section of criticism of United States imperialism by such United States authors as Scott Nearing, Ernest Gruening, Carleton Beals, Samuel Guy Inman, and others. The Monroe Doctrine was represented as intended initially to preserve the political independence of the new nations of the Western Hemisphere. Subsequently, however, its character changes: "the Monroe Doctrine means that the right of intervention among the weakest neighbors, and the privilege to exploit them, is reserved to the United States. The Monroe Doctrine has been converted into an economic declaration."[49]

The hegemony over the world exercised by a few great powers had resulted in a "moral chaos" in international affairs and in a

---

from booksellers in major European or United States cities. It probably was the hold upon Lombardo of idealist philosophy which restrained his initiative in seeking out Marxist works.

47. Mexico, 1927.
48. *Ibid.*, p. 28.
49. *Ibid.*, p. 33.

"perpetual economic crisis for the peoples" of the world. A new force, however, had been counterpoised to the imperialists: "the clamor of the proletariat of the world which demands a revision in the present [world social] organization, on the basis of justice."[50] Lombardo then, oddly enough, proceeded to heap praise upon Section XIII of the Treaty of Versailles for what he considered its advanced labor provisions respecting such things as shorter hours and higher wages, and for its general statement that true world peace could be achieved only by means of a revision in social structures on the basis of social justice. Lombardo, evidently, was still thinking in terms of a gradual transition to socialism. Nevertheless, he displayed a matured conception of working-class tactics when he maintained that both national and international working-class unity were of greatest importance in the combat against imperialism. In this respect, however, he praised the labor of the mild Pan American Federation of Labor, dominated by the American Federation of Labor (AFL).

Lombardo continued to express the nationalist sentiment revealed in his previous writings as he warned against not only foreign economic but also foreign cultural penetration into Mexican life. A budding sense of internationalism was present, though, not only in his concern for the international unity of workers but also in his conclusion reached early in the work that world political development had lagged behind world economic development in that the various regions of the earth were mutually interdependent economically, whereas politically they were divided into autonomous nations.[51]

At the end of the work, Lombardo said: "We are Marxists; but we consider that there are more things in the world than that thought of in the philosophy of Marx. We think that without being someone, without having a personality, without working for the elevation of a class, one cannot effectively contribute to world freedom."[52] Although this seemed to promise something more than Marx, in his succeeding statements he merely stressed the need for unity within the proletariat (evidently including the peasantry under this category).

In 1928, Lombardo served as a member of the Mexican delega-

50. *Ibid.*, p. 58.
51. *Ibid.*, pp. 7-35, 39-56, 59-61, 63.
52. *Ibid.*, p. 64.

tion to the Sixth Inter-American Conference meeting in Havana.[53] He played a major role in originating the resolution introduced by the Mexican delegation (and adopted by the conference) to the effect that future conferences consider problems related to the material improvement and to the raising of the living standards of the workers of the hemisphere. Writing about this resolution a few months later, Lombardo said: "The socialist concept has been triumphant step by step, constantly rendering its program clearly and evidently, making the justice of its cause seen."[54]

Thus, by 1928, Lombardo still may be considered an evolutionary socialist in the tradition of the Second International. There is clear evidence, nonetheless, that a profound transformation was occurring in his thinking.

In summary, Lombardo's thought included a number of distinctive features. He expressed strong nationalistic and (non-philosophical) idealistic sentiments as well as the desire to realize humanistic values in practice. He stressed the social, corporate nature of modern life and wrote of the importance of social duty. At the same time, he rejected traditional liberalism with its concept that human rights, legal principles, the forms and objectives of education, and property rights were absolute in nature. In its place he developed a conception of the social origin and constant mutability of human institutions and of human ideas. His increasing class consciousness and personal identification with the proletariat was expressed in a strong interest in both general and militantly class-oriented education of the working class. In contrast to his early (1918) apparent acceptance of foreign capitalist penetration into Mexico, he now stressed the necessity for both national and international unity of the working class in order to combat imperialism, which he identified as the major obstacle to human progress. In contrast to his declaration in 1918 that it was economically impractical to eliminate the private profit motive, he now thought it essential that the Mexican working class attain political power and that Mexico be socialized. In his intellectual and practical activities he emphasized a combination of thought and action, of the theoretical and the practical, of study and struggle, but always with a readiness to achieve practical re-

53. U.S. Department of State, Correspondence from U.S. Embassy, Mexico City to U.S. State Department, Washington, D.C., Dec. 27, 1927.
54. Vicente Lombardo Toledano, "El Derecho Internacional Americano y El Movimiento Obrero," *Derecho Obrero*, II, xiv (1928), 7.

sults even if this necessitated deviation from strict intellectual honesty (as revealed in his role in the CROM, especially in his failure to criticize the corruption and reformism of the leaders). He displayed a budding sense of internationalism and his thought had developed from a complete antagonism to Marxism to a generally favorable attitude toward the concepts of historical materialism.

Conflicting with these concepts were others, including those of philosophic idealism, of gradualism in revolutionary social change, and of a middle-class form of nationalism (reflected especially in his rejection of some Marxist and other leftist ideas and parties as foreign and alien to Mexican realities).

What perhaps might have restrained Lombardo from a rejection of the latter concepts and a transformation of the former into a unified Marxist framework of thought was a personal difficulty, both intellectual and emotional, of realizing that material necessity is primary to free will. Once Lombardo accepted this, the change of his thought should have been rapid.

Several phenomena were associated with Lombardo's intellectual transformation. First, there was Lombardo's long and continuous association with the Mexican working class. Initially he was associated with the labor movement as secretary of the Universidad Popular; he soon became a leader of organized labor when, in 1920, he organized and directed the League of Professors of the Federal District. In 1923 he was appointed to the Central Committee of the CROM, and in 1927 served as secretary general of the National Federation of Teachers. In these positions he was in constant contact both with the material and moral needs of the workers and with the betrayal of those needs by corrupt and reformist labor leaders and politicians.

Second, by the late 1920's the nation had experienced more than a decade of the consequences of the political rule of revolutionary military chieftains and of the economic and social domination by the bourgeoisie and the petty bourgeoisie. Corruption was general and restraints were placed upon the rapid development of democracy and social justice. Revolutionary reforms were occurring, particularly in regard to land distribution, promotion of a program of rural education, restriction of the powers and privileges of the Catholic church, assertion of national sovereignty over subsoil rights, implementation of the right of the national government to determine the forms of property holding permissible in the nation, and extension of health improvement programs. But most of these programs were moving comparatively slowly. For example, a total of 7,666,877 hectares of land were distributed from 1917 to 1934; Cárdenas distributed 17,889,791 hectares from 1934 to 1940.[55] Some programs, such as the reclamation of national subsoil rights from foreign owners, had come to a standstill. Furthermore, the revolutionary leaders (Plutarco Elías Calles and his followers) gave every indication after 1926 (and especially after 1928) that some of the major ideals of the revolution—such as national independence from foreign economic control, popular democracy, and increasingly higher levels of living—were to be abandoned in favor of the private interests of a small group of politicians and of foreign and national property-owners.[56]

Little wonder, then, that such events and experiences should have had a profound influence upon Lombardo, possessed as he was of a highly developed social consciousness and of a strong sense of idealism and humanism. Lombardo's answer to the problems of the Mexican Revolution was Marxian socialism.

Lombardo's militant Marxian socialism was bound to lead him into conflict with the men in power who increasingly abandoned the precepts of the Constitution of 1917. His criticisms of the spiritualist-idealist orientation of instruction at the National University led to his expulsion from that institution in 1933 and to his subsequent founding of a new, Marxist-oriented university.

In 1928, Lombardo unsuccessfully proposed the dissolution of the PLM, the corrupted political arm of the CROM.[57] Division within the ranks of the CROM increased from this date until 1932 when Lombardo resigned from the labor confederation after having his policies publicly repudiated by its secretary, Luís Morones. As has been suggested, Lombardo always had eschewed the role of "a 'great' leader solitarily throwing down leaflets

55. I. A. Langnas, "Mexico Today: Aspects of Progress Since the Revolution," *World Today*, XVII (April, 1961), 164.
56. For general surveys of the Obregón-Calles period see Gruening, pp. 146-167, 211-664; J. M. Puig Casauranc, *El Sentido Social del Proceso Histórico de México* (Mexico, 1936), pp. 155-217; Parkes, pp. 371-399; and Dulles, pp. 79-604.
57. U.S. Department of State, Correspondence from U.S. Embassy, Mexico City to U.S. State Department, Washington, D.C., Dec. 11, 1928; Clark, pp. 135-136.

from the summit of Popocatepetl'"[58] in favor of constant association with the workers and their problems. This policy now bore fruit as the majority of the syndicate's members followed Lombardo into a new labor organization, the "Purified CROM." In 1933, this labor confederation was reorganized into the larger Confederación General de Obreros y Campesinos de México (CGOCM).

Lombardo's speech of resignation from the CROM made on September 19, 1932, revealed his position as a labor leader and the strength of his Marxist views. In his speech, Lombardo complained, referring to Luís Morones's critical speech, that this was the first time in his career in the CROM that one of its members had deprived his action of authority. He had always been free, he claimed, to express himself as he wished, guided only by the principles of the CROM constitution which accepted the concepts of class struggle and historical materialism sustained by Karl Marx. For this reason, Lombardo continued, he had overlooked the opinions and the manner of living of many of his companions which were not in accord with his own views or philosophy of life and had worked enthusiastically within the CROM, attempting to serve the workers and not their leaders.

Lombardo went on to claim that his many years of study and struggle in the labor movement had led him to the conclusion that socialist concepts must be spread among the Mexican people and that only by accepting these concepts as its guide to action could the Mexican proletariat achieve "a sense of its social force and of its historic responsibility." The labor unions should act as permanent judges of the state and union leaders should not try to prevent the workers from making constant demands for justice before government functionaries.

Lombardo announced that he would continue to be a "radical Marxist, although not a Communist," that he would remain an internationalist and an opponent of chauvinistic nationalism and that he would work for a change in Mexico's bourgeois social system and for a better life for the Mexican people.

He concluded by warning the labor movement that if it should deviate from the path of profound social transformation and seek compromises with a government which had arrested social change, then that movement would lose its value as a perennial revolu-

---

58. Quoted in Ramírez y Ramírez, *La Obra y la Lucha*, p. 9.

tionary force and convert itself into a satellite of the bourgeois state.[59]

Positivistic thought in Mexico had emphasized material progress through scientific investigation. Spiritualism had stressed the realization of man's spiritual potential for truth, justice, beauty, and goodness through the moral uplifting of humanity by means of proper education. As a Marxist, Lombardo's goal remained that of realizing the finest of human potentials. This realization, though, he did not conceive as being essentially dependent upon education—although this was important—but rather contingent upon progressive industrialization and upon the reordering of human social relationships to eliminate social classes, which inevitably have antagonistic interests. The realization of man's spiritual capacities depend upon the solution of man's material problems of production and of social relationships; the solution of man's material problems would permit increasing realization of his spiritual capacities. Realization of man's spiritual capacities in turn would provide for more rapid solution of man's material problems. Thus, the two problems—the material and the spiritual—were indissoluably linked into an organic whole. Lombardo's ideals remained but the means to achieve them became more direct.[60]

The character of Lombardo's practical activities changed as he developed from an idealist into a dialectical materialist. Early in his career, when his emphasis was upon moral improvement through education as a means of realizing human ideals, Lombardo gave popular lectures on humanistic themes at the Universidad Popular and he taught ethics in the National Preparatory School. As he came to adopt the Marxist view that the realization of human ideals depended fundamentally upon changes and improvements in the material conditions of human beings, Lombardo became increasingly active in the labor movement. As shall be demonstrated in subsequent chapters, his new intellectual orientation led him to become a prominent labor leader, the leader of a socialist political party, and the director of a Marxist-oriented worker's university.

59. Speech quoted in part in Ramírez y Ramírez, ''Vicente Lombardo Toledano,'' p. 39.
60. This is a general interpretation of Lombardo's thought; Lombardo agrees that it is accurate.

II. New Orientation: Marxist Philosophy

Vicente Lombardo Toledano's thought has remained within a Marxist framework from the early 1930's to the present. He subscribes without reservation to all the basic concepts of dialectical and historical materialism, as well as to those concepts contained in Marx's and Lenin's economic analyses of the structure of capitalism and imperialism. In regard to contemporary Marxist thought, Lombardo has accepted modern Soviet additions to and modifications of the body of ideas and concepts known as Marxism-Leninism, such as the conception that world war between the capitalist and socialist states is not inevitable.

Lombardo has summarized the basic concepts of historical materialism as:

> (a) the incorporation of social evolution in the general process of the universe; (b) the physical structure of society, the regime of economic production, as that which determines the form adopted by the other social realities; and (c) the antagonism between the always changing productive forces of society and the juridical institutions which though created by these same forces do not follow them in their development. In summary: the materialist conception of history [arises from] a materialist conception of the universe, and [basic to historical materialism is the concept of] "class struggle" as the mover of the historical process.[1]

In his economic analyses, Lombardo repeated the Marxist-Leninist concepts on capitalism and imperialism. On capitalism, Lombardo has said:

> The internal contradiction of the capitalist regime consists of the contradiction between the ever greater development of production which by means of the division of labor is converted into a collective phenomenon, and the individual appropriation of that which is produced, which benefits only a minority. [The contradiction between collective produc-

---

1. Vicente Lombardo Toledano, Xavier Icaza, *et al.*, *Marxismo y Anti-Marxismo* (Mexico, 1934), p. 42.

tion and private appropriation of the product] is aggravated by the development of the capitalist regime itself; the periodicity of the crises in which the contradiction manifests itself is reduced and the crises become more profound.[2]

In social terms, this contradiction manifests itself in class struggles which in turn are the practical basis for the elimination of capitalism and its final stage, imperialism. On the elimination of capitalist imperialism Lombardo has written: "There are three principal internal causes which contribute to the historical liquidation of the capitalist regime: the class struggle within nations of great industrial development, the inter-imperialist antagonisms, and the rebellion of the colonies against the imperialist powers."[3] In these as well as in other statements Lombardo has employed an individuality of terminology which indicates his basic understanding of Marxist concepts.

Dialectical materialism influenced Lombardo's thinking on all other subjects. Thus, Lombardo states that historical materialism is but dialectical materialism applied to the study of human society. The contradictions inherent in capitalism and imperialism are the conceptual products of the application of historical materialism to analyses of capitalist economics.

According to Lombardo, dialectical materialism contains, among others, the following basic concepts: Reality exists objectively apart from human thought, although thought, of course, is a part of reality. Reality (including thought) consists fundamentally of matter in motion whose various manifestations are organically interconnected in reciprocal relationships of cause and effect. These manifestations of reality are in a constant state of change (motion) produced by the interactions of antagonistic forces and the resolution of these antagonisms into new manifestations. This resolution involves the sudden transformation of quantitative change to qualitative change. Man's existence is not determined by his knowledge, but rather his knowledge is determined by his existence. Human reason, however, can understand reality on the basis of experience proved in practice. This ability to understand the nature of reality enables man to control and

2. Vicente Lombardo Toledano, *La Rebelión del Mundo Colonial Contra el Imperialismo* (Mexico, 1950), p. 23.
3. *Ibid.*, pp. 5-6.

transform his existence.[4] Lombardo summed up the import of dialectical materialism to mankind (and also to Lombardo's personal thought and action) in the following statement: "In conceiving nature as a whole and as a process and human reason as possessing the capacity for knowing all that exists, Dialectical Materialism promises man the possibility of taking advantage of nature to his own benefit. It discloses the laws of historical progress and also provides man with the possibility of transforming social life into another more advanced."[5]

As the concepts of dialectical materialism expressed by Lombardo reveal, the contrast between his new and his past intellectual orientation could not be greater. Lombardo commented upon the contrast on several occasions. In an article published in 1935 as a sequel to a philosophical debate with Antonio Caso, Lombardo criticized the philosophically idealistic orientation of the education he received at the National Preparatory School. This instruction, he claimed, taught him many inaccurate concepts, such as the following: A fundamental, unbridgeable duality exists between the inorganic and the organic worlds as well as between the material and the ideal aspects of reality. Evolutionary progress in this dualistic reality occurs simply and without contradictions. Knowledge of the essences of the various manifestations of reality, of "things in themselves," could be determined only through intuition because science informs only as to the external aspects of these manifestations. Human salvation in this dualistic world depends upon God. The spiritual world guides human and natural destinies through the actions of great men possessed of divine inspiration. Mankind can feel assured that the goodness of God will triumph.[6]

Lombardo, alluding to his designation by Antonio Caso as a "renegade," stated that he was freely able to reject these concepts, and added:

For the satisfaction of Don Antonio Caso and of myself, I declare, then, that I reject what I received as exact, as con-

---

4. Vicente Lombardo Toledano, *Escritos Filosóficos* (Mexico, 1937), pp. 123-215; *La Batalla de las Ideas en Nuestro Tiempo* (Mexico, 1959), pp. 18-20; *La Filosofía y El Proletariado* (Mexico, 1962), pp. 75-91.

5. Lombardo Toledano, *La Batalla*, p. 20. For additional elaborations of the themes of historical and dialectical materialism, see his *Lenin, el Genio* (Mexico, 1942), pp. 5-9, *passim*, and his *La Perspectiva de México: Una Democracia del Pueblo* (Mexico, 1956), pp. 83, 86-89.

6. Lombardo Toledano, *Escritos Filosóficos*, pp. 208-210.

tradictory, as false in every one of its parts, as having awakened doubt in me in respect to the veracity of all principles and as having inclined me during my adolescence to accept the unfruitful and mentally lazy positions embodied in [the theory of] the spiritual solution of historical conflicts and the theory that compromise is the definition of justice.[7]

The debate, carried on through the newspaper articles, centered upon the subjects of idealism and materialism.[8] Lombardo revealed himself in the process as an excellent polemicist. The heart of Lombardo's argument consisted of the concept of the unity of matter, space, and time. This concept, Lombardo claimed, is sustained by the findings of modern science. Caso, on the other hand, maintained the existence of a non-material reality, of which such things as sensation, will, thought, and conscience were expressions. Lombardo insisted upon scientific proof of this duality and maintained that the only refuge of the idealists is in metaphysics or in a relegous affirmation of faith.[9]

On several occasions during the debate Caso criticized his own ideas. That is, he criticized concepts which he ascribed to Lombardo but which in fact were arguments which he himself had used previously in the debate. At one point, Caso "commits suicide," Lombardo stated, by accepting the basic concept of materialism that matter exists in space and time and space and time exist in matter—and thus leaving no dimension for the existence of the ideal.[10] Lombardo concluded the controversy by stating:

> I leave, then, Don Antonio Caso at the gates of Heaven, and declare the constroversy concluded. Before the sanctuary of religious metaphysics I stop, as, in its place, I have noted: the defense of the bases of socialism is scientific and philosophic, and not mystical. The refuge in which my impugner has confined himself does not have any importance for the ideas of those who are constructing a society better than

7. *Ibid.*, p. 210.
8. The entire debate has been published recently in Vicente Lombardo Toledano and Antonio Caso, *Idealismo vs Materialismo Dialéctico: Caso-Lombardo* (Mexico, 1963).
9. *Ibid.*, pp. 123-215.
10. *Ibid.*, p. 179.

the present: it belongs more to the repentance of man than to his action upon history.[11]

In spite of his complete intellectual reorientation, Lombardo still retained respect for his early education and educators. For example, he claimed at one time that the intellectuals of the Generation of 1910 opened new horizons in the sterile cultural medium of Mexico. Students of these intellectuals had received an invigorating and optimistic insight into the breadth and depth of human capabilities. Sentiments were aroused of creative rebellion, of the possibility of surmounting obstacles in life, and of personal responsibility for the realization of justice.[12] Indeed, there seems little doubt that Lombardo's ample humanistic and idealistic sentiments owe much to the stimuli he received from his early educators.

Lombardo, in 1959, examined the history of modern philosophy in the light of the concepts of dialectical materialism in his paper, *La Batalla de las Ideas en Nuestro Tiempo*.[13] As his principal theme, Lombardo developed the concept that bourgeois philosophical thought has come increasingly to rely upon idealism and irrationalism in its struggle with proletarian philosophical thought (dialectical materialism). The negation or restriction by bourgeois ideologists of the power of reason as a means to knowledge and progress serves to bolster the perpetuation of capitalism and imperialism.

This negation in modern times of the full potential of human reason had its beginning in the conception by Immanuel Kant that reason is incapable of conceiving the "thing in itself." This trend of thought was continued by Fichte, Hegel, and especially Schelling.

According to Lombardo, Arthur Schopenhauer can be considered "the first philosopher of an idealism typically bourgeois."[14] He removed man from determinative social influences, denied the existence of progressive social development, and affirmed that only by annulling his will could man free himself.

11. *Ibid.*, p. 203.
12. Vicente Lombardo Toledano, "El Sentido Humanista de la Revolución Mexicana," *Universidad de México*, I (Dec., 1930), 102, 104.
13. Pp. 8-18. Lombardo briefly traces the history of philosophical thought in Mexico from colonial to modern times in his *Las Corrientes Filosóficas en la Vida de México* (Mexico, 1963).
14. *La Batalla*, p. 9.

Schopenhauer was followed by other philosophers "now frankly placed in the camp of mysticism and of rejection of all evolutionary theory of history, and also of rejection of the thesis of the material and ideological evolution of society."[15] The two most prominent of these thinkers were Soren Kierkegaard and Frederich Nietzsche. The former, with his dictum that the only essential event in history was the salvation of the soul by the appearance of Christ, in effect claims that history does not exist and reduces reality to the subjective. The latter denies evolutionary progress, affirms that the will to power is the only validity in life, proclaims the natural and perpetual division of society into masters and slaves, and proclaims his well-known thesis of the superman.

These philosophers, according to Lombardo, can be considered "the precursors of the reactionary philosophy of recent years."[16] This reactionary philosophy, comprehended in the philosophical tendency known as the Philosophy of Life, is the bourgeoisie's answer to dialectical materialism.

Lombardo discussed the ideas of some of the participants in this trend, including those of Wilhelm Dilthey, Georg Simmel, Oswald Spengler, Max Scheler, Martin Heidegger, Karl Jaspers, and of the prominent fascist ideologist, Alfred Rosenberg. He summed up his general interpretation of this school of thought in two paragraphs:

> What is the essence of the Philosophy of Life? It consists in taking agnosticism, the "impossibility" of reason to know the "thing in itself," as Kant said; in transforming it into mysticism and in making a myth of subjective idealism, created by man's own consciousness....[17]

> It is interesting to notice that all these philosophers are equally characterized by the negation of rational knowledge. By the negation of progressive historical development. By the affirmation of the exceptional character of conscience in the midst of nature, and by their implacable fight against Dialectical Materialism.[18]

Existentialism he characterized as "nothing but a new adapta-

---
15. *Ibid.*, p. 10.
16. *Ibid.*, p. 11.
17. *Ibid.*
18. *Ibid.*, p. 12.

tion of the Philosophy of Life to the necessities of the decadent post-war capitalist regime."[19] It serves as a refuge from reality for mediocre middle-class intellectuals who are afraid to accept socialism yet at the same time realize that the forces of reaction will be defeated.[20]

Finally, pragmatism "is simply a variation of irrationalism,"[21] as it affirms that reason cannot grasp the essence of things and declares that action is of most importance in human development.

Lombardo went on to discuss the nature of dialectical and historical materialism and to emphasize what he believed to be the proven superiority of dialectical materialism over the antirational philosophies. With the triumph of dialectical materialism and the restoration of the value of reason as a means of human development, the prospects for humanity will be greater than they ever have been in history. A new humanism is contained in these concepts, one which promises concretely to improve the material and spiritual existence of each and all.[22]

Two topics associated with Lombardo's Marxist orientation remain to be considered. One concerns Lombardo's concept of nationalism, the other his relationship as a Marxist to the Mexican Communist party and to the international Communist movement.

In common with Marxist socialists in underdeveloped countries, Lombardo has manifested powerful nationalistic sentiments. He has praised the exaltation of nationalism as one of the few positive features of the Mexican Revolution. There is considerable continuity between his early and his later thought concerning nationalism; his mature sentiments, however, are more consciously anticapitalistic and pro-proletarian. Lombardo expressed the essence of his concept of nationalism in a speech given in Mexico City before the National Committee of Proletarian Defense in 1936, wherein he defended himself and the workers against the charge that they were traitors to the nation. The nation, he claimed, was really in the hands of a limited number of private Mexican and foreign interests whose concern was only for private profit. These propertied classes identified their selfish interests

19. *Ibid.*, p. 15.
20. *Ibid.*, pp. 15-17; Vicente Lombardo Toledano, *Diario de un Viaje a la China Nueva* (Mexico, 1950), pp. 217-219.
21. Lombardo Toledano, *La Batalla*, p. 18.
22. *Ibid.*, pp. 18-23. For additional brief surveys of modern philosophy see Lombardo's *La Perspectiva de México*, pp. 86-89 and *La Filosofía*, pp. 109-116.

with those of the Mexican nation, and hence the origin of their charge of "traitors" against those who struggled for the liberty and well-being of the Mexican masses. It is the latter, actually, who have the interests of Mexico at heart, who are the genuine patriots.[23]

In other speeches, Lombardo frequently has elaborated with pride upon the cultural heritage of Mexico. While occasionally he has shown favoritism for its Indian heritage,[24] he has given the Spanish tradition its due: among the "great creators of Mexico" were Bartolomé de las Casas, Sor Juana Inés de la Cruz, and Carlos de Sigüenza y Góngora as well as Cuauhtémoc, Benito Juárez, and Emiliano Zapata.[25] Lombardo has been especially concerned with promoting the diffusion of knowledge of and pride in this cultural heritage among the Mexican workers; this activity is one of the special functions of his worker's university. The diffusion of knowledge of Mexico's cultural heritage is important as a counterbalance to the threat of United States imperialism, because the threat is not only economic and political, but also cultural. United States imperialism, he has stated, is bent upon destroying native Mexican culture and "yankeefying" the nation as part of its drive towards hemispheric domination.[26]

In spite of his pronounced adherence to Marxist-Leninist views, Lombardo has never been a member of the Mexican Communist party (PCM). In fact, he has been consistently critical of the tactical policies of this party. According to Lombardo, the PCM was founded (in 1919) in a climate favorable for its development on a large scale. That it did not was owing largely "to the lack of ideological preparation, to the sectarianism which moved it, and to its forgetfulness of the great national problems and of the study of the concrete recovery of rights by the working class."[27] He

23. Vicente Lombardo Toledano, "La Bandera Mexicana y el Proletariado," *Futuro*, III (Feb., 1936), 24.
24. Lombardo began his campaign as candidate for the presidency of Mexico in 1952 by rendering homage before the tomb of the Aztec chief Cuauhtemoc. Source: Victor Alba (pseud.), *Historia del Frente Popular* (Mexico, 1959), pp. 243-244.
25. Lombardo Toledano, *La Perspectiva*, pp. 101-102.
26. *Ibid.*, pp. 102-103. Lombardo's proposals for the solution of the problem of Mexico's ethnic minorities will be considered later, pp. 65-66.
27. Vicente Lombardo Toledano, *La Evolución de México durante la Primera Mitad del Siglo XX* (Mexico, 1956), p. 14.

believes that these shortcomings still characterize the party.[28]

Lombardo has criticized the tactics of the Mexican Communist party in the 1930's as demagogic and as characterized by opposition for the sake of opposition. These tactics, rather than helping the proletariat, he feels actually served the interests of the reactionaries. The PCM in 1935 criticized the proposed reform of Article 3 of the Constitution of 1917 to provide for "socialist" education as a useless gesture because it was fantastic to think that education could be genuinely socialist in a society which was dominated by the bourgeoisie. Lombardo agreed that education could not be completely socialist in contemporary Mexican society, yet he thought education could be given a socialist bent that would help to develop the class consciousness of the proletariat. Therefore, according to Lombardo, the PCM's opposition to the reform of Article 3 served to hinder the attainment of minimum rights by the working class.

Similarly, according to Lombardo, the PCM's blind promotion of strikes whenever and wherever it could without regard for legal requisites did not serve, as it thought, to increase the militant class consciousness of the defeated workers, but rather promoted cynicism, rejection of the revolutionary movement, and the acceptance of company unions.[29] Its attempts to gain unilateral control over the Mexican labor movement threatened the popular-front unity of leftist elements against the reactionaries in 1935-1936. Specifically, the PCM refused to co-operate with the National Committee of Proletarian Defense organized by Lombardo in 1935 to support President Cárdenas in his conflict with rightist ex-President Calles. Again, in 1936, the PCM withdrew its representation from the newly organized Confederación de Trabajadores de México (CTM) when it was unable to gain control of that labor confederation. Although the breach was healed in 1937, permanent harm resulted, according to Lombardo, because the seats abandoned by the Communists on the National Council of the

28. Opinion expressed personally to the author by Vicente Lombardo Toledano in April 1962.

29. Vicente Lombardo Toledano, *La Doctrina Socialista y Su Interpretación en el Artículo 3º* (Mexico, 1935), pp. 22-23; *En Qué Consiste y a Cuánto Asciende la Fortuna de Vicente Lombardo Toledano* (Mexico, 1940), no pagination.

CTM were taken by moderates, much to the detriment of the future political and tactical orientation of the CTM.[30]

Lombardo relates a story from this period of the 1930's to illustrate the "infantile and ridiculous" tactics of the PCM. Shortly after the formation of the "Purified CROM" in 1932, Lombardo and his companions organized a meeting in a Mexico City theater in honor of Karl Marx. Lombardo was surprised upon his arrival at the meeting to discover that the theater was full of placards signed by the PCM which read "Marx is ours!" Groups of Communists started fights in an unsuccessful attempt to break up the meeting.[31]

To this day, according to Lombardo, the tactics of the Mexican Communist party have continued to hinder unity within the working class and among the leftist political parties. Its infantile radicalism still serves the counterrevolution more than the revolution. This is evidenced by its support of the anarchistic tactics employed by the Sindicato de Trabajadores Ferrocarrileros during the 1959 strikes and by Section IX of the Sindicato Nacional de Trabajadores de la Educación (SNTE) in its attempts to gain control of the national union. Those tactics served to divide rather than to unite the labor movement.[32] (See Chapter V.)

In 1961, Lombardo summed up his attitude toward the PCM and, at the same time, expressed hope that unity on the Left might sometime be achieved in two statements made in response to questions which followed a conference he gave on the theory and tactics of the labor movement in Mexico:

> In Mexico there are three groups which have adopted Marxism-Leninism. The Partido Popular Socialista [Popular Socialist Party of which Lombardo is Secretary General], the Partido Comunista Mexicano [Mexican Communist Party] and the Partido Obrero-Campesino [Workers Peasants Party]. But until the present they have not achieved unity because the Communist Party says it is the the only proprietor of Marxism-Leninism, and accuses the other two of not being able, without its consent, to utilize the Marxist-Leninist philosophy. (Laughter).[33]

30. Lombardo Toledano, *Teoría y Práctica del Movimiento Sindical Mexicano*, pp. 69, 81-82, 186-187.
31. *Ibid.*, pp. 146-147.
32. *Ibid.*, pp. 90-95, *passim*.
33. *Ibid.*, p. 146.

Referring to the PCM, Lombardo said:

You have heard the principal experiences of the union movement of our country. What has happened to these companions is that in thirty years they have not done what they should have done to have [properly] organized their party. It is the same attitude of all times that bears little relationship to Marxism-Leninism. Their alliance with the Trotskyites and with the agents of the clergy in their support of divisive ultraradical tactics, is the consequence of abandonment of revolutionary theory. As to what must be done we have already spoken. I hope that someday they will correct their errors for good in the sake of unity and of the quantitative and qualitative growth of the working class.[34]

Lombardo's role in the international Communist movement has been the subject of considerable dispute. Some authors claim that Lombardo was a direct agent of the Comintern—or of the U.S.S.R. after the Comintern's dissolution.[35] Others suggest that Lombardo ardently supports the international Communist movement from personal conviction rather than on direct orders from Moscow.[36] Still others beg the question.[37]

Lombardo has ridiculed the charge that he is an agent of Moscow. His tactical policies, he has claimed—such as the creation of a national front in the 1930's and the organization of the Partido Popular in 1947-1948—have been dictated by the national

---

34. *Ibid.*, p. 166. For a variety of comments on the relationship of Lombardo to the Mexican Communist party, see Robert J. Alexander, *Communism in Latin America* (New Brunswick, N.J., 1957), pp. 14, 332-335, 343-344, 346-348; Randall Pond, "Toledano and Mexico," *The Commonweal*, XXIV (June 12, 1936), 174; Harry Sylvester, "A Revolution Doesn't Come Off," *The Commonweal*, XXVIII (June 24, 1938), 232; "Communications" section, *The Commonweal*, XXVIII (Aug. 5, 1938) 389-390; "Communications" section, *The Commonweal*, XXVIII (Aug. 19, 1938), 430; "Toledano Faces Labor Revolt," *World Report*, Dec. 31, 1946, p. 30; Alba, *Historia del Frente Popular*, p. 248. Lombardo expresses himself further on the PCM and on the characteristics and history of the political Left in Mexico in his recent work, *La Izquierda en la Historia de México* (Mexico, 1963).

35. Article by Will Lissner, New York *Times*, June 22, 1950, p. 1; Betty Kirk, *Covering the Mexican Front* (Norman, Okla., 1942), pp. 81-82, 231-232, 265, 272.

36. Article by Milton Bracker, New York *Times*, Sept. 23, 1946, p. 7.

37. Alexander, pp. 36, 39-41; James Riley Hayes, "The Mexican Labor Movement, 1931-51" (M.A. thesis, University of California, 1951), pp. 191-192, 201-203.

necessities of Mexico and not by any foreign power.[38] Articles 5 and 6 of the statutes of the Partido Popular prohibit everyone but Mexican nationals from membership and expressly forbid the party "for any reason... to subordinate its action to any international organization" or "to maintain ties of dependence with foreign parties," although it will maintain "relations of friendship and solidarity, in accordance with the principles of proletarian internationalism, with all movements and foreign parties which have similar ends, in accordance with its Declaration of Principles and its Program."[39]

In brief, Lombardo has consistently supported the actions and policies of the U.S.S.R. and other socialist nations. In questions of policy and theory, he has followed the interpretations expressed by the Soviet Union. This writer, for one, completely rejects the charge that Lombardo is a paid agent of the U.S.S.R. or of any other power. The charge is belied by Lombardo's modest level of living and by the limited financial resources of the Universidad Obrera and the Partido Popular Socialista, which Lombardo directs. Neither institution has sufficient funds to maintain a newspaper or a news magazine. In the author's opinion, Lombardo's actions are the result of his freely formed conceptions of the tactics he must follow in order to help achieve socialism in Mexico and in the world.

In summary, Lombardo's Marxist concepts contrast drastically with his early philosophically idealistic concepts. He had conceived that a fundamental duality existed between the material and the ideal, as well as between the organic and inorganic aspects of reality. As a Marxist he considered reality to consist fundamentally of matter in motion whose various manifestations are organically interconnected in reciprocal relationships of cause and effect. Rather than thinking as before that changes in this reality are simple and non-contradictory, Lombardo conceived that reality changed constantly through a process in which the interactions of fundamentally antagonistic forces were constantly being resolved into new manifestations, which likewise contain contradictory forces of their own. Therefore, rather than being solely and forever gradual and quantitative, changes also are rapid and

38. *El Popular*, Oct. 30, 1947, p. 5; *El Frente Único en México*, ed. Marcos Díaz (Habana, 1938), pp. 30-31.

39. Partido Popular, *III Asamblea Nacional Ordinaria del Partido Popular; Materiales de Estudio* (Mexico, 1960), p. 40.

qualitative. The essence of reality could not be determined by intuition, as he previously thought, but only by human reason which avails itself of proven, practical experience to test its theoretical representations of the nature of reality. Human salvation depends not upon God or the divine guidance of human destinies, but rather upon man's use of his reason by which he understands and hence controls and transforms his existence. It may be implied from Lombardo's thought that if mankind merely awaits the realization of the will of God in order to improve its life, the wait will likely be long.[40]

40. Lombardo recently expressed the quintessence of his thought on man, his prospects and problems, in his *Summa* (Mexico, 1964).

III. Imperialism and the Mexican Economy

Capitalist imperialism is the major obstacle to the material, cultural, and democratic development of the people of Mexico and of other semicolonial and colonial countries of the world; and the chief source of modern imperialism is the United States of America. This has been the principal theme of the thought of Vicente Lombardo Toledano and also of the program and actions of the Partido Popular Socialista. Lombardo's statements upon the nature of capitalist imperialism indicate that he has accepted without modifications the official Soviet viewpoints on the subject.

In the modern world, according to Lombardo, the distinctive feature of imperialism is not territorial control but rather economic domination by means of foreign capital investments. Economic domination leads to strong direct and indirect pressures for control in the interests of the imperialist power of the domestic and international policies, both political and military, of the underdeveloped, semicolonial nations. Therefore, whereas a large number are juridically independent, only a few nations of the world are genuinely independent because most are in positions of economic dependence upon a foreign power.

Since the end of World War II, Lombardo maintained in *Carta a la Juventud*, the United States has been the dominant world imperialist power. Its ideologists claim that this century was to be the "American Century" and its government promoted a national and international anticommunist campaign in the form of the Cold War as a cover and justification for its imperialist policies. The Marshall Plan and the NATO alliance had their origins in the desire of United States monopolists to dominate the European economy. Similarly, the Truman Plan, the Havana Charter, and the Alliance for Progress are devices to prevent the attainment of complete autonomy and full industrialization by the Latin-American nations in order to maintain the region as a safe area for the extraction of private profits by American monopolies.

But, says Lombardo, the United States has not been able to achieve its goal of world hegemony and, in its frustration, threatens the world with a third world war. Three factors, he contends, rising from the contradictions within the capitalist mode of production itself serve to undermine capitalist imperialism: (1) the class struggle within the highly developed capitalist nations, stimulated by the unavoidable cyclical economic crises and the permanent unemployment of capitalism; (2) continued inter-imperialist rivalries over markets, sources of investment, and raw materials; and (3) the continuing rebellions for independence in the colonial and semicolonial world engendered by imperialist penetration itself.

These contradictions within capitalism, Lombardo argues, have served to promote the advance of socialism. The world is now divided into two camps: the socialist—which includes not only the socialist nations but also the democratic, pacifist, and anti-imperialist elements of the capitalist-dominated world—and the capitalist. It is the strength of the former which is the primary force preventing war and promoting human development in the world today.[1]

According to Lombardo, defeats suffered by United States imperialism in Asia and in Europe have increased the United States' desire for hegemony in the Western Hemisphere, which it regards as its peculiar sphere of domination. The United States stands ready to intervene as necessary to prevent the victory of any truly democratic, popular, pacifist, and national-sovereignty movement in Latin America. Thus confronted by United States imperialism, Latin-America has but two choices—either submit to the domination of imperialism and its native allies and remain immersed in poverty, ignorance, and economic and political backwardness, or reject this domination and move toward national sovereignty, economic development, higher levels of living, and political democracy.[2] The Cuban Revolution has shown the way,

1. Lombardo Toledano, *La Rebelión del Mundo Colonial Contra el Imperialismo*, pp. 5-6, 42-44, 73-78, *passim*; *Diario de un Viaje a la China Nueva*, pp. 141-144; *La Perspectiva de México: Una Democracia del Pueblo*, pp. 17-18; *Carta a la Juventud* (Mexico, 1960), pp. 39-42.

2. Vicente Lombardo Toledano, *Mensaje al Proletariado de la América Latina* (Mexico, 1936), pp. 15-16; *Objetivos y Táctica del Proletariado y del Sector Revolucionario de México en la Actual Etapa de la Evolución Histórica del País* (Mexico, 1947), pp. 26-27, 35; *La Tercera Devaluación del Peso Mexicano en los Últimos 15 Años* (Mexico, 1954), pp. 3-6; *La Perspectiva*

yet he contends that not all popular movements in Latin America need follow exactly Castro's tactics to achieve victory.[3]

Lombardo has made many specific criticisms of foreign activities in Mexico. In the past, foreign investments have developed some of Mexico's resources, but always at considerable expense to the Mexican nation.[4] Mexican railways were developed by foreign capital but at the cost of large subsidies to the investors. Moreover, this railway system was not constructed for the purpose of promoting the integrated economic development of Mexico, but was built to serve the interest of foreigners who exploited Mexico's natural resources. Foreign investors monopolized huge tracts of land in the Díaz era (1876-1910) to the detriment of agricultural development. In the interests of private American investors, the United States government burdened the Mexican nation during the revolution of 1910-1920 with two military interventions, with demands for payment for property damages, and with opposition to revolutionary reforms that were meant to enhance Mexican national economic sovereignty. Foreign companies, Lombardo contends, for a century and a half have exploited Mexico's mineral resources to the point of exhaustion, have hindered the industrialization of metals produced by companies other than their own, and have left in Mexico nothing but "low taxes and miserable salaries which even today still depend, in their principal sum, upon the price of metals in the international market dominated by North American enterprises."[5] Previous to its recent nationalization by purchase by the Mexican government, the electric energy industry was monopolized by foreign investments. High rates were charged while at the same time the supplies of electricity were not expanded rapidly enough to keep pace with the growing demand. Furthermore, the Mexican government sold energy at low cost to the foreign monopoly which in turn resold the energy at high prices and with large profits. Foreign investors in the petroleum industry (nationalized in 1938) exported most of the product in crude form. The investors showed no concern for the govern-

---

de México, pp. 16-17; Partido Popular, *Razón Histórica, Programa y Estatutos del Partido Popular* (Mexico, 1948), pp. 36-37.

3. Vicente Lombardo Toledano, *Al Pueblo Mexicano: Defender a Cuba es Defender a México y a la América Latina* (Mexico, 1961), pp. 9-11, *passim*.

4. Partido Popular, *Tesis sobre México* (Mexico, 1958), pp. 19-22; Lombardo Toledano, *Carta*, pp. 42-45.

5. Partido Popular, *Tesis*, p. 22.

ment's plans for the over-all development of the economy. Their only interest was in unlimited exploitation of Mexico's resources for private profit. They were ready to defend these interests to the point of engaging in "spoliation, assassination and the formation of a private army."[6]

According to Lombardo, foreign investments in Mexico more than doubled between 1938 and 1950. The United States' share in the investments increased from 61.6 per cent to 67 per cent. In the early 1950's, American capital controlled 41 per cent of the most important industries of Mexico. American investments have been directed increasingly into Mexican industry and commerce while at the same time maintaining their traditional control of the mining industry. Substantial increments in American investments in the Mexican economy have continued to the present.[7]

Mexico's dependence upon American and European investments has had many deleterious effects upon the nation's development, Lombardo argues. Currently, some 80 per cent of the profits earned by foreign investments are sent out of the country. This impedes the formation of national capital and the development of Mexican private and governmental investments. The foreign monopolies with their tremendous economic resources enter into fierce competition with native enterprises for complete control of the domestic market. The advantage usually goes to the former who then have complete control over the pricing of their products. The flood of products which enters from the United States as a consequence of inadequate tariff barriers has similar harmful effects upon native business. The need for foreign exchange—especially for the purchase of capital goods for which Mexico is almost completely dependent upon imports—has contributed to the orientation of part of the agricultural section of the economy toward the production of commercial crops (cotton, coffee) for export. At the same time, much of the total agricultural production has been left at or near the subsistence level. The primary product exports are subject to market fluctuations and to the pricing policies of international monopolies.

It is not only the primary commercial agricultural products which are dependent upon foreign monopolies and foreign pricing,

6. *Ibid.*
7. Vicente Lombardo Toledano, *La Evolución de México durante la Primera Mitad del Siglo XX*, p. 9; *Carta*, pp. 60-61.

for approximately 80 per cent of both the imports and exports of Mexico are dominated by United States monopolies. Mexico, in brief, must depend upon this market dominated by foreign monopolies for the sale of low-cost primary products and the purchase of high-cost manufactured goods. Balance-of-payments difficulties arise which require devaluations of the peso; devaluations in turn cause domestic price inflations. That Mexico does not have even greater difficulties with its balance of payments is the result of two fortuitous circumstances: the expenditures of American tourists and the earnings of Mexican *braceros* in the United States. These compensations, however, are acquired at the expense of exposing Mexican culture to a crude "yankeefication" and of encouraging the draining of part of the lifeblood from the nation.

The distorted development of agriculture has left the mass of rural Mexicans with low incomes and hence with limited purchasing power. Domestic price inflation has inhibited their demand for commodities further and also has restricted the purchasing power of urban workers. The combined effect of these restrictions upon demand has impeded the industrialization of Mexico because of the lack of a flexible, expanding domestic market. Mexico is forced to rely increasingly upon foreign trade and foreign capital —the very elements which serve to promote its economic difficulties.

In summary, as Lombardo has interpreted it, the total effect of this economic process has been to increase Mexico's dependence upon foreign capital, to restrict the rapid industrialization of Mexico—especially the development of the capital goods industry —to distort and to unbalance the over-all economic development of the country, to lower the level of living of the majority in the interests of a minority, and to orient the Mexican economy to serve the needs of United States' monopolies for mineral, agricultural, and semifinished products and for markets for the investment of capital and the sale of capital goods. It is the conscious intention of the American monopolies and the American government to maintain this semicolonial orientation of the Mexican economy and to prevent the independent industrialization of the nation the better to maintain Mexico as a source of cheap raw materials and as a market for the sale of industrial goods.[8]

8. Lombardo Toledano, *Objetivos y Táctica*, pp. 47-49; *La Tercera Devaluación*, pp. 1-2, 4-9, 12-13, *passim; El Drama de México; Nuestros Grandes Problemas Económicos* (Mexico, 1954), pp. 9-13; *La Evolución de México*, pp. 9-12; Partido Popular, *Tesis*, pp. 22-27.

The solution to these problems, Lombardo believes, lies in increased economic nationalization and state planning.⁹ The López Mateos regime (1958-1964) took some steps in this direction. In 1960, for example, the government nationalized by purchase the electric energy industry, a measure which was applauded by Lombardo and the Partido Popular Socialista.¹⁰ In addition, Lombardo and the PPS call for a federal law regulating foreign capital in Mexico.¹¹ Such a law, he advocated, should delimit all economic activities susceptible to foreign investments, establish rates of profit, prohibit the export of profits, and, in short, establish the conditions which would place foreign investments "in the role of supplementary credit to the national economy, under the control of the state power."¹²

In short, the *sine qua non* of Mexican economic development is freedom from the overriding influence of United States imperialism. Lombardo made this abundantly clear in his *El Drama de México; Nuestros Grandes Problemas Económicas*. He claimed that Mexico could not pursue a policy to raise the level of living of the Mexican people and at the same time permit the subordination of the Mexican economy to foreign monopolies. Nor, he continued, is it possible to defend the nation's economic independence from foreign imperialism and at the same time increase the economic exploitation of the Mexican people. These policies are contradictory. Mexico needs a program for national economic development which has as its focal point Mexican, not foreign, interests. Mexico needs a program which considers the Mexican people the supreme wealth of the nation and which devotes all the nation's material and financial resources to the development of that human wealth.¹³ "The drama that Yankee imperialism represents for Mexico is the dilemma of choosing between being a colony of the United States, with the help of imperialism, or of

9. Lombardo Toledano, *Carta*, pp. 65-66; Partido Popular, *III Asamblea Nacional Ordinaria del Partido Popular; Materiales de Estudio*, pp. 24-27, 61-63.
10. *Ibid.*, p. 61; "Conferencia de Prensa del Secretario General del P.P.S.," *Avante*, XXV (May, 1962), 12-13.
11. Lombardo Toledano, *La Tercera Devaluación*, pp. 13-22; *Carta*, pp. 61-62; Partido Popular, *III Asamblea*, p. 62; "Conferencia," *Avante*, p. 13.
12. Lombardo Toledano, *Carta*, p. 62.
13. Lombardo Toledano, *El Drama de México*, p. 13.

being a prosperous and independent nation, against the will of imperialism and the consequences of its opposition...."[14]

Lombardo succinctly summarized his attitude toward American imperialism in *Un Nuevo Partido para la Defensa de México y de su Pueblo*: "In the same measure as we come to depend less on the exterior, the Revolution will have fulfilled its most important historical objective."[15]

Lombardo has made a variety of detailed analyses and criticisms of the Mexican economy and of its development in accordance with the principles of the Mexican Revolution. He has devoted special attention to agriculture as the key to Mexico's economic development.[16]

Article 27 of the Constitution of 1917 set forth three fundamental principals of the revolution: (1) the nation has the right to modify the forms of private property in the public interest; (2) the national lands, waters, and subsoil are the property of the nation; (3) rural villages will be granted usurped lands or will be given new lands sufficient for their needs. With these principles as bases, the agrarian reform has developed through three stages. First, communities received lands in quantities sufficient only to augment the incomes of the villagers: the villagers still had to depend on wage labor. Next, the size of parcels granted was increased so that the recipients could live upon the production of their land alone. Finally, under President Lázaro Cárdenas, the lands were given to agricultural workers as well as to members of village communities, and agricultural co-operatives were formed. In 1950, *ejidos* (semicollective and collective landholding communities) accounted for 53 per cent of the cultivated lands in Mexico and for 43 per cent of total agricultural production.

This process of agrarian reform, according to Lombardo, has had two primary virtues: (1) parcels were granted in usufruct

14. *Ibid.*, p. 12.
15. (Mexico, 1947), p. 21.
16. Lombardo's ideas on Mexican agriculture which are summarized in the following discussion are presented in several of his works, including *Qué Ha Sido la Reforma Agraria Ayer y Qué es Durante el Régimen Actual* (Mexico, 1952), pp. 2-11, *passim;* *El Régimen Actual Ha Hecho de Matamoros un Gran Monumento contra el Agrarismo* (Mexico, 1952), pp. 7-9, 15-20; *La Reforma Agraria en China y en México; Semejanzas y Diferencias* (Mexico, 1954), pp. 26-45; *El Drama de México*, pp. 1-9; Partido Popular, *Tesis,* pp. 42-62.

only and thus re-alienation of the land was avoided, and (2) the reforms were achieved as a direct result of the militancy of the peasants. This militancy, which continues to this day, provides the hope for renewed agrarian reform in the future.

The positive benefits to the Mexican nation of the agrarian reform have been considerable. The redistribution of some 38 million hectares of land between 1915 and 1958 has definitely ended the old feudal relationships of land tenure and opened the way for a considerable increase in the productive forces of agriculture. Agricultural production and rural income have increased as a consequence of the extension of irrigation and colonization projects, the increased use of machinery, improved seeds, and scientific methods of cultivation, and the extension of credit. A national market has been created and industrial production has been stimulated owing to the increase in the purchasing power of the rural masses since the revolution.

The agrarian reform, however, is burdened with many negative aspects. The over-all underdeveloped nature of Mexican agriculture can be seen from the fact that in 1956, according to the Bank of Mexico, the 58 per cent of the economically active population which was devoted to agriculture produced only 16.4 per cent of the national income. Furthermore, the average daily income of the worker in agriculture was only Mex$3.05, whereas for the industrial worker it was Mex$19.85, and for those engaged in commerce, Mex$47.76.[17]

Lombardo contends that although considerable land has been redistributed, much more must be divided. Many of the rural dwellers are landless and lack means of support while others have parcels that are too small for their needs; altogether, some two million heads of families are either landless or possess less than one hectare. Except for the northwest and the southeast, this insufficiency of land prevails in all regions of the nation, including those areas in which communal *ejidos* predominated in the past, such as in the La Laguna region centering around Torreón. The nature of the agrarian reform law aggravates this problem because it limits expropriable land to that within a perimeter of seven kilometers around a given village; the basic law remains unchanged even though little land of this character remains to be expropriated. Furthermore, not all affectable hacienda lands have been ex-

17. Lombardo Toledano, *La Evolución de México*, p. 10.

propriated. More important, a new *latifundismo*[18] has arisen as the major portion of the choice lands in the new irrigation districts have gone not to needy peasants but rather to a favored few with political influence. This new rural bourgeoisie, enjoying credit and other resources of the government, does not directly cultivate the land itself (and frequently does not even know exactly where it is) but rather employs others to do the work. Certificates of inaffectability from expropriation have been extended generously to these and other private owners, whereas few of the certificates have been granted which guarantee a peasant the right to work land (and hence help to prevent the usurpation of his rights).

The governments of Manuel Ávila Camacho, Miguel Alemán, and Adolfo Ruíz Cortines (1940-1958) turned away from agrarian reform and promoted the development of private interests in agriculture and particularly the interests of the new capitalist landlords. The López Mateos government (1958-1964) returned to land reform but, Lombardo contends, many presidential measures were thwarted by state officials acting in the interests of foreign and native landlords.[19]

Particularly violent and constant have been the attacks upon the collective *ejidos*. These *ejidos* (which numbered some 500 and existed throughout Mexico but were located particularly in the areas of commercial crop production) made enormous advances in output of production and in returns to their members in spite of their inexperience and lack of political knowledge and professional education. Government bureaucrats and others, nevertheless, conducted an intensive propaganda campaign against the collectives. The *ejidos* were called communistic and copies of Russian methods alien to Mexican needs. Peasant leaders were bought off and rank-and-file *ejidatarios*[20] were pressured, confused, and deceived with promises. Finally, many of the collective *ejidos* (especially those in the northwest) were broken up. As a consequence of these actions, *ejido* lands have been rented contrary to constitutional provision, land has been abandoned, misery and peonage have returned in some areas, and all but a few of the most stalwart peasant leaders have become mere bureaucrats of one or the other of the two government banks of rural credit.

18. The process of organizing land into latifundia or large landed estates.
19. Vicente Lombardo Toledano, ''Reforma Agraria,'' *Siempre!*, CDLXVI (May 23, 1962), 22-23.
20. Members of *ejidos*.

One of the major concerns of the rural masses is the problem of credit. The two government banks created to meet the credit needs of the *ejidatarios* and the small proprietors—the Banco Nacional de Crédito Ejidal and the Banco Nacional de Crédito Agrícola—have extended credit sufficient to meet the needs of only some 10 to 13 per cent of their charges. As a consequence, the peasants have been forced to accept loans from usurers who extort the major portion of the peasant's crops with their high interest rates. The new rural bourgeoisie, on the other hand, enjoys to the full the benefits of government credits.

In addition to insufficient credit, the countryside suffers from inadequate water resources as the many government irrigation projects still have not fully provided for the needs of the majority of rural dwellers. Furthermore, as noted above, much of the land opened by these publically financed irrigation projects has gone not to needy peasants but rather to non-farmers with political influence.

Although northern Mexico enjoys peace and security in the countryside, the central and the southern parts of the nation lack such guarantees. Cattle thieves, gunmen, and corrupt authorities "have made agriculture for the poor people a veritable drama."[21]

The lack of means of self-support for many in the rural areas, owing to the insufficiency of land, water, and credit resources, has resulted in the annual flight of workers who seek work in the United States. Mexico, Lombardo has argued, is losing her greatest wealth—her human wealth—and also is weakening her sense of national distinctiveness as the experiences of the *braceros* turn these workers unconsciously "into partisans of the perpetual submission of our country to the nation to the north."[22]

Production in the export-oriented cattle industry in Mexico is almost completely extensive rather than intensive in nature. Few scientific methods are used, yields are low, and the cattle are subject to a variety of diseases. As a result of the agrarian reform, most of the cattle are raised by small farmers. While this organization of cattle production has had the positive effect of increasing the small farmers' incomes, it also has tended to perpetuate unscientific methods.

The sugar industry especially has been criticized by Lombardo.

21. Lombardo Toledano, *Qué Ha Sido la Reforma Agraria*, p. 7.
22. Partido Popular, *Tesis*, p. 56.

The National Association of Sugar Producers, composed of workers, owners, and representatives of the government, has been turned into a private monopoly to the benefit of a portion of the owners of *ingenios de azúcar* (sugar mills). As a consequence of the activities of this monopoly, new mills have been opened in regions distant from the more favorable tropical areas of the nation where low yields and high production costs predominate. In order to sustain these inefficient mills, the government has had to lend its full political and financial support to the owners, even to the extent of forcing the country people in these regions to plant sugar cane—because the peasants, if free to make their own choice, would plant crops with greater returns. As a consequence, many of the peasants "are living as peons of the *ingenio*."[23] Furthermore, credit frequently is denied the more productive mills in the tropical regions.

Some of the *ingenios de azúcar* are organized as co-operatives. They are co-operatives in name only, however, as they are not directed by and for the producers but rather are monopolies controlled by and for the benefit of political favorites. Finally, sugar is exported even though sugar production does not meet national consumption needs. At the same time foreign sugar is imported to make up the deficiencies in supplies on the domestic market.[24]

Lombardo summed up the condition of the sugar industry in a speech delivered in Ciudad Mante, Tamaulipas, in 1952. According to Lombardo, the sugar industry was characterized by low output, high costs, insufficient credit, super-exploitation of the cane growers "who live like peons in the days of Porfirio Díaz," poverty of the growers, and enrichment of politicians and others in the government favor.[25]

The internal government of the *ejidos* is not democratic. Most *ejido* leaders have submitted to the political leaders of their region; they hold their offices for as many years as they continue to serve the interests of these politicians rather than of their communities. Furthermore, politicians ranging from local authorities to members of the national congress place pressures upon the

---

23. Vicente Lombardo Toledano, *El Fracaso Actual de la Industria Azucarera y las Estupendas Perspectivas para su Triunfo* (Mexico, 1952), p. 10.
24. *Ibid.*, pp. 7-12, *passim*.
25. *Ibid.*, p. 12.

rural population to support certain candidates at political rallies and at the polls.

Finally, one of the most serious shortcomings is the lack of planned co-ordination between agricultural and industrial production. This lack of synchronization together with the general underdeveloped nature of most of the nation's agricultural production has contributed to the increasing alienation of the city from the country and of the working class from the peasantry. It has obstructed the development of industry—especially of heavy industry—and thereby has contributed to the extension of foreign ownership in the manufacturing industry.

As a solution to these problems, Lombardo does not suggest the immediate socialization of the means of production in agriculture. This should come later after the proletariat has assumed political power, he argues. At that time a planned, socialized agriculture would be co-ordinated with the development of heavy industry. For the present, Lombardo insists upon a continued and genuine realization of the precepts of the Mexican Revolution embodied in the Constitution of 1917—the precepts which provided for a democratic, antifeudal, and anti-imperialist revolution. Land distribution to *ejidos* and to small- and middle-scale proprietors should be pursued to a conclusion; there should be no more latifundia or "agriculture at long distance" of the politically privileged. Agricultural development must be planned so that production will satisfy the domestic demand for food, clothing, and industrial raw materials. Export-import controls must restrict competition from foreign products and prevent the export of products needed on the domestic market. Only processed rather than crude raw materials should be exported.

The policies of opening centers of agriculture in the tropical regions of the nation and of promoting internal colonization should be pursued vigorously. A number of techniques, services, and benefits must be extended in rural areas more rapidly than at present. Agriculture must be mechanized; irrigation projects must be extended; fertilizers and advanced techniques of modern science must be employed increasingly; experimental stations must be spread; agricultural prices must be fixed and protected; a firm, adequate, and equitable system of credit and of crop insurance must be created; the cheap and efficacious transportation of agricultural products must be insured by adequate measures; and a number of services must be extended, including such services as social security, modern housing, modern sanitation, medical care and health information, rest and health camps, educational facilities of all types, libraries, theaters, and movies.

Only if agriculture has a sane, over-all, planned development, Lombardo has reasoned, will the nation have the basis for a sound industrialization. For only by means of industrialization will Mexico become a truly independent nation.[26]

Vital to the industrialization of Mexico is the development of transportation and communications and the extension of credit facilities. Lombardo has praised government accomplishments in transportation and communications, especially in the construction by 1960 of over 43,000 kilometers of roads and highways and in the construction of national telegraph and telephone networks.[27] He also has listed a number of shortcomings which have persisted over the years in these fields: persistence largely in its original pattern of a railroad network constructed to serve the needs of foreign enterprises exploiting Mexico's exportable raw materials; reduction of rates for the transportation of certain exportable commodities; shortages of equipment aggravated by failure of national industry to supply the needs of the railroads; construction of too many large highways for Mexico's needs "in accordance with a plan suggested by the interests of the United States";[28] lack of sufficient highways and railroads connecting the Gulf and Pacific coasts of Mexico; "lack of coordination between the highways and railroads which serve principally the production and the distribution of goods in the interior of the country";[29] shortage of connecting roads; insufficiently developed merchant marine; shortage of ports for Mexican coastal trade; and monopolization of telephone communications by an international corporation.[30]

Progress, he admits, has been made in the field of banking and credit. In 1925, the government-controlled Bank of Mexico was created with the power to issue money and to control money supplies, foreign exchange, and interest rates. Subsequently, a num-

26. Cogent summaries of Lombardo's proposals for improved agricultural development are to be found in his *Qué Ha Sido la Reforma Agraria*, pp. 11-18 and in his *La Reforma Agraria en China y en México*, pp. 43-45.
27. Lombardo Toledano, *Carta*, pp. 48-49.
28. Partido Popular, *Tesis*, p. 71.
29. *Ibid.*, pp. 71-72.
30. *Ibid.*, pp. 71-75.

ber of banks were created to provide credit to *ejidatarios* and small proprietors and to town and state governments. Investments made by the Nacional Financiera, or government investment institution, have helped to industrialize the nation.[31] On the other hand, the control of money and credit by state institutions has not been complete enough to direct all public and private credit into productive activities so as to prevent usurious and superfluous extensions of credit. The state has not established, he argues, a general control over the activities of the many private banks of the nation, nor has it prevented the foundation of banks devoted exclusively to "lucrative transactions."[32] Finally, as noted previously, credit facilities are completely inadequate for the great mass of Mexico's farmers.[33]

The development of industry in Mexico has proceeded rapidly in the last generation. In 1950, for the first time in the history of Mexico, the value of industrial production was greater than that of agricultural and mining production combined.[34] The industrial revolution in Mexico, however, suffers from two primary defects which threaten to detain its development: a limited and inelastic domestic demand for industrial products (due partially to the limited development of agricultural production) and a severe competition from foreign products.[35]

In regard to the lack of effective demand, Lombardo has noted that the process of industrialization has benefited materially only a minority of the population composed mainly of the bourgeoisie, the urban petty bourgeoisie, and some sectors of the rural petty bourgeoisie. The remainder of the population "only very occasionally consumes the multiple products of national industry."[36] In brief, there has been little improvement in the level of living of the majority of the Mexican people since the revolution. Increasing costs of living (especially since 1940) have caused a loss of real wages to many Mexicans.[37] An example of the great inequality in income distribution is provided in the following data: In 1955, the average annual income per family of 50,000 families

31. Lombardo Toledano, *Carta*, pp. 52-54.
32. Partido Popular, *Tesis*, p. 69.
33. *Ibid.*, pp. 68-71.
34. Lombardo Toledano, *Carta*, pp. 45-46.
35. Lombardo Toledano, *Objetivos y Táctica*, p. 48; *El Fracaso Actual*, pp. 14-15.
36. Lombardo Toledano, *Objectivos y Táctica*, p. 48.
37. Lombardo Toledano, *La Perspectiva de México*, pp. 46-50.

was more than Mex$300,000; of 200,000 families, between Mex$50,-000 and Mex$100,000; of one million families, between Mex$5,000 and Mex$15,000; of 7 million families, between Mex$1,000 and Mex$3,000.[38] The distribution of income constantly is becoming more unequal.[39]

This decline in the resources of the Mexican masses in recent years is the direct result primarily of the decline in the purchasing power of the Mexican peso because of successive devaluations. The devaluations have occurred as a consequence of Mexico's situation as a semicolonial country—as an exporter of raw materials and an importer of capital goods and investment capital. Mexico suffers a balance-of-exchange crisis whenever there is a serious decline in prices of Mexican raw-material exports, especially if the decline is accompanied by a rise in import prices and a flight of capital from Mexico. The peso is devalued as a measure to solve the crisis.[40]

The second factor which threatens Mexican industrial development, that of foreign competition, has been an increasing source of danger. The competition comes from two sources: goods produced in the United States and imported into Mexico at low cost as a consequence of inadequate tariff barriers, and goods produced in Mexico by American-owned enterprises. These enterprises threaten to dominate the domestic market. Furthermore, they hinder the national capitalization of industry as the major portion of their profits are exported.[41]

An additional obstacle to industrial development lies in the government's financial policies which have failed to divert sufficient public and private credit from speculative investments to reproductive investments.[42]

Lombardo has made specific criticisms of some of Mexico's industries. His major and often-reiterated criticism is that Mexico's heavy industry has but a limited development. Unless there is a planned and rapid development of a capital-goods industry Mexico will never achieve economic independence from foreign nations nor will it ever achieve the mechanization of agriculture or

38. Partido Popular, *Tesis*, p. 77.
39. *Ibid.*, pp. 75-77.
40. Lombardo Toledano, *La Tercera Devaluación*, pp. 1-13, *passim*.
41. Lombardo Toledano, *Objetivos y Táctica*, p. 48; *El Fracaso Actual*, pp. 14-15; *Carta*, pp. 60-62.
42. Lombardo Toledano, *Objetivos y Táctica*, p. 48.

an advanced development of manufacturing, transportation, and communications.[43]

Although the Mexican petroleum industry has developed rapidly, it has not kept pace with the growing national demand for petroleum derivatives. The inequality between production and demand threatens the entire development of the national economy. Several factors have contributed to this inefficiency: the superabundance of employees in the industry owing to political favoritism; the lack of integration within the industry as some of its functions, such as exploration and distribution, are in private hands; and the necessity of purchasing abroad at high cost machinery, equipment, and primary materials required by the industry.[44]

Except in coal and iron, foreign capital still completely dominates the mining industry; hence Mexicans can only play the role of secondary and subsidiary producers. "If this situation should continue, the industrialization of Mexico will be difficult or impossible."[45] There are no extensive geologic surveys of mineral deposits of the nation and there is no national bank especially designed to stimulate the mining industry.[46]

Lombardo cogently summarized the problems of Mexican industry as follows:

> Now industrial production is more important, by volume, than mineral and agricultural production combined. But its rhythm has descended in recent years.
>
> Because the poverty of the countryside has restricted the internal market.
>
> Because the lowering of the purchasing power of the working class and of the sectors of fixed income also has restricted the domestic market.
>
> Because we have begun to industrialize without producing machines.
>
> Because we have to acquire capital goods from outside and we do not totally pay for them with what we export.

43. Partido Popular, *Tesis*, pp. 40-42.
44. *Ibid.*, pp. 27-34.
45. *Ibid.*, p. 34.
46. *Ibid.*, pp. 34-36.

Because, in short, we want to progress without the progress of the people and without the progress of the nation. This is the great drama of our productive system.[47]

Mexico's increasing state capitalism, on the other hand, has been a progressive force in developing the nation's productive forces, in supplying capital for investment in areas where private capital resources are insufficient, and in promoting national economic independence. A number of industries have been nationalized: electric energy, petroleum, petrochemicals, agricultural fertilizers, coal and iron supplies, the major part of the iron and steel industry, and railroad-car manufacturing. In addition, the government owns many manufacturing and assembly plants, including sugar mills and textile and newsprint factories. Transportation and communications facilities, railroads, telecommunications, and part of civil aviation have been nationalized. The state stepped into the field of social insurance with the formation of the Administration of Civil Pensions for government employees in 1925 and extended its activities in 1944 with the founding of the Mexican Institute of Social Security. The latter serviced 3,547,769 registrants in 1960.[48]

According to Lombardo the solution to the many problems of Mexican industry (as well as of other areas of the economy) lies in increased state planning and nationalization. This is necessary in order to co-ordinate the development of agriculture and industry, to co-ordinate the growth of consumer income and production, to have available ample supplies of capital to be invested in the areas of the economy most critical to over-all development, and to free Mexico from its semicolonial status by ending the nation's dependence upon foreign investment capital and upon the sale of raw materials and the purchase of capital goods in foreign markets.

47. Lombardo Toledano, *El Drama de México*, p. 11.
48. Lombardo Toledano, *Carta*, pp. 50-52.

IV. The Social and Political Structure of Mexico

Vicente Lombardo Toledano conceives Mexican society to be divided into seven social classes.[1] A social class, according to Lombardo, is "fundamentally an economic category.... One can affirm that the strength of social classes can be measured by the [amount of] property or [the right of] appropriation which each has in respect to the instruments of economic production and exchange."[2]

The first and dominant social class is the "bourgeoisie in power"[3] which controls the state and sustains Mexico's system of state capitalism. Second, there exists the bourgeoisie which is independent of the state and dedicated to private agricultural, pastoral, and industrial production. Thirdly, there is the private banking and large commercial bourgeoisie, "the bourgeoisie which manages the credit of private individuals by way of deposits and of commercial operations and of the transactions on the Stock Exchange and, also, through the means which it uses in the commercial affairs of the internal market."[4] The fourth and fifth social classes in Mexico, Lombardo maintains, are the rural petty bourgeoisie composed of *ejidatarios* and small proprietors and the urban petty bourgeoisie of small industrialists, professionals, artisans, and others. The working class constitutes the sixth. The seventh is composed "of the agents of the foreign enterprises which operate in our country."[5]

Lombardo has stressed the importance to working class revolutionaries of understanding the true nature of the portion of the bourgeoisie which represents state capitalism. He emphatically denies that this class is merely a representative of imperialism or similar to the comprador bourgeoisie of the Chinese republic.

1. Partido Popular, *III Asamblea*, pp. 72-73; Vicente Lombardo Toledano, *Democracia y Partidos Políticos* (Mexico, 1957), pp. 7-8.
2. Partido Popular, *III Asamblea*, pp. 72-73.
3. *Ibid.*, p. 73.
4. *Ibid.*
5. *Ibid.*

Rather, it is "timorous, vacillating, contradictory"[6] and therefore it is not a revolutionary social class.[7] "Sometimes it yields to the pressure of internal democratic opinion and takes advanced steps. Other times it yields to the pressure of imperialism and restrains the process of the independent development of the country."[8] From this analysis stems the long-established policy of Lombardo and the Partido Popular Socialista to support what are considered the positive policies of the Mexican government and to criticize the negative policies.[9]

The "agents of imperialism" include some members of the political bureaucracy and "businessmen dedicated to foreign commerce and to the exploitation of the natural resources of the country."[10] The activities of United States imperialism and its agents Lombardo sees as having stimulated a strong sense of anti-imperialist unity among the other sectors of the population.[11]

The various elements of the middle class, the small industrialists, the artisans, the public employees, the small merchants, and their like, "receive nothing but injuries; no advantage, no stimulus, no protection; [they are] exploited by the more powerful, [and are] despised by those below them."[12] These elements are especially in need of ample and easy credit and lower taxes.[13]

Middle-class intellectuals have been the subject of frequent critical characterizations by Lombardo. On one occasion, for example, Lombardo claimed that many intellectuals realize that the future of humanity lies in socialism, but they wish to achieve socialism "quickly and without obstacles...without personal sacrifices, without exposing their possessions or their lives." Lombardo went on to note that the mediocre intellectual is characterized by concern for his personal security. Consequently, he wants to be a revolutionary with the applause of the bourgeoisie, an anti-imperialist with the approval of the United States government; an anticleric without provoking the wrath of the church; and a

6. *Ibid.*, p. 76.
7. *Ibid.*, pp. 76-77; Lombardo Toledano, *Objectivos y Táctica*, p. 45.
8. Partido Popular, *III Asamblea*, p. 76.
9. *Ibid.*, p. 20; Lombardo Toledano, *Teoría y Práctica*, p. 112.
10. Vicente Lombardo Toledano, *La Evolución de México*, pp. 23-24.
11. *Ibid.*
12. Vicente Lombardo Toledano, *Por Vez Primera en la Historia Contemporanea de Nuestro País la Revolución está en la Oposición al Gobierno* (Mexico, 1952), p. 19.
13. *Ibid.*; Partido Popular, *Tesis*, pp. 91-93.

militant leader of the working class without endangering his social relationships with the exploiters of the working class. The mediocre intellectual is concerned over the future when his concern is futile and is "a fugitive from the struggle when the fight against reaction requires soldiers who give something more than their biological presence: the example of intellectual honesty."[14]

These and similar criticisms centering around the instability and unreliability of middle-class intellectuals as socialist revolutionaries have been directed by Lombardo against some of his former associates, such as Enrique Ramírez y Ramírez and Victor Manuel Villaseñor, and most of the members of the leftist Movimiento Nacional Revolucionario (MNR) and the Mexican Communist party.[15]

The working class is the only genuinely revolutionary class in the nation, Lombardo holds; its task is to advance Mexico to socialism. The labor union in capitalist nations is the principal form of organization of the working class in its daily struggles for its rights. Lombardo conceives labor unions as united fronts of the working class independent of state and business control. The united front of labor includes workers of all varieties of political and religious belief who have joined together and democratically elected leaders to defend their common interests against the capitalist class. The workers are organized in unions according to their peculiar branch of production or of service; these unions are in turn united into labor centrals. Organized thus, the collective power of the workers is qualitatively greater than the quantitative sum of the powers of the individual workers. Finally, unions are centers of political education and orientation, of sharpening of class consciousness. They are not, however, and should not pretend to be, political parties, although they may and should make political demands and manifestations. The ultimate attainment of political power by the working class is the function of an organized proletarian political party (the PPS) which is distinct from the unions.[16]

The ideal of working-class unity of which Lombardo speaks

14. Vicente Lombardo Toledano, *Ante la Crisis de Hungria* (Mexico, 1956), pp. 52-53.
15. Opinions expressed to the author by Vicente Lombardo Toledano in April 1962.
16. Lombardo Toledano, *Teoría y Práctica*, pp. 44-46, 95-98, 101-102, *passim*.

was approached in the 1930's with the formation of the Confederación de Trabajadores de México (CTM) in 1936 and of the Confederación de Trabajadores de América Latina (CTAL) in 1938. Both labor centrals were headed by Lombardo and both were independent from government control. The CTM, possessed of a great unitary and combative spirit, seriously concerned itself with thoroughly examining the real problems of Mexico and with contributing to their solution. It lent its full support to the formation of the popular front political party, the Partido de la Revolución Mexicana (PRM), and to the promotion of the revolutionary policies of the Cárdenas regime (land reform, formation of agricultural and industrial co-operatives, nationalization of petroleum).[17]

This unity and revolutionary militancy was gradually destroyed, however, Lombardo states, by the combined actions of "the employer's class, the betrayer politicians... the agents of imperialism,"[18] and the press as part of the "anticommunism" campaign of the Cold War. The long conditioning to paternalism of the peasants and workers contributed to the success of the campaign. These elements traditionally had looked to the president rather than to their own independent class struggle for the satisfaction of their wants and the protection of their rights.[19]

According to Lombardo, a beginning to the antilabor movement was made during World War II as Mexico's conservative elements took advantage of wartime policies of national unity and of Lombardo's frequent absences from Mexico to promote allied unity in Latin America to further their own selfish interests. Later the rightists achieved their greatest successes during the presidency of Miguel Alemán (1946-1952). The government openly intervened in internal union affairs and imposed union directors of its choosing; labor leaders became corrupted pawns of the government. Laws were passed (such as the amendment to the law of "social dissolution")[20] which enabled the government to persecute militant, class-conscious labor leaders. As a consequence, the labor movement was divided into a number of mutually

17. *Ibid.*, pp. 70-80; Lombardo Toledano, *La Evolución de México*, p. 21; Betty Kirk, *Covering the Mexican Front*, pp. 83-84.
18. Vicente Lombardo Toledano, *La Evolución de México*, p. 21.
19. *Ibid.*, p. 23.
20. See Vicente Lombardo Toledano, "Alegato en Favor de Siqueiros," *Siempre!*, CDLXVII (May 30, 1962), 20.

hostile fragments. This division persisted in spite of the subsequent attempt to unite labor into a progovernment labor central, the Bloque de Unidad Obrera (BUO).[21]

The break in the unity of the labor movement, Lombardo argues, resulted in loss of union democracy, in the corruption of most union leaders, in the disorientation of the unions from their objective of class struggle, in the constant decline in the real income of workers, and in the loss by the working class of its former powerful influence in stating and in meeting national problems and popular demands.[22]

In 1957, Lombardo summarized the conditions which had prevailed in the labor movement for many years. These conditions included lack of unity and of democratic practices in the internal functioning of the unions; the perennial domination of the unions by a handful of leaders who muzzle the workers' demands; control of the workers through threats of loss of work if they protest their leaders' actions; obligatory participation of the workers in the official party, the Partido Revolucionario Institucional (PRI); forced attendance of workers of all categories at important state-sponsored ceremonies; constant decreases in the workers' real incomes; limited struggle for economic demands; and the imposition in labor-capital relationships of the concept that an augment of 10 per cent in nominal wages is adequate whenever collective contracts are renegotiated, regardless of the fact that the cost of living generally has increased by a much greater percentage.[23]

A spirit of militancy and of desire for unity was renewed within the labor movement during the López Mateos administration (1958-1964). The new combativeness was evidenced in the railroad strikes of 1959 (broken by the government with the arrest of its leaders, some of whom were still in jail in 1962) and in the inner turmoils of the Sindicato Nacional de Trabajadores de la Educación (SNTE). Lombardo, however, is very critical of the tactics employed by the union leaders in these affairs. Their tactics, he has claimed, were anarchistic, opportunistic, and ultraradical to the point of harming the workers' struggle and serving the cause of reaction. Thus, he argues, the railroad union was thoroughly smashed as a consequence of its extreme action in dis-

21. Lombardo Toledano, *Teoría y Práctica*, pp. 82-95.
22. *Ibid.*, pp. 290-291.
23. Partido Popular, *Tesis*, p. 82.

regarding the government declaration that its strike was "illegal."

The newly elected radical leadership of Section IX of SNTE was defeated in 1960 and alienated from the other sections of the labor central when it attempted immediately to usurp by fiat the authority of the entire national union. In neither case was the major need of the labor movement served: the need for unity.[24]

In 1962, Lombardo summarized his view of what should be the major characteristics and goals of labor unity. A unified labor movement should be characterized by independence from the state and the capitalists; acceptance of the principle of class struggle and defense of the interests of all the workers regardless of their political, religious, or other beliefs; democratic practices in internal union affairs; promotion, vigilance, and protection of nationalized industries and services; struggle for the economic development of Mexico with independence from foreign control; and establishment of relations with the labor unions of the world regardless of their political affiliations.[25]

The tactics which best promote unity are relatively simple, Lombardo maintains, but they require honesty, perserverance, responsibility, and complete devotion to the cause of labor in those who would pursue them consistently. The only way to replace reformist and opportunist union leaders and to revive the militant revolutionary orientation of the unions is to work from within the unions with patience and determination until the mass of the union members, as a consequence of an increase in their class consciousness, act to remove their false leaders and replace them with revolutionaries who genuinely represent their interests. Not by manipulations or by suicidal strikes but only by this hardearned democratic mass movement of the workers can genuine revolutionary unity be achieved.[26]

Unity within the working class is an essential step toward unity among all the popular, democratic, anti-imperialist elements in Mexico. The action of a unified popular front is necessary in order to establish a People's Democracy in Mexico. The People's

24. Lombardo Toledano, *Teoría y Práctica*, pp. 91-95, 125-131, *passim*; Partido Popular, *La Situación Política de México con Motivo del Conflicto Ferrocarrilero* (Mexico, 1959), pp. 31-52.
25. Vicente Lombardo Toledano, "No es la Hora de Buscar Culpables," *Siempre!*, CDLXV (May 16, 1962), 19.
26. Lombardo Toledano, *Teoría y Práctica*, pp. 95-98, 102-105, 148-149, 150, 167, *passim*.

Democracy will serve as the basis for the construction of socialism.[27] Lombardo has emphasized that "with the exception of the banker bourgeoisie and of the agents of foreign enterprises, the social classes in our country, in greater or lesser proportion and within them only some of the sectors which form them, are susceptible of contributing to the formation of the Democratic and Patriotic National Front."[28] It is important to note that Lombardo considers that sectors of the "bourgeoisie in power" (representing state capitalism) are capable of participating in the popular front. This interpretation—which as noted previously leads to the policy of supporting the positive and criticizing the negative actions of the government—is a major source of contention between Lombardo and the Mexican Communist party.[29]

Related to Lombardo's interpretations of Mexican society are his opinions on women's rights, the protection of Indian communities, the problems of youth, and the problem of population growth. Considerable progress has been made recently in women's rights as women have been accorded the ballot in local (1952) and in national (1958) elections. Inequalities persist, nevertheless, which Lombardo thinks should be rectified, such as the discriminatory features of the Code of Commerce which require a married woman to have the formal authorization of her husband in order to engage in business.[30]

Official government policy is one of protection and promotion of the interests of the Indians. In practice, however, this policy has been limited largely to the promotion of folklore. Most of the Indian communities have been abandoned completely by the government and progress is slow in the few regions where they are helped. Mexico continues to be what it always has been: a country in which a dominant minority oppresses a number of native communities. The government, Lombardo contends, should act vigorously to prevent encroachments upon the rights of the Indians to land and to local self-government.[31] The problem of suppressed

27. Partido Popular, *III Asamblea*, p. 20.
28. *Ibid.*, p. 74.
29. *Ibid.*, pp. 76-78. A recent publication of Lombardo's, *El Frente Nacional Democrátic* (Mexico, 1964), reproduces a number of speeches, articles, and interviews in which Lombardo elaborates upon his concept of the national, anti-imperialist front.
30. Partido Popular, *Tesis*, pp. 99-101.
31. *Ibid.*, pp. 87-88; Lombardo Toledano, *Por Vez Primera*, p. 18; Vicente Lombardo Toledano, *Un Viaje al Mundo del Porvenir* (Mexico, 1936), p. 118.

communities will not be solved completely, however, until there exists in Mexico "a proletarian government similar to that of the Soviet Union."[32]

Beyond the sovietization of Mexico, Lombardo has made five proposals for a solution to Mexico's problem of native communities.[33] (1) A political reorganization must be undertaken in order to eliminate artificial divisions and to organize ethnic groups into homogeneous districts. (2) The ethnic groups must be granted complete political autonomy under native authorities. (3) The various ethnic groups must become literate in their respective native languages, to which end alphabets must be constructed for those languages for which this has not yet been done. (4) The sources of economic production in areas inhabited by ethnic groups must be developed. (5) Private property in land must be eliminated and agricultural production must be completely collectivized and mechanized in areas inhabited by ethnic groups. Outsiders must be prohibited from residing in these zones, and the aesthetic, physical, and military education of these ethnic groups must be promoted "under the protection of the industrial proletariat."[34]

Lombardo made a practical contribution to the realization of the third proposal when in 1931 he completed work on his doctoral dissertation, entitled: *Geografía de las Lenguas de la Sierra de Puebla*.[35] Lombardo became especially interested in this topic when he was told by a rural school teacher that Indians learned much more slowly than others. This, the teacher claimed, was due to their natural stupidity. Lombardo thought otherwise; he undertook his study in order to contribute to an effective technique for instructing the Indians. The technique, similar to that used by Spanish missionaries in the sixteenth century, consisted in provided alphabets for the native languages in order to make the Indians literate in their own tongues, at the same time teaching them Spanish.[36]

The problems of youth have not only not been attended to but it is officially denied that such problems exist. A great restlessness

32. Lombardo Toledano, *Un Viaje al Mundo del Porvenir*, p. 119.
33. *Ibid.*, pp. 119-120.
34. *Ibid.*, p. 120.
35. Vicente Lombardo Toledano, *Geografía de las Lenguas de la Sierra de Puebla* (Mexico, 1931).
36. Information supplied personally to the author by Vicente Lombardo Toledano in April 1962.

and anxiety has come over Mexican youth in recent years owing to the insecurity of life, especially in regard to the future. There are few opportunities available to youths either in the *ejidos*, in the factories, in government service, or in the crafts. Educational facilities are inadequate. Thousands can attain neither work nor education and therefore remain, often in great destitution, dependent upon their parents. The great majority of youth lives completely without facilities to stimulate and to develop their aesthetic sense, their intelligence, and their physical health.[37]

Lombardo has pointed out that the rate of population increase in Mexico has become one of the highest in the world. The annual rate of increase advanced from an average of 1.4 per cent from 1895 to 1910 to 2 per cent from 1930 to 1940, to 3.1 per cent from 1941 to 1950, to 3.4 per cent from 1950 to 1960.[38] Lombardo has emphasized that "if the rhythm of production does not exceed, with ample margin, the demographic increase and does not anticipate the future, the economic progress of the country will be detained, creating grave problems of every order."[39]

Lombardo has continued to the present his lifelong concern for the problems of Mexican education. He has praised some aspects of the work of the revolution in education, such as the organization and extension of rural and secondary schools, the creation of the Instituto Politécnico Nacional in 1937, and the implementation of Article 3 of the Constitution of 1917 which prohibits religious corporations from establishing or directing primary schools.[40] Lombardo staunchly supported the amendment of this article in 1934 to provide that education must be "socialist" in character. His arguments indicated his new Marxist orientation: educational systems are historical products determined in each case by a given set of property relationships. They serve to help perpetuate these relationships and hence also to preserve the domination of the ruling social class. Therefore education in a capitalist society cannot be completely socialist in character in the sense that it teaches dialectical materialism, the materialist conception of history, and the theory of class struggle. It can, however, achieve a semisocialist orientation in such a socie-

37. Partido Popular, *Tesis*, pp. 101-104.
38. Lombardo Toledano, *Carta*, pp. 59-60.
39. *Ibid.*, p. 60.
40. *Ibid.*, pp. 55-58.

ty. It is of crucial importance that revolutionaries promote such an orientation, because education can play a basic role in creating proletarian class consciousness—a fundamental prerequisite to the establishment of a proletarian regime. At the same time, the promotion by some of a peculiar "Mexican socialism" must be thwarted as this "socialism" is really only a form of fascism.[41]

In 1946, Article 3 was amended again; the proviso that education be "socialist" was removed. Lombardo is lenient in his judgment of this action, though, because the new amendment retained the sanctions against the imparting of religious doctrines in education and reasserted the predominant role of the state in establishing the educational norms of the nation.[42]

In spite of his praise for its achievements, Lombardo has criticized Mexico's system of education from top to bottom: Mexican education has lost both its revolutionary orientation and the professional dedication of its teachers; it has become merely an administrative and bureaucratic function. Mexico lacks a scientific pedagogy to serve as a basis for action and development. This is particularly evidenced by the general Mexican practice of uncritically copying from the United States system. Lombardo has pointed out that the needs of Mexico in respect to national development and also the psychology of the Mexican students are different from those of the United States. He has criticized the use of American-developed tests in Mexican schools and, further, has questioned the value of such tests in themselves. In this regard, he especially has questioned the value of multiple-choice, fill-in, and true-and-false tests as means for developing the critical powers and the creativity of students. Furthermore, he has claimed that American education is itself in a crisis and hence serves as a poor model. Among other things, American education is unable to develop adequate numbers of excellent scientists and is falling behind the Soviet Union in this respect.[43]

Mexican primary education has long been superficial and inferior; it has become more so as United States pedagogical methods have been copied, Lombardo mentions. There is an acute shortage

41. Vicente Lombardo Toledano, *La Doctrina Socialista y su Interpretación en el Artículo 3°*, pp. 4, 12-13, 23, 25-27, 41-42.
42. Lombardo Toledano, *Carta*, pp. 57-58.
43. Vicente Lombardo Toledano, *Una Ojeada a la Crisis de la Educación en México* (Mexico, 1958), pp. 4-7, 10-12; Lombardo Toledano, *Teoría y Práctica*, pp. 142-143.

of schools and teachers: there were only 75,000 primary school teachers in 1958, whereas double that number were needed. Some 50,000 of the 88,850 villages of Mexico lack schools and teachers. Textbooks—and this applies to all levels of education—frequently are selected and changed not in order to meet the criteria of scientific planning but rather in order to favor certain authors "for reasons not exactly pedagogical."[44]

Beginning in the 1920's, secondary schools were developed in Mexico on the model of the American high school. The model, however, Lombardo claims was not adapted to Mexican needs nor, what is worse, was it integrally linked "pedagogically and functionally"[45] with the primary school. The subjects taught were not tied rationally with one another nor were they offered to the student in a logically integrated sequence. The decline in the quality of primary education has necessarily caused a decline in that of secondary education; both suffer from a superficiality which is compounded by use of poor testing methods. The manual training offered in secondary schools is totally inadequate to prepare the student for any practical occupation.[46]

The inadequacies of primary and secondary education can be seen in the facts that only 11 per cent of those students who finish primary school enter secondary school; that 76 per cent of those registered do not complete more than one year of secondary education; and that only 37 per cent of those who complete secondary education enter preparatory school.[47]

Rural schools are insufficient in number and are lacking in personnel. Lombardo objects to the fact that rural teachers do not have the revolutionary missionary spirit of earlier days; rather, many are corrupted spiritually and for personal—frequently monetary—ends are leagued with regional politicians. They have lost consciousness of their high duty as educators.[48]

The National Preparatory School, a distinctive Mexican institution created by Benito Juárez in 1868, is used to complement the six years of primary education with five years of study preparatory to university training. The school once provided a broad education, including a solid founding in the sciences. This advanced

44. Lombardo Toledano, *Una Ojeada*, pp. 4-7, 32, 35.
45. *Ibid.*, p. 8.
46. *Ibid.*, pp. 4, 8-12, 32.
47. *Ibid.*, pp. 9-10.
48. Lombardo Toledano, *Teoría y Práctica*, pp. 142-143.

nature of the preparatory school has been lost as its curriculum has been changed to emphasize the arts and to make the subjects of the sciences secondary and elective. Its specialists in disciplines have been replaced by specialists in methodology and its standards have been lowered to meet those of the primary school. The preparatory school degree (the Bachillerato) has not been standardized nationally. As a consequence, considerable variations have arisen in the quality of the education imparted in the preparatories of the various states owing to the differing (and usually inadequate) financial and personnel resources of the schools.[49]

The defects in primary and secondary education derive not only from the shortage of schools, teachers, and economic resources, but also from a prolonged crisis in the normal school system, says Lombardo. The normal schools are of low caliber. They impart to the students an imperfect knowledge of nature, social life, science, and technology; methodology is emphasized at the expense of knowledge of the disciplines to be taught. The methodology tends to emphasize routine and memorizing in the learning process, both of which underestimate and stultify the powers of abstract and original thought of the students. Furthermore, teaching as a profession lacks sufficient attraction in terms of economic rewards and social prestige. As a consequence, many use the normal school and teaching merely as a stepping stone to the professions; only those who cannot so aspire remain in the elementary school. Finally, the federal government partially has given up the control over the nature and forms of education warranted it by Article 3 of the constitution in that it permits (in 1958) some 43 private normal schools, generally religious in nature, to operate upon their own standards and methods; the state has but 29 schools.[50]

The improvement of technical education requires not only a reorganization of the Instituto Politécnico Nacional (the major technical school in Mexico) but also a planning and co-ordination of the functions and of the development of the various types of technical schools in the nation. These schools exist presently in a state of anarchy. Some are run as private enterprises while others are under the authority of various departments and institutions of the national government or of provincial governments. All these

49. Lombardo Toledano, *Una Ojeada*, pp. 13-17, 32.
50. *Ibid.*, pp. 18-21, 32.

institutions must be co-ordinated directly with the developmental needs of Mexico.[51]

The facilities of universities and other institutions of higher learning generally are inadequate and are available only to the socially privileged.[52] This situation has not been alleviated by the establishment—in imitation of the United States—of a number of universities throughout Mexico. If judged by the criteria of a genuine university, however, then "being generous" only two or three of these new schools may be considered true institutions of higher learning. These criteria are: a high level of instruction, a superior caliber of teachers, and an ability to stimulate and develop the intellectual activities and capabilities of its students in pace with the most advanced development of human thought. Instead of permitting the creation of numerous universities of low quality and few economic resources, the national government rather should plan with the states for the establishment of five or six universities of high quality. The national government must take charge because it is the only source with funds adequate for the task.[53]

In summary, Lombardo criticizes Mexican education for its lack of a scientific theory of education based upon Mexican realities; for the turning of education into an administrative and bureaucratic function; for the loss by many teachers of their revolutionary orientation and professional devotion to the cause of educating the people; for excessive copying of American methods inapplicable to Mexican needs; for the lack of co-ordination between the various educational levels; for a general lowering of educational standards; for a general insufficiency of facilities; for the shortage of rural schools and teachers and for the loss of professional dedication by the latter; for the increased role of the church and of private enterprise in education; for the lack of opportunities for many Mexicans to attain an education, particularly for the limitation to the socially privileged of opportunities for higher education; and for the inadequate training and remuneration of teachers.[54]

The solution to Mexico's crisis in education, Lombardo argues,

51. *Ibid.*, pp. 22-26, 32.
52. Lombardo Toledano, *Por Vez Primera*, p. 19.
53. Lombardo Toledano, *Una Ojeada*, pp. 27-31.
54. *Ibid.*, pp. 32-35; Partido Popular, *Tesis*, pp. 88-91; Lombardo Toledano, *Teoría y Práctica*, pp. 142-143.

lies essentially in the development of a scientific pedagogy adjusted to Mexican needs and in the reassertion by the national government of its constitutional prerogative and obligation to administer, control, and orient Mexican education in the light of the most advanced knowledge of the times. The national government must cease its practice of seeking to increase the number of schools available by the device of permitting religious and other private sources to operate freely in Mexican education. In order to have sufficient financial resources effectively to control and promote education and to develop a scientific pedagogy, the Mexican nation must rapidly industrialize its economy on the basis of the promotion of a heavy industry oriented toward Mexican interests. This basic industrialization will in turn serve to develop agricultural production, light industry, and the services.[55]

Lombardo also has analyzed the characteristics of Mexico's major political parties. Partido Acción Nacional (PAN), Mexico's major rightist and clerical party, represents, in his opinion, the private bankers, the large merchants, and the foreign capitalists and their Mexican associates. The Unión Nacional Sinarquista is a satellite of PAN which serves it "as a note of popular color and as a tribune for demagogic agitation."[56] The Partido Revolucionario Institucional (PRI), which has controlled the government since it was organized in 1946 as the official government party, represents the new bourgeoisie arisen since the revolution. A part of the bourgeoisie, however, is not represented by any party. This includes the Mexican industrialists and a part of the farmers and ranchers; the latter, nevertheless, serve the PRI "circumstantially." The Partido Popular (Socialista) (PP[S])—Lombardo's party—and the Partido Comunista Mexicano (PCM) represent the working class. With the collaboration of elements of other parties, the PP(S) seeks to form a popular front representing the rural and urban working class, the peasantry, the revolutionary intellectuals, the industrialists, the farmers, the cattlemen, and the "progressive elements among the new bourgeoisie leagued with

55. Lombardo Toledano, *Una Ojeada*, pp. 33-35.
56. Lombardo Toledano, *Democracia*, p. 8. In Lombardo's *La Constitución de los Cristeros* (Mexico, 1963), he has made public the constitution which the rightist, Catholic rebels of the late 1920's wished to impose upon the Mexican people. The constitution, together with Lombardo's preliminary remarks, throws much light upon the essence of traditional reactionary and clerical political thought in Mexico.

the Public Power."⁵⁷ Such a political union is feasible because although there are differences within these groups, they nevertheless all share a common antagonism to the operations of imperialist monopolies in Mexico. The object of the union would be to promote national independence, economic development, and political democracy.⁵⁸

Lombardo has contrasted the PP(S) with the PRI and with the PAN. In the former case the difference between the two parties is one of degree; the PP(S) seeks firmly to hasten the development of the revolution while the PRI hesitates and obstructs. In the latter case, however, the difference is one of kind; it is the difference between the revolution and the counterrevolution, "between Morelos and Iturbide, between Juárez and Maximilian, between Zapata and Porfirio Díaz, ... between the mining workers and American Smelting."⁵⁹

Referring to the presidential election in 1958, Lombardo made a statement concerning the PRI which is still valid:

> The PRI must define itself forever prior to the presidential election. We shall see its program, its goals and its candidates. There will prevail in its direction—not officially, of course—either the current of the bourgeoisie which has not surrendered itself to imperialism nor which wishes to liquidate the work of the Reform and thereby politically rehabilitate the clergy, or [there will prevail the current which wishes to] declare that the Revolution has concluded. In the latter event, the better elements of the PRI will add themselves, sooner or later, to the revolutionary opposition, on the side of the parties and the authentic leaders of the people.⁶⁰

Lombardo is severely critical of the corrupt and undemocratic political practices of Mexico. He is most critical of contemporary practices. With the exception of the second period of national control by Calles (1928-1934), the presidents from Venustiano Carranza through Manual Ávila Camacho are not too harshly judged. Cárdenas (1934-1940), he regards as a great man for his promotion of national independence, of higher levels of living, and of demo-

57. Lombardo Toledano, *Democracia*, p. 9.
58. *Ibid.*, pp. 8-10.
59. *Ibid.*, p. 10.
60. *Ibid.*

cratic liberties. Ávila Camacho (1940-1946) is well regarded because of the roles he played in supporting the Allies in World War II and in continuing the Cárdenas tradition of limiting the political activities of the army.[61]

The presidency of Miguel Alemán (1946-1952) marks the end of the age of military *caudillos* and the beginning of the rule of the bureaucratic bourgeoisie (or the "bourgeoisie in power" representing state capitalism). This bureaucratic bourgeoisie, "composed of public functionaries and political, labor union and agrarian *caciques*,"[62] is—with but a few honorable exceptions—thoroughly corrupt. Indeed, it has "made corruption the official method of government."[63] Many public functionaries form business enterprises to which they grant public contracts over which they have official control. They borrow public funds and use the men and machines under their control to develop cattle ranches or agricultural estates on rich lands obtained at little or no cost through their political influence. Many of the newly irrigated lands have fallen under their control. Members of the bureaucratic bourgeoisie have bought shares in all the most lucrative business enterprises in the nation; political favorites own most of the important buildings in Mexico City. In short, either through "the direct sacking of public coffers or by utilization of the state apparatus to facilitate the attainment of their purposes, the parasitic bourgeoisie has obtained fabulous fortunes which would have horrified previous rulers."[64] The wealth, luxury, and ostentation of the numerically small bureaucratic bourgeoisie is contrasted sharply by the poverty and sobriety of the mass of the Mexican people.[65]

Corruption, he complains, extends everywhere. Labor leaders have generally been bought (or persecuted) as the government has moved to control the labor movement. The peasant communities no longer have democratic reunions to discuss common problems. Rather, the peasants are dominated by leaders who, instead of being renewed periodically in accordance with the Agrarian Code,

61. Lombardo Toledano, *La Perspectiva de México*, pp. 64-67.
62. *Ibid.*, pp. 69-70.
63. *Ibid.*, p. 67.
64. *Ibid.*, p. 70.
65. *Ibid.*, pp. 69-72; Lombardo Toledano, *El Régimen Actual*, pp. 5-9; *Por Vez Primera*, pp. 19-20.

stay in office for many years at the service of political bosses and their cohorts.[66]

The administration of justice is thoroughly corrupt. "Justice has to be bought: first, from the gendarme, then from the public ministry, then from the judge, then from the mayor (*alcalde*), then from the deputy, then from the governor, then from the minister, then from the Secretary of State."[67]

Mexico has the forms but not the content of a bourgeois democracy. Lombardo is critical of the practice of bourgeois democracy which on the one hand exalts the citizen as the base, source, and object of state institutions but on the other propagates the idea that politics is the business of a few professionals in the field and consequently is out of the immediate hands of the ordinary person. Many of these professional politicians look upon politics not as a public service but rather as a field for gaining personal advantages of some sort.[68] Lombardo, however, does recognize merit in the advanced bourgeois democracies of the United States, England, and other western European nations, although he criticizes the attack upon traditional liberties in some of these countries. Mexico would do well to follow the example of these nations because it would represent at the least an improvement upon its present system.[69]

Referring to Mexican elections, Lombardo has stated: "The principal defect... of the electoral system... consists in that votes are never counted."[70] Election results are known as soon as the PRI announces its candidates.[71] The Mexican government, in short, "in spite of the constitutional declaration that we are a federal, representative and democratic Republic, is a government of one person, the President of the Republic."[72] The president names the state governors "as if they were confidential employ-

66. Lombardo Toledano, *El Régimen Actual*, pp. 8-9; *La Perspectiva de México*, pp. 68-69.
67. Lombardo Toledano, *Por Vez Primera*, pp. 19-20.
68. Vicente Lombardo Toledano, *El Llanto del Sureste* (Mexico, 1934), pp. 59-61.
69. *El Popular*, June 24, 1950, pp. 3-4.
70. Vicente Lombardo Toledano, *La Sucesión Presidencial de 1958* (Mexico, 1957), p. 31.
71. *Ibid.*, p. 32.
72. Vicente Lombardo Toledano, *Menoscabar la Libertad de Creencia Religiosa es Conspirar contra el Progreso Democrático de México* (Mexico, 1952), p. 10.

ees."[73] The state governors name the deputies to the state legislatures; the state deputies and the governors name the *alcaldes* and *regidores* of the municipal governments (*ayuntamientos*). The deputies to the national congress and the members of the judiciary are designated by the president, by the ministers, or by the governors.[74] The one-man dictatorship is actually becoming worse than in the past as the president through the secretariat of Gobernación increasingly names directly the members of the state legislatures and the municipal councils.[75]

Furthermore, this principal of one-man rule (*caudillismo* or *caciquismo*) extends throughout Mexican society. Union, peasant, and government leaders of all degrees are little *caciques* (chiefs) who dominate their subordinates absolutely and jealously defend their domains against potential usurpers.[76]

As one might expect, there is little freedom for parliamentary criticism in such an undemocratic system, nor is there effective division of governmental powers. The national congress merely ratifies the initiatives of the executive power not only without any opposition but even without any debate so as to improve the initiatives. Similar rubber-stamp policies characterize the other branches of the state organization.[77]

Obstacles are placed upon the development of independent political parties—such as the requirement that in order to be legally registered a political party must have a minimum of 75,000 members. This requirement operates in practice to prevent the Mexican Communist party from officially putting up candidates for political office. Mexico, in reality, is "in a transition stage between the hegemony of caudillos and the development of permanent political parties."[78]

Lombardo and the Partido Popular Socialista make three basic suggestions for the immediate improvement of Mexico's political system. First, they call for a constitutional amendment to lay the foundations for municipal autonomy. Municipal freedom was

73. Lombardo Toledano, *El Régimen Actual*, p. 10.
74. *Ibid.*; Lombardo Toledano, *Por Vez Primera*, pp. 15-17; *La Perspectiva de México*, p. 74.
75. Vicente Lombardo Toledano, *En Torno al XX Congreso del Partido Comunista de la Unión Soviética* (Mexico, 1956), pp. 249-251.
76. Lombardo Toledano, *La Sucesión*, p. 33.
77. Lombardo Toledano, *El Régimen Actual*, p. 10.
78. Lombardo Toledano, *La Sucesión*, p. 35.

one of the most profoundly sought objectives of the revolution, but it was never achieved. The *municipios* must be made more independent economically and granted greater control over local taxation as well as complete control over local elections, which must be free from intervention by state authorities. Second, the public administration should be reorganized to rationalize the uncoordinated maze of government departments and agencies which frequently duplicate and often contradict one another's efforts. Third, the electoral system should be reformed to provide for political democracy on the basis of proportional representation, that is, representation in accordance with the percentage of the total votes received by each political party.[79]

The long-run solution to Mexico's political problems lies in the creation of a proletarian socialist democracy, Lombardo holds. In describing on one occasion how such a system should function, Lombardo claimed that a one-party system would prevail; the single party would be the party of a class, the party of the majority. (Lombardo evidently referred here to a situation in which the working class formed the majority of the population.) In such a system, continued Lombardo, the program of the party serves as a measure of the conduct of the government; the party is always alert to see that its program is followed. Government officials are instruments which the working class utilizes to transform the social system. No public functionary, therefore, has less freedom of action, less chance to err, and less opportunity to betray than the socialist functionary. Not only does the socialist political leader have his path and his goals clearly laid out for him by the party and the workers, but, as an integral member of the revolutionary movement, he should on his own accord seek to realize these goals with greater zeal and conviction than other members of the party.[80]

Associated with the problems of the state are those of the church. Lombardo, personally, is an atheist.[81] He, however, does recognize considerable value in early Christianity. "The philosophy of pristine Christianity, made by slaves, is the first truly humanist conception of history: but it contrasts principally with

79. Partido Popular, *Tesis*, pp. 97-99, 104-113.
80. Lombardo Toledano, *El Llanto del Sureste*, pp. 23-24.
81. Vicente Lombardo Toledano, *Vicente Lombardo Toledano en Nicaragua* (Managua, 1943), p. 32; Lombardo Toledano, *Menoscabar la Libertad*, p. 9.

the Greek because it is a subjective flight from reality."[82] The essence of this Christian humanism is the concept of social justice. Christian charity is but a means to attain social justice in the world. The original concepts of Christianity were corrupted, however, as the religion was institutionalized and became a prop for ruling classes. Christian beliefs were used to justify the continuation of the status quo in class relationships; justice would be meted not in this world but in the life after death. The concept of social justice, nevertheless, has remained an important element of Christian thought. It is the basic unifying link between Christian and socialist thought, even though the former considers the attainment of social justice as fundamentally a moral problem whereas the latter considers it essentially an economic problem—a question of social relationships of production. During World War II, Lombardo used this common desire for social justice as the basis for an appeal for unity among Christians and socialists against fascism and the fascistic "New Christian Order."[83]

Lombardo has been highly critical of the past and present activities of the Catholic church in Mexican politics and education. He has indicated that throughout Mexican history there has been conflict between the church and the state and between the church and broad popular movements. Thus, the church opposed the movements of independence, reform, and the Revolution of 1910. "The Church always has been the enemy of these revolutions, because it always has been the enemy of the progress of Mexico...."[84]

The constitutional restrictions upon the church are the product of this long conflict. The church is forbidden to own property because past experience has demonstrated that economic life is stagnated when the church owns large amounts of real estate. Public religious ceremonies are forbidden because previous experience has shown that they were used as political demonstrations. Church control of primary and secondary schools is prohibited because in the past such schools were used as political instruments

82. Vicente Lombardo Toledano, *Causas de la Elevación del Espíritu Humano* (Mexico, 1960), p. 11.
83. Vicente Lombardo Toledano, *Cristianos y Socialistas Unidos contra la Regresión* (El Paso, Tex., 1943), pp. 14-19, *passim*.
84. Vicente Lombardo Toledano, *El Estado y la Iglesia: La Revolución y la Religión: Progreso y Retroceso* (Mexico, 1943), p. 13.

to indoctrinate students against the lay state and against revolutionary progress.

All of these constitutional norms are being violated. There are many convents in the nation, the church operates a number of schools, public religious processions occur in all parts of the nation, and the church is associated sympathically with the rightist political party, the Partido Acción Nacional (PAN). The objective of this latter alliance is the conquest of political power by all the rightist, antirevolutionary forces in Mexico.[85]

As a solution to the problem of illicit religious activities, Lombardo and the Partido Popular Socialista have proposed merely that the state enforce the constitutional norms which prohibit such activities. They are particularly insistent that the proscriptions against the church in education be obeyed.[86]

One of the principal propaganda weapons of the church and PAN has been the charge that the revolution and religion are diametrically opposed. This has been emphatically denied by Lombardo. Church and state have struggled throughout Mexican history with the consequence that, by the will of the nation, limitations have been placed upon the political activities of the church. Neither the long struggle nor the restrictions were directed against religion per se or against freedom of conscience. This assertion is supported by the fact that the constitution guarantees freedom of conscience and by the fact that many of the leaders of the independence, the reform, and the revolution—such as Hidalgo, Morelos, and Juárez—were believing Catholics.[87] Lombardo summed up his attitude in the following sentence: "In the same manner that there has been a perpetual struggle between Church and state, there has never existed a struggle between the Revolution and Religion."[88]

Lombardo personally has declared his complete respect for freedom of conscience and for the free functioning of the Catholic church in Mexico as a religious association of the faithful. Speaking before a crowd of over 100,000 people in Mexico City in 1943 on the occasion of the thirty-third anniversary of the Mexican revolution, Lombardo summed up the position of the Confedera-

85. *Ibid.*, pp. 10-11, 15-16.
86. Partido Popular, *Razón Histórica*, pp. 13-14.
87. Lombardo Toledano, *El Estado y la Iglesia*, pp. 12-16, *passim*.
88. *Ibid.*, p. 13.

ción de Trabajadores de México on freedom of conscience as follows: "the Mexican Revolution should defend freedom of conscience today, tomorrow, always. If one day a sectarian government should be organized in Mexico which attacks freedom of conscience, the organized Mexican proletariat would fight and would give its blood to reconquer freedom of conscience in our country."[89] Again, speaking in Mazatlán during the 1952 presidential campaign, Lombardo said: "I, who am an atheist, who have no religious belief, have declared on one occasion and now I repeat it, that on the day in which in my country there should be a government that tries to abolish freedom of religious conscience, I would take up arms to restore religious freedom...."[90]

There is, of course, no contradiction between Lombardo's atheism and his staunch defense of freedom of religious conscience. The latter is one of the fundamental human rights without which there could be no genuine social democracy.[91] Lombardo, as a Marxist, thinks that religion gradually will fade away as science progresses and as social relationships are improved in a socialist society.[92]

89. *Ibid.*, p. 15.
90. Lombardo Toledano, *Menoscabar la Libertad*, p. 9.
91. *Ibid.*
92. Lombardo Toledano, *Escritos Filosóficos*, pp. 169-170.

V. A People's Democracy and Socialism: The New Humanism

As we have seen, Vicente Lombardo Toledano has made many specific criticisms of the Mexican Revolution. This chapter will examine Lombardo's general views on the positive and negative aspects of the revolution and on the means for continuing the pursuit of the revolutionary ideals. These views are gathered from expressions of opinion made by Lombardo over a period of time. Lombardo agreed in 1962, however, that they were representative of his thinking at that time.

Lombardo believes that the Mexican Revolution is essentially a bourgeois revolution. Its major achievements, such as the adoption of the Constitution of 1917, were attained as a consequence of the alliance between the governing revolutionary petty bourgeoisie and the workers and peasants. The revolution, however, is not completely comparable to the bourgeois revolutions of the eighteenth and nineteenth centuries because it occurred in the twentieth century during the era of capitalist imperialism. Capitalist imperialism had penetrated Mexico to a considerable extent in the latter nineteenth and early twentieth centuries. As a consequence, the Mexican Revolution was not only democratic and antifeudal, but also was anti-imperialist. In this sense it is linked with all the anticolonial movements of this century.[1]

The goals of the revolution—democracy, national independence, higher levels of living through economic development—have not yet been achieved. The revolution has gone through periods of progression and retrogression. But the revolution continues, as it must, because it is the "genuine and direct fruit of the popular demands of our country."[2]

The positive achievements of the revolution, he has recognized, have been many. The semifeudal hacienda system has been destroyed and great amounts of land have been distributed to the

1. Lombardo Toledano, *Carta*, pp. 38-44; *La Evolución de México*, pp. 4-7; *Teoría y Práctica*, pp. 112-113.
2. Lombardo Toledano, *La Reforma Agraria*, p. 1; *Por Vez Primera*, pp. 1-8.

peasants and agricultural workers. Agricultural production has been increased and diversified. Domestic demand has increased as the level of living of the rural masses has increased. New industries have been developed and railroads and modern highways have been constructed. Health and sanitation services have been extended and a social security program has been established. The number of schools has increased and programs have been undertaken for the construction and extension of rural and secondary schools. The nation's population has increased rapidly. The national income and governmental revenues have grown considerably. Direct promotion of production by the national government has increased to the extent that the government provides 40 per cent of all investments made in Mexico. The working-class movement has been developed and the peasants have been organized.[3]

In spite of the progress made, Lombardo claims, the goals of the revolution are far from achieved. Mexican national life is far from democratic. Electoral freedom does not exist, for the president and the official party control all elections; hence, holders of public office are really appointees of those in power rather than popularly elected representatives. *Caciques* dominate most Mexican organizations from labor unions to peasant organizations to government departments and offices. There exists neither effective separation of governmental powers nor free and critical parliamentary debate. Corruption is rampant in all branches of the state organization, including the judiciary.

Economic development has brought but limited increases in the level of living of the masses. Indeed, in recent years, economic development has been proceeding at the expense of the general level of living of most Mexicans. The Mexican economy suffers from many liabilities. Latifundia still exist in Mexico as a new class of capitalist landlords has arisen; more than a million peasants are landless. Archaic methods still persist in much of agricultural production and water and credit resources are inadequate. Hundreds of thousands of rural Mexicans, he claims, are forced yearly to travel to the United States to find work. A profound and critical disequilibrium exists between the development of industry and of agriculture, between city and country. Domestic purchasing power is too small and inflexible to stimulate

3. Lombardo Toledano, *La Evolución de México*, pp. 7-8; *Carta*, pp. 44-59.

the rapid and sound industrialization of the nation, and the development of heavy industry has but a limited beginning.

Complete national independence is yet to be achieved as Mexico still is dependent economically upon foreign nations—especially upon the United States. This dependence is manifested in several ways. In its attempts to achieve stability in its balance of payments, Mexico depends upon the United States for three major sources of foreign exchange: the sale of agricultural and mining raw materials exported to the United States, the earnings acquired by Mexican workers in the United States, and the expenditures of American tourists in Mexico. Further, Mexico is dependent upon the United States for loans and for investment capital as well as for the purchase of capital goods. As one would expect from the foregoing, the great majority of Mexico's foreign trade is controlled by the United States. American monopolies dominate Mexico's mining industry and own the greater portion of the major manufacturing enterprises.[4]

Ever greater American investments seek to control the Mexican economy, "denaturalizing the economic development of our country, impeding its true industrialization, hindering our international commerce and seeking to make the nation a colony dependent on the monopolies of the northern potency."[5]

The United States government interferes in Mexican affairs in several ways. The Federal Bureau of Investigation (FBI) operates freely in Mexico. The Organización Interamericana de Trabajadores (ORIT), promoted by the U.S. government and "directed by the reactionary leaders of the American Federation of Labor"[6] interferes in the Mexican labor movement in order to control it in the interests of American imperialism. As part of the Cold War hostilities, the United States government directs a campaign against all Mexican leftists who struggle for national independence and for international peace. Finally, in order to control Mexico's destiny more easily, the U.S. government seeks to isolate Mexico from its Latin-American neighbors.[7]

4. General summaries of Vicente Lombardo Toledano's criticisms of the negative aspects of the Mexican Revolution can be found in his *Carta*, pp. 59-74; *El Drama de México*, pp. 1-13; *La Evolución de México*, pp. 9-12; *La Reforma Agraria*, pp. 37-45.
5. Lombardo Toledano, *En Torno al XX Congreso*, p. 229.
6. *Ibid.*, pp. 229-230.
7. *Ibid.*

Major obstacles to the continued development of the Mexican Revolution are presented by the self-interested activities of United States monopolies which are supported by the United States government and are leagued with elements of the Mexican bureaucratic and private banking bourgeosie. Elements of the private banking bourgeoisie and other supporters and agents of American economic imperialism have joined with traditionalist conservative survivors of the revolution (such as members of the clergy and lay religious fanatics), Lombardo charges, to form the Partido Acción Nacional. The aim of this party is the destruction of the revolution.[8]

Lombardo insists that, in the face of this opposition, national unity against imperialism must be sought as the basis for continuing the movement towards the revolutionary goals of democracy, higher levels of living through economic development, and national independence. Fundamental to the formation of a popular anti-imperialist front is the achievement of solidarity and revolutionary class consciousness within the working class. The class-conscious workers can unite politically with most of the other social classes of Mexico on the basis of common opposition to imperialism. Thus, the popular front would represent the vast majority of the Mexican people, including the urban and rural petty bourgeoisie (which includes the peasantry), the national bourgeoisie, and elements of the bureaucratic bourgeoisie (the bourgeoisie in power representing state capitalism). It was pursuit of such a popular front that led Lombardo in 1947-1948 to initiate the organization of the Partido Popular. The Partido Popular (whose name was changed in 1960 to the Partido Popular Socialista) has continued as the popular front, anti-imperialist party par excellence in Mexican history.[9]

Mexico, Lombardo is convinced, cannot achieve its revolutionary objectives on the basis of the capitalist system. Rather, the popular anti-imperialist front must establish a Popular (or People's) Democracy as a means for constructing socialism in

8. Lombardo Toledano, *Objectivos y Táctica*, p. 51; *Un Nuevo Partido*, pp. 12-14, 18-20.
9. Lombardo Toledano, *Mensaje al Proletariado*, pp. 4, 16-19; *Objectivos y Táctica*, pp. 51-54; *En Torno al XX Congreso*, pp. 245-251; *Partido Popular, III Asamblea*, p. 20; Lombardo Toledano, *Teoría y Práctica*, pp. 1-46, 99-120, *passim*. Lombardo's *El Frente Nacional Democrático* reproduces a number of speeches, articles, and interviews in which Lombardo elaborates upon his concept of the national, anti-imperialist front.

Mexico. Only by this means shall Mexico realize its revolutionary goals.[10] Lombardo's views on the anachronistic nature of capitalism in modern underdeveloped nations, although lengthy, are worthy of notation. In his work, *En Torno al XX Congreso del Partido Comunista de la Unión Soviética*, Lombardo pointed out that to think that Mexico and other Latin-American nations can establish capitalist regimes of the nineteenth-century variety (which exist nowhere in this age of monopoly capitalist imperialism) "is to believe that people can elevate to an ideal category of social organization a system of life which belongs to the past."

New concepts are abroad in the world, continued Lombardo, which are replacing the old way of viewing things. The new are the concepts that political systems must be democratized in order to permit access to representative institutions by new and better human elements; that enormous human and material forces exist throughout the world waiting to be tapped for the benefit of all mankind; that economic production is a means, not an end, and that it should serve all the people and not only the privileged few who expropriate the fruits of collective labor; that the majority of the people, the workers, do not have to limit themselves to making demands for immediate economic improvements which, once attained, are quickly lost, but can seek to put an end to the division of society into antagonistic classes and thereby eliminate the consequences of that division: unequal distribution of wealth, unemployment, economic crises, suppression of individual and social guarantees, and war.

These new concepts contrast with old views and institutions which are disappearing. The old includes "bourgeois democracy, which, under the mask of economic, political and juridical equality of all individuals proclaimed in the abstract, conceals the dictatorship of a class which exploits the majority." The old, continued Lombardo, include the concepts that underdeveloped nations can be developed by foreign monopolies which seek only maximum profits and deform the economic and political development of these nations; that the real incomes of the people can be augmented by granting freedom of action to private monopolies; that a nation can industrialize without creating an extensive basic industry which produces machinery vital to the development of the rest of the economy. In summary, concluded Lombardo, the old is the

10. Lombardo Toledano, *La Perspectiva de México*, pp. 77-80.

view that economic development is an end in itself, that "progress is valid even at the cost of the economic and political sacrifice of the popular masses, or of national independence."[11]

The Popular Democracy which he hopes to establish is defined as "a government composed of workers and members of the bourgeoisie and petty-bourgeoisie of the city and the country who are insubornable by the reaction and by imperialism, under the direc- of the working class."[12] The principal task of the Popular Democracy is the construction of socialism.

Is the transition to a Popular Democracy (as the basis for the construction of socialism) to be effected peacefully or violently? Lombardo has emphasized that there are many roads to socialism and that Mexico must choose the path which best fits its circumstances. The Cuban Revolution must be studied, but it must not be assumed that Mexico should follow exactly Fidel Castro's methods. Just as the Mexican Revolution has distinctive characteristics which mark it apart from other Latin-American experiences, so also will Mexico's socialist revolution have its distinctive features. The important thing to realize, Lombardo stresses, is that the objective and subjective conditions for revolution must exist before it will occur. It is the task of the revolutionary sectors to help prepare these conditions.[13]

The circumstances for the socialist revolution can be created in two essential manners. (1) By promoting in every way the economic development of Mexico. This development will sharpen the basic contradiction between social production and private appropriation, which is expressed in Mexico essentially as contradictions between the development of agriculture and the development of industrial production and between imperialist monopoly penetration and national economic development. (2) By promoting the revolutionary, class-conscious solidarity of the working class and the unity of this class with other social classes in a broad anti-imperialist popular front.[14]

Once the objective conditions exist, Lombardo insists, the revo-

11. Lombardo Toledano, *En Torno al XX Congreso*, pp. 234-236.
12. Lombardo Toledano, *La Perspectiva de México*, p. 79.
13. *Ibid.*, pp. 81-84, 109-111; Lombardo Toledano, *En Torno al XX Congreso*, pp. 176-178; *Teoría y Práctica*, pp. 164-165.
14. Vicente Lombardo Toledano, *La Revolución Rusa—la Revolución Mexicana: Pasado, Presente y Porvenir* (Mexico, 1943), pp. 39-42; *La Rebelión del Mundo Colonial*, pp. 5-6; *Teoría y Práctica*, pp. 164-165.

lution will occur in spite of attempts by the dominant groups at repression and division of the popular forces. The actual period of change from Mexico's semicolonial, state-capitalist economy pregnant with socialism to a Popular Democracy will be brief. This prediction is supported by the concept of dialectical materialism that once the critical transition point is reached, change-overs from quantitative to qualitative states occur rapidly.[15]

The transition, however, Lombardo predicts, will be peaceful—or at least it can be. He has expressed this view on several occasions. In his address to the National Council of the Partido Popular in 1955, published as *La Perspectiva de México: Una Democracia del Pueblo*, he argued that a peaceful revolution is necessary because of Mexico's proximity to the throne of international reaction—the United States. American imperialism would establish a repressive reactionary regime in Mexico if an armed revolution occurred—or even if an attempt to organize one was undertaken. Lombardo developed the "many roads to socialism" theme and emphasized that he did not reject the possibility of violent revolution in Mexico's future for fear of being imprisoned if he did otherwise, but rather because he feared to be anti-Marxist if he came to any other conclusion.[16] That is to say, Lombardo apparently thought that Marxist analysis led inevitably to the conclusion that the transition to socialism in Mexico would be peaceful. The following year, 1956 Lombardo, in his book *En Torno al XX Congreso del Partido Comunista de la Unión Soviética*, used the emphasis by the Twentieth Congress of the Communist party of the Soviet Union upon the "many roads to socialism" theme and upon the possibility of peaceful transition to socialism to bolster his own opinions about the possibility of peaceful change.[17] Finally, one can infer from Lombardo's report made in 1960 to the National Committee of the Partido Popular that the possibility of a peaceful change is reinforced by the likelihood that elements of the ruling bureaucratic bourgeoisie representing state capitalism will join the broad anti-imperialist popular front in a future move towards a Popular Democracy.[18]

In other writings, however, Lombardo appears to conceive the

15. Vicente Lombardo Toledano, "La Evolución del Movimiento Obrero," *Futuro*, XLVIII (Feb., 1940), 15; Selden Rodman, *Mexican Journal*, p. 154.
16. Lombardo Toledano, *La Perspectiva de México*, pp. 81-84.
17. Lombardo Toledano, *En Torno al XX Congreso*, pp. 176-178.
18. Partido Popular, *III Asamblea*, pp. 67-94.

possibility of a violent revolution. Thus, he has spoken of rejecting violence "in this historic moment"[19] of Mexican development and he has warned of civil war if the needs of the Mexican people are not satisfied "in a patriotic manner."[20] Again, he has warned that "one cannot think of peaceful forms of Revolution in arriving at a popular democracy except when the people have the right to have their voice heard in the legislative power of the nation and in the organs of municipal administration."[21] Lombardo, in October 1962, expressed to the writer the opinion that the attitude of the Mexican bourgeoisie will be crucial. If the bourgeoisie uses force to prevent revolutionary change, the proletariat will employ force to compel change. If the bourgeoisie accepts change, the proletariat, of course, will not employ force.

Lombardo, in brief, evidently considers that the specific form the future revolution shall take will depend upon the particular correlation of internal and international forces which exists at the time of revolutionary crisis. The revolution can be peaceful, and Lombardo both thinks and hopes that it shall be. On the other hand, it may be violent. Mexico's popular revolutionary elements must promote the conditions prerequisite to the change (economic development and popular anti-imperialist unity) and then must be prepared to act decisively and with wisdom as future exigencies demand.[22]

Lombardo's faith in the advent of socialism in Mexico—and in the world—is absolute and unshakable.[23] As he has put it: "I belong to an imperishable cause."[24] The cause is human fulfilment. Socialism is but a means to that end.

Therefore, the broadly humanistic and amply (non-philosophic) idealistic sentiments of Lombardo's youth have continued into his mature years. Indeed, the mainspring of Lombardo's entire life of study and action has been his desire to promote improved human social relationships so as to permit an unrestricted flourishing of human potentials. Lombardo's idealism is very evident in

19. Lombardo Toledano, *La Perspectiva de México*, p. 109.
20. Lombardo Toledano, *En Torno al XX Congreso*, pp. 231-232.
21. *Ibid.*, p. 251.
22. See Lombardo Toledano, *Teoría y Práctica*, pp. 164-165.
23. Lombardo Toledano, *Lenin, el Genio*, p. 23; *Un Viaje al Mundo del Porvenir*, p. 158; *La Perspectiva de México*, p. 112.
24. Lombardo Toledano, *Escritos Filosóficos*, p. 215.

his speeches and writings, and in a speech delivered in 1940, he confessed:

> I have preferred to be a man to being a litigator; I have preferred to be a man to being a lawyer; I have preferred to be a man to being a university professor; because of this I am in the arroyo with my own, fighting against the reaction for the autonomy of Mexico, for the Mexican Revolution....
>
> ... what our enemies do not know is that all we militants of the proletariat are permanently young; not only does our faith in the struggle not die within us but, on the contrary, it increases as the historic process places the capitalist regime in one of its great crises, and the coming dawn already illuminates our spirits, our eyes, and indicates to us that soon for all of humanity and not only for the proletariat there will have to come the compensation for so many sacrifices.[25]

Speaking in 1942, after explaining that the U.S.S.R. must be defended and the forces of fascism defeated, Lombardo added:

> All this must be spread about, it must be explained; but first it is necessary to feel it. And the only ones who can feel it are those who also, like Lenin, love the human species; these men are capable of wanting to give their lives over to a greater cause. The petty are not, nor can they be Leninists. Those who tire of giving, or those who have given and consider that they have given much, cannot be Leninists. On the other hand, those who give and feel that they have never given anything, those who work tirelessly even when they are dying materially; those who live with the illusion, which will never be quenched, of a great future for all men; those who dream of a better world; those who glimpse imperfectly in their consciences a world without exploited nor exploiters; those who have been able to sense the efficacy of a regime which really corresponds to the will of the people ... these will be the vanguard that the people needs to be able to mobilize successfully.[26]

Finally, Lombardo's idealism shines forth in his poem, *Presente y Futuro*, which he wrote in 1950 while attending the Warsaw

---

25. Lombardo Toledano, *En Qué Consiste y a Cuánto Asciende la Fortuna de Vicente Lombardo Toledano*, no pagination.
26. Lombardo Toledano, *Lenin, el Genio*, p. 17.

Peace Conference. The poem presents an optimistic, joyful view of the prospects for human progress and human happiness as the socialist movement develops. The last three stanzas read:

> I am the richest of men
> because my ideal is superior
> to all human beings
> And my love is a love
> greater than life and death
>
> I give all that I have
> and I do not tire of giving
> because the more I give
> the more I receive
> And my ideal grows
> And my love shines
> beside the other loves
> as a star shines
> in the midst of the night
>
> How great is the happiness
> thus to live
> How easy thus is
> the road of life.[27]

Socialism is a means to an end. It is a means to human fulfilment, to the realization of the humanistic values stressed throughout human history. "Socialism," he insists, "is not a religion.... Socialism is pure humanism, the vindication of man, redeeming him from the shadows of ignorance and from his original religious fears."[28] Florescences of humanism have occurred in the past, but the human values realized in practice have always been partial and attenuated because man has remained divided against nature and against himself. Bourgeois society has been unable to achieve the humanistic ideals it has professed. Men still are divided into mutually hostile social classes and still are alienated from their own persons as they are forced to sell their labor power as a commodity. Furthermore—and perhaps to him the greatest shortcoming—a part of mankind considers that bourgeois society is a perpetual form of social organization. Many forms of brutal repression are employed to maintain it.

27. Vicente Lombardo Toledano, *Presente y Futuro* (Mexico, 1952), p. 10.
28. Lombardo Toledano, *Escritos Filosóficos*, p. 214.

Socialism, Lombardo points out, will eliminate the antagonistic class divisions of society and will end the sale of human labor power for the production of private profits. Based upon co-operative, planned production for use, the new social relationships will offer the possibilities for rapid economic development. Economic progress will provide goods and services in abundance ample to satisfy man's basic material necessities. Thereby freed from predominant concern with his physical requisites, man will be able to develop to the full his intellectual and spiritual potentials.[29]

Lombardo frequently has expressed the view that socialism is a means to the end of human fulfilment. In 1930, he wrote that only "the myopic or the ignorant believe that socialism is an end in itself." Socialism, continued Lombardo, is a means rather than an end; a means to realizing man's "spiritual power" which capitalism has suffocated. It is this spiritual power which alone "makes life worth living and turns every human being into a happy and indefatigable worker."[30]

And, in 1960, Lombardo wrote that socialism would not be a decisive influence in the liberation of mankind if it could offer man only improved material conditions of life, increased real incomes, better housing, and the like. Socialism is more than that. "Socialism is a means and not an end. A means to emancipate man from his material sufferings, but with the purpose of transforming him into a true man free in the midst of the world."[31]

For the first time in history man will dominate himself and nature; the forces within man which have struggled throughout history to elevate the human spirit shall be released. The new humanism will embrace not a part but all of mankind.[32]

> The new humanism embraces
> for the first time in history
> all men on earth
> The yellow and the white
> the black and the red

29. Lombardo Toledano, *Causas de la Elevación*, pp. 87-94; *Escritos Filosóficos*, pp. 115-119; *Judíos y Mexicanos ¿Razas Inferiores?* (Mexico, 1944), p. 42; Lombardo Toledano, *La Filosofía*, pp. 93-122.
30. Vicente Lombardo Toledano, "El Sentido Humanista de la Revolución Mexicana," *Universidad de México*, I (Dec., 1930), 107.
31. Lombardo Toledano, *Causas de la Elevación*, p. 90.
32. Lombardo recently expressed the quintessence of his thought on man, his prospects and problems, in his *Summa*.

There is no East nor West
nor north nor south
in the eagerness to live
with the same ideal
and with the same hope.

Now the beings of all nations
are truly brothers
and in the tongue characteristic of each
all sing in imposing chorus
the same hymn of liberty.[33]

33. Lombardo Toledano, *Presente y Futuro*, p. 5.

VI. *International Affairs*

A handful of capitalist-imperialist nations dominated the world when the Mexican Revolution began. Vicente Lombardo Toledano points out that in the mid-twentieth century, however, this situation no longer exists, as the world is divided into two systems: the capitalist and the socialist. Lombardo's thoughts upon the nature and the interrelationships of these two systems indicate he has accepted and repeated without reservations or modifications the official Soviet viewpoints on the subject.

According to Lombardo, three predominant features characterize the capitalist world: (1) intensified class struggles in the highly industrialized capitalist nations caused by business crises and permanent unemployment; (2) continued rebellion of the colonial and semicolonial countries for national independence; and (3) continued interimperialist rivalries which threaten the solidarity of action among the capitalist nations. The major contradiction within capitalism, he states without further explanation, which leads to the superannuation of the capitalist mode of production and to its supersedure by socialism consists in the ever greater contrast within capitalism between collective production and private appropriation of that which is produced.[1]

In the socialist world, he concludes, there are no class struggles and production increases continuously without crises; moreover, there are no serious rivalries between the socialist nations, and there are no colonies. The correlation of world forces favors socialism.[2]

The capitalist nations, says Lombardo, are making preparations for a third world war in order to destroy socialism and re-establish capitalism on a world scale—"A resurrection theoretically impossible, historically absurd and practically unrealizable."[3] Peaceful coexistence and the avoidance of another major war are possible, however, because of the preponderance of strength of the forces for peace. These forces include the Soviet Union and

---

1. Lombardo Toledano, *La Rebelión del Mundo Colonial*, pp. 5-6, 23; *La Perspectiva de México*, p. 17.
2. Lombardo Toledano, *Carta*, pp. 41-42.
3. Lombardo Toledano, *La Perspectiva de México*, p. 18.

the other socialist nations as well as the most advanced popular elements in the capitalist nations. Thus, while the economic impulse to war exists, war may nevertheless be prevented by the energetic and unified actions of the forces for peace.[4] "The key to peace rests on the decisions that people make in the face of existing conflicts and controversies, because... man is a product of history, but he acts upon reality and builds his own future."[5]

The whole world will some day be socialist, he is convinced. But the road to socialism will be long and difficult, for the capitalist nations progress unevenly toward the inevitable transition. Intercapitalist leagues and the continued technical progress of many capitalist nations help to maintain and to prolong the life of the capitalist system. Furthermore, the transition in each nation awaits the union of the workers and other popular elements into a revolutionary force which consciously seeks political power. The transitions, when they occur, may be peaceful or violent; each will assume peculiarities of its own. They will result from popular national movements and cannot and should not be imposed from outside. The real transition to socialism can occur only when the state is under the control of the working class.[6]

Lombardo claims the greatest obstacles to the development of socialism in the world are the actions of United States imperialism. Latin-America, especially, is suffering under the hegemony of capitalist—essentially United States—economic imperialism. The development of Latin-America has been subjected to the dictates of American and European needs for food and for industrial raw materials; the prices of these primary commodity exports are subject to foreign manipulation. The ultimate objective of this foreign economic exploitation has been the production of profits for a few private monopolies. Rather than submit to the exigencies of foreign monopolies, Latin-America must have a planned development controlled by and suited to the interests of the Latin-American nations.[7] The conflict between private profit and national well-being in Latin America has reached the point that "the struggle is being delimited more and more, in a profound

4. Lombardo Toledano, *En Torno al XX Congreso*, pp. 171-176; *El Neonasismo: Sus Características y Peligros* (Mexico, 1960), p. 56.
5. *Ibid.*
6. Lombardo Toledano, *En Torno al XX Congreso*, pp. 171-176.
7. Vicente Lombardo Toledano, *Los Principales Problemas de la Agricultura y de la Economía del Continente Americano* (Mexico, 1942), pp. 70-79.

manner, into two camps: that of national independence and the functioning of democratic liberties on the one hand, and that of political oppression and the submission of the country to the dictates of North American imperialism."[8] The victory will go to the former.[9]

In spite of his criticisms of American imperialism, Lombardo has praised the American people and the traditional functioning of American political democracy.[10] In a speech delivered in 1950, Lombardo noted with admiration the tradition of permanent political criticism in the United States—a criticism between the three branches of government and a criticism of the government by all United States citizens regardless of their social class. Mexico would do well to follow this example rather than to continue to classify all political critics as traitors to the nation. He pointed out though that these traditional liberties have been under attack since the end of World War II and, as a consequence, the United States is entering into a period of decline in its democratic political regime.[11]

Lombardo has noted both the positive and the negative aspects of the historical relationships between the United States and Latin-America. Among the former he has included the favorable attitude the United States assumed toward the Latin-American countries in their struggles for independence from Spain, such as Henry Clay's support of recognition by the United States of the independence of Spain's former colonies; the Monroe Doctrine "at the moment in which it was proclaimed, and with the intention given it by its author"; Abraham Lincoln's speech in the House of Representatives on January 12, 1848, in which he criticized the aggressive, annexationist character of the Mexican War; the support of Juárez by the United States government during the French intervention; and Franklin D. Roosevelt's Good Neighbor Policy which led to declarations against interventionism at the Inter-American Conferences held in Montevideo in 1933 and in Buenos Aires in 1936; the abrogation of the Platt Amendment in

8. Lombardo Toledano, *La Perspectiva de México*, p. 16.
9. *Ibid.*, pp. 16-17; see also Lombardo Toledano, *Objectivos y Táctica*, pp. 26-27.
10. See "Toledano Faces Labor Revolt," *World Report*, I (Dec. 31, 1946), 30-31.
11. *El Popular*, June 24, 1950, p. 3.

1934; and the ending of intervention and the declaration against any future intervention in Nicaragua and Haiti.[12]

Among the negative aspects which Lombardo has noted in the United States' relations with Latin-America are its failure to lend sufficient support to the Panama Congress of 1826; its war with Mexico; its doctrine of Manifest Destiny; the Olney doctrine (which in effect proclaimed United States hegemony over Latin-America); its "big stick" and dollar-diplomacy policies which led in the latter part of the nineteenth and early part of the twentieth centuries to many American interventions—armed and otherwise—into the internal affairs of Latin-American nations;[13] and its revival of interventionism following World War II, especially in regard to the American activities in Guatemala and in Cuba.[14]

Lombardo has noted the similarities between the histories of the United States and Latin-America. In the past both regions served to attract settlers in search of economic opportunities and of refuge from persecution. Since the 1860's, however, basic differences have arisen between the two regions. The United States developed into an industrial capitalist nation while Latin-America remained agrarian and feudal.[15] As a consequence of these different developments, the Latin-American nations became economic tributaries of the United States and Europe. Instead of serving as a complement to the American capitalist economy, Latin-America should, he advances, develop independently on the basis of her own requirements.[16]

Lombardo devoted a large section of a speech delivered in El Paso, Texas, during World War II to emphasize that the differences between the levels of material development of the United States and Latin-America were the result of social and historical rather than racial circumstances. To accept racial interpretations was to accept the point of view of the fascists against whom the war was being waged. Lombardo eulogized the Indian, Negro,

12. Vicente Lombardo Toledano, *The United States and Mexico: Two Nations—One Ideal* (New York, 1942), pp. 13-19.
13. *Ibid.*, pp. 10-13.
14. Lombardo Toledano, *La Perspectiva de México*, pp. 14-17; *Al Pueblo Mexicano*, pp. 5-11.
15. *El Popular*, July 6, 1943, p. 6.
16. Lombardo Toledano, *Los Principales Problemas*, pp. 70-79.

and mestizo ethnic groups for their contributions to the material and cultural development of Latin-America.[17]

In the same speech, Lombardo stressed that the Latin-American people have always made a distinction between the American people and the regimes of imperialist exploitation from which Latin-Americans have suffered. "None of the peoples of Latin America is an enemy of the United States, nor of the North American people. On the other hand, all the people are enemies of imperialism."[18]

In short, Lombardo considers the United States the major imperialist power in the world and the chief obstacle to the rapid and independent development of many of the world's peoples. The American people, however, should not be considered directly responsible for the imperialist policies of the United States government; these policies are undertaken in the interests of a handful of United States monopolies. The contradictions within capitalism and imperialism some day will lead the American people themselves to reject capitalism and establish a socialist system. On that day, he implies, the whole world will heave a sigh of relief.

Mexico must respect the power of the United States, Lombardo stated in 1957, but he pointed out that Mexico also must realize that it not only can but must follow an independent domestic and foreign policy. The power of the United States is limited by the force of the socialist nations and by the contradictions within capitalism. These contradictions are expressed in economic crises, interimperialist rivalries, and colonial rebellions. "Governments which truly represent and defend their people take advantage of these contradictions in order to advance by their own route."[19]

Mexican foreign policy, however, Lombardo lamented in 1958, does not avail itself of opportunities to pursue an independent policy. Noteworthy affirmations of the principles of non-intervention have been made in support of weak Latin-American nations. In its daily practice, nevertheless, Mexican foreign policy is submissive to the interests of the United States. United States and other foreign capital is permitted to flood the nation. The Mexican government restricts trade and cultural exchange with the socialist nations. United States institutions are allowed to intervene freely

17. *El Popular*, July 6, 1943, p. 6.
18. *Ibid.*
19. Lombardo Toledano, *La Sucesión*, p. 9.

in Mexico's cultural life. Mexico tolerates "humiliating restrictions" placed upon the freedom of Mexicans to visit the United States while at the same time it permits all Americans to enter Mexico and it allows (and assists) the American political police—the Federal Bureau of Investigation (FBI)—to operate freely in Mexico. In order to please the United States, Mexico refrains from establishing diplomatic relations with the Peoples' Republic of China.[20] Finally (and notoriously), attacks are made against communism in the belief that in reward "our uncles are going to heap gifts upon us."[21]

Lombardo has outlined a truly Mexican foreign policy:

> Our international policy can be none other than friendship with all peoples, without political discrimination; of close relations with nations similar to ours; of cordial, sincere and dignified relations with the United States free from inferiority or sacrificial complexes; of systematic diffusion of our commerce with all possible markets; of cultural interexchanges with the great peoples of the world which, while conserving and extoling our national characteristics, enable us to incorporate into our mind the progresses of science and the highest expressions of universal art.[22]

The leading socialist nation of the world, the Union of Soviet Socialist Republics, he stated in 1956, is developing rapidly and evenly in all aspects of its life. The uniform and peaceful progress of that nation is contrasted sharply by the unresolved structural contradictions and the impulses toward war which exist within the United States and other capitalist nations. The Soviet Union is now the second industrial power of the world and, together with the other socialist nations, is the primary force for world peace and for assistance to the world movement toward socialism.[23]

These opinions, stated in 1956, are expressions of a highly favorable attitude Lombardo has maintained toward the U.S.S.R. since the early 1930's. He has confirmed and reinforced his views by many visits to the Soviet Union from 1935 to 1961. His initial

20. *Ibid.*, pp. 48-50.
21. *Ibid.*, p. 49.
22. *Ibid.*, p. 50.
23. Lombardo Toledano, *En Torno al XX Congreso*, pp. 171-176.

visit led to the publication of two works: *50 Verdades sobre la U.R.S.S.*[24] and *Un Viaje al Mundo del Porvenir.*[25]

As the title suggests, *50 Verdades sobre la U.R.S.S.* lists fifty statements of fact and of interpretation concerning the socialist regime in the Soviet Union. The tone of these statements is very idealistic; no real criticism is made. Lombardo seemed impressed especially by the highly social orientation of the ethics and attitudes of the Soviet people. Lombardo's idealization of the Soviet regime is evidenced particularly by the following "truths":

> 5. The dictatorship of the proletariat consists in government of the workers, by the workers and for the workers: it is true democracy....
>
> 12. No one has imposed upon the people of the U.S.S.R. the perfect discipline in which it lives; the rhythm of their own labor has converted each man and each woman into notes of a great social symphony. . . .
>
> 22. In the majority of the capitalist countries one can be assured that almost all the individuals who travel in their own cars are exploiters of their fellows. In the U.S.S.R. for each individual who owns an automobile the people have a smile of sincere gratitude....
>
> 39. Premeditated political propaganda is foreign to the esthetic doctrine of the Soviet regime....[26]

Un Viaje al Mundo del Porvenir is a compilation of four public lectures by Lombardo and two by Victor Manuel Villaseñor delivered in Mexico City in 1935 on the subject of the Soviet Union. Lombardo's lectures included: "The Political Structure of the U.S.S.R."; "Present Conditions of the Soviet People"; "How the Soviet Regime Resolved the Problem of Suppressed Nationalities"; and "The World of the Future." The idealistic interpretations of Soviet realities presented in *50 Verdades* is continued in these lectures. The U.S.S.R., said Lombardo, is the greatest democracy in history because the effective political unit is the working man. Soviet society is oriented toward human needs and aspirations which he claims it is rapidly and directly satisfying, whereas capitalist society is directed toward the private profit of a few.

24. Mexico, 1935.
25. Mexico, 1936.
26. Lombardo Toledano, *50 Verdades*, pp. 1, 2, 4, 7.

The Russian experience in constructing socialism is not alien to Mexican realities for scientific laws of human society apply to men everywhere. Indeed, this Russian experience should serve as an example to help guide Mexico toward the solution of its problems through the construction of socialism.[27]

Lombardo continued to be an ardent and uncritical supporter of the domestic and foreign policies of the Soviet Union.[28] In a speech delivered in 1942, Lombardo praised the genuineness of Soviet democracy and Soviet justice. "The U.S.S.R. is the only country in which justice is law, true law, law which never is violated, law which is applied inflexibly."[29] In an address delivered the following year, Lombardo praised three consequences of the Russian October Revolution, reasoning that (1) it ushered in a new epoch in human history in which man scientifically controls his own social development; (2) it has "saved humanity" in that the Red army, product of the revolution, has saved the world from fascism; and (3) it has helped to guarantee world peace in that it has created a strong counterforce to the source of modern wars—imperialism.[30] In the same speech, Lombardo defended the Soviet interventions in Finland, Poland, and the Baltic states as measures undertaken solely to defend weaker peoples against fascism.[31]

Since World War II Lombardo has supported the Soviet position on all major international issues of the Cold War, ranging from opposition to the Marshall Plan[32] to condemnation of United States intervention in the Korean war[33] and to support of the policies of peaceful coexistence and universal disarmament.[34] Respecting Soviet domestic affairs, Lombardo continued an ardent admirer of Stalin and his policies during his lifetime. In 1949, Lombardo wrote a short article in the Soviet newspaper *Trud* in honor of Stalin's birthday.[35] The following year he praised Stalin as one

27. Lombardo Toledano, *Un Viaje al Mundo del Porvenir*, pp. 9-34, 70-96, 97-120, 145-159.
28. Lombardo's attitudes toward the Soviet Union and World War II will be considered later in this chapter.
29. Lombardo Toledano, *Lenin, el Genio*, p. 12.
30. Lombardo Toledano, *La Revolución Rusa—la Revolución Mexicana*, pp. 10-14.
31. *Ibid.*, p. 25.
32. James Riley Hayes, p. 202.
33. Lombardo Toledano, *La Rebelión del Mundo Colonial*, pp. 63-74.
34. Lombardo Toledano, *La Perspectiva de México*, pp. 18-22.
35. Lombardo Toledano, *Diario*, p. 225.

of the three greatest men of the century—along with Lenin and Mao.³⁶

Lombardo, nevertheless, accepted the criticisms of Stalin made in 1956 in the Twentieth Party Congress of the Communist party of the Soviet Union. Likewise, he supported the emphasis by the Congress upon the themes that there are many roads to socialism and that a third world war can be prevented. He praised the self-criticisms of the Congress as a sign of strength rather than weakness and declared that a party in power in the capitalist nations would never engage in such realistic self-appraisal—all criticism comes from opposition and usually non-revolutionary parties.³⁷ Lombardo, nevertheless, still retained much respect for Stalin. Joseph Stalin, he wrote in 1956, "is one of the great men of world history. [He is] an eminent revolutionary thinker and one of the principal constructors of the first socialist state. In order to be objective and valid, judgements upon his work must take into account his positive acts as well as his errors. To indicate the latter—as did the XXth Congress—is useful and necessary, because the experience [of analyzing past mistakes] will enable us to avoid them in the future."³⁸ Lombardo accepted the explanation of the Twentieth Party Congress that the errors committed by Stalin were the consequence of the "cult of personality." Similar errors may be avoided in the future by insuring the functioning of collective leadership within the Soviet Communist party.³⁹

In regard to the relationships of the Soviet Union with the eastern European socialist nations, Lombardo has said:

> The supposed subordination to the Soviet Union of the nations with people's democracies is nothing but a natural, historical, necessary and legitimate alliance among the peoples who have abolished the capitalist regime in order to form the socialist world. [The socialist world in creation] is based on internal planning and on the future international planning of the economy, without the fetters of private property and the contradictions of interests which exist between the capitalist nations themselves.⁴⁰

36. *Ibid.*, pp. 161-162.
37. Lombardo Toledano, *En Torno al XX Congreso*, pp. 168-171.
38. *Ibid.*, pp. 170-171.
39. *Ibid.*, pp. 175-176.
40. Lombardo Toledano, *Diario*, p. 29.

He has denounced Yugoslavia for its "theoretical and tactical discrepancies" and for its "treason" in pursuing its "autarchical conception of a socialist economy in such a small nation."[41]

Lombardo has written and spoken a good deal about the 1956 Hungarian Revolution. His thoughts on the subject have been compiled in the work, *Ante la Crisis de Hungria*.[42] The essence of Lombardo's views are as follows: The Hungarian rebellion resulted partly from serious mistakes committed by the Popular Democratic Government of Hungary and partly from agitations and revolutionary organizing undertaken by foreign imperialisms in league with rightist elements located both within and without Hungary. Although the Hungarian government had warnings of great popular discontent for two years prior to the revolt, very mistakenly it did not act promptly to alleviate genuine grievances —such as the complaint against low wages. Rightist elements took advantage of this popular unrest to organize—with foreign moral and material support—a *putsch*. These rightist elements began the revolt. Most of the population wanted genuine, progressive reforms which would aid the country in its movement toward socialism, and workers' declarations attest to this fact. The rightist elements, however, gained the upper hand in the revolt. They could count on the support of 10,000 ex-officers of the Hungarian fascist army which fought for Hitler who were awaiting—along with other reactionary elements of the old order—the opportunity to return to Hungary. Under these circumstances, the Hungarian government asked for assistance from the U.S.S.R. under the Warsaw Pact's provisions for mutual defense.

Neither Hungary nor any other of the eastern European countries are satellites of the Soviet Union, nor, he states, is the Soviet Union imperialistic. The Soviet Union wishes other nations freely to become and remain socialist because socialism is a more advanced stage of human development and because the increase in the number of socialist nations helps guarantee the security of Russian socialism. The Soviet Union does not want a return to pre-World War II conditions when it was surrounded by hostile semifeudal states dominated by foreign capitalist-imperialist neighbors.

Apart from the Soviet Union, Lombardo reasons, none of the

41. *Ibid.*, pp. 28-29.
42. Mexico, 1956.

popular democracies has yet achieved socialism. They are all trying to do so and in the process are committing many mistakes. The transition from feudalism to capitalism also took time—a century and a half—and was marked by error and war. The important thing, he insists, to keep in mind is that these nations are constantly developing a higher stage of civilization. Attempts by capitalist nations and native reactionaries to take advantage of difficulties encountered and mistakes committed within the popular democracies in order to restore capitalism will not be successful because the restoration of capitalism is contrary to the best interests of the people of these nations. History is on the side of socialism; eventually, in spite of all obstacles, it will triumph everywhere.[43]

Lombardo has devoted considerable attention to the origins and construction of socialism in the People's Republic of China. Lombardo visited China in 1949 (shortly after the victory of the revolution) as representative to the Peking regional conference of the World Federation of Trade Unions. Two works resulted from his journey: *Diario de Un Viaje a la China Nueva* which describes in dated entries his observations while traveling in China, the Soviet Union, and Czechoslovakia, and *Victoria de la Revolución China*[44] which outlines the course of modern Chinese history, including the development and victory of the revolution. The tone of the works is summarized in a statement made by Lombardo in an article published in a Chinese review and quoted in his *Diario*: "I brought to the Chinese people the message of millions of workers represented by the Confederation of Latin American Workers. Now I carry to these workers a message from the workers and people of China: the message of their example."[45]

As the previous quotation might indicate, Lombardo now speaks more about China than of the Soviet Union as an immediate example for Mexico to follow. He believes that the problems of underdeveloped, predominantly agrarian China are closer to Mexican realities than are those of the now highly industrialized Soviet Union. In a talk given in 1954 and printed under the title, *La Reforma Agraria en China y en México, Semejanzas y Diferencias*,[46] Lombardo presented a detailed analysis of the revolution and of the stages of the agrarian reform in China. He did not

43. *Ibid.*, pp. 14-21, 24, 27-28, 33-38, 40-44, 49, *passim*.
44. Mexico, 1950.
45. Lombardo Toledano, *Diario*, p. 212.
46. Mexico, 1954.

suggest that Mexico immediately follow the Chinese example. Rather, Mexico should pursue to a conclusion the program of agrarian reform embodied in its constitution. But the inference is clear that if it is genuinely to progress in the future, Mexico must follow the Chinese example and unite a thoroughgoing land reform with an industrial revolution as part of a planned program for the construction of socialism.[47]

Lombardo's well-written *Causas de la Elevación del Espíritu Humano*,[48] published in 1960, consists of a record of an imaginary series of conversations sustained in various parts of China between the author and Chinese citizens. The book is based upon Lombardo's experiences in China. Lombardo records conversations with representatives of various social classes of old China whose manners, customs, and ideas have changed and progressed with the social and material transformations brought by the Chinese Revolution. These representatives include former nomadic pastoralists, primitive farmers, slaves, serfs, and enfeoffed peasants, together with their former masters. In addition, oral exchanges with young leaders of the social revolution, with artisans, with farmers who also are manufacturers, and with industrial workers are recorded. In all, a panorama is presented of the vast material, social, and psychological transformations that have occurred and which continue to occur in revolutionary China.[49]

This gigantic process of change, of improvement, and of increasing strengthening of human dignity which Lombardo sees within China indicate to him the possibilities for infinite human improvement, for the ending of exploitation of man by man, for satisfying in abundance basic human material wants, and for the flowering of human potentials in all their variety.[50]

To the author's knowledge, Lombardo has not commented publicly upon Soviet-Chinese policy disputes.[51] He did, however, make an indirect reference to the disputes in an article published in the review *Siempre!* in December 1962, in which he said "the

47. *Ibid.*, pp. 44-45.
48. Mexico, 1960.
49. *Ibid.*, pp. 17-85.
50. *Ibid.*, pp. 87-94.
51. Since this was written Lombardo has published a detailed analysis of the Sino-Soviet ideological dispute in which he unequivocally supported the Soviet positions. See Vicente Lombardo Toledano, *¿Moscú o Pehin? La Vía Mexicana hacia el Socialismo* (Mexico, 1963).

debate between the parties and the governments which preside over the march of the socialist states around the principles which inspire them and around the great [world] problems, such as that of peace and that of the coexistence of all social regimes, [although] harsh at times, is a sign of affirmation of guiding ideas and of methods for achieving the common objectives.'"[52]

Lombardo, of course, is a staunch defender of the Cuban Revolution. Cuba has begun the second Latin-American revolution. The first was for political independence from Spain; the second is for economic independence from the United States.[53] At the time of the American-sponsored invasion of Cuba in April 1961, Lombardo issued a stirring appeal for volunteers to defend the Cuban people. The struggle of the Cuban people, Lombardo claimed, is one with that of the Mexican people. If the United States should be successful in the invasion of Cuba, he wrote, it would mean the Mexican people have suffered a defeat in their aspirations for the continuation of their democratic and anti-imperialist revolution. It would imply that United States imperialism and the forces associated with it are able to dominate the hemisphere and to dictate the major policies of the Latin-American nations.[54]

Lombardo noted in the following paragraph the United States' desire to split Mexico from support of the Cuban Revolution:

> Yankee imperialism and other forces of exploitation of weak peoples seek to flatter us saying that Mexico is the model of America, when they themselves know that our country is a paradise but for a national privileged minority and for North American monopolies, and that the forward march of our society is full of daily contradictions and of problems still unsolved. Their praise has no purpose other than to try to disassociate us from what happens in Cuba and to cause us to ignore the popular movements which exist in the Continent against the most primitive and bloody tyrannies. [Their praise seeks] even to cause us to condemn all popular manifestations of inconformity and the rebellions of the peoples who arise against misery, lack of democratic liberties and the surrender of the vital interests of their country to foreign imperialism.[55]

52. Vicente Lombardo Toledano, ''Las Grandes Lecciones de 1962,'' *Siempre!*, CDXCV (Dec. 12, 1962), 19.
53. New York *Times*, July 13, 1960, p. 3; Lombardo Toledano, *Al Pueblo Mexicano*, pp. 10-11.
54. Lombardo Toledano, *Al Pueblo Mexicano*, pp. 5-11.
55. *Ibid.*, p. 9.

In spite of his praise and staunch support of the Cuban Revolution, Lombardo does not advocate that Mexican leftists employ methods exactly similar to those of the Cuban revolutionaries. Mexico's road to socialism should be in accord with her own special circumstances.[56] (See also Chapter VIII.)

Lombardo devoted detailed attention to the problem of neonazism in the German Federal Republic in his scholarly book published in 1960 under the title: *El Neonazismo; Sus Características y Peligros*.[57] The work is divided into three chapters respectively entitled "From the Democratic-Bourgeois Revolution in Germany to German Imperialism," "Nazism: Its Economic Bases and its Political Consequences," and "The Rebirth of Nazism in the German Federal Republic and the Perspectives." Appendixes include an account of the names and the brief biographies of twenty-five generals of the Bundeswehr "who held high posts in Hitler's Wehrmacht and who participated in crimes against the European nations"; an account of the names and the brief biographies of nineteen members of the Federal Republic's foreign service "who held high posts in the Nazi Government and in the National Socialist Party"; and an account of the past and present offices of sixty-two West German judges who held posts in Czechoslovakia during World War II, together with the serial numbers on the list of war criminals of thirty of these judges.

The major themes of the book include the proposition that Germany's financial and industrial capitalist oligarchy was primarily responsible for bringing Hitler to power, for fascism was "the dictatorship of finance capitalism and constitute[d] the social philosophy of imperialism."[58] Since the war the capitalist oligarchy again has become predominant in West Germany; similar motivations—as well as similar propaganda and preparations—for imperialist expansion exist as before the war because these expansionist motivations arise from the structural nature of capitalism. The concatenation of world forces, he reasons, is unfavorable to the budding revival of German militarism. Factors which serve to prevent the success of German neonazism include the number and strength of the socialist nations, the existence of the Warsaw Pact, the division of Germany into two parts, the unity and

---

56. Lombardo Toledano, *Teoría y Práctica*, p. 165.
57. Mexico, 1960.
58. *Ibid.*, p. 31.

strength of the French and Italian working classes, the limited areas in the world remaining available for colonial exploitation, and the opposition to remilitarization within the West German working class itself. The only real solution of the German question is the confederation of the two Germanies on the basis of the free choice of the German people. Lombardo implies that this reunification will occur only on the basis of a socialist Germany.[59]

Lombardo has written a number of other works on foreign nations and international problems, including *La Revolución del Brasil*,[60] *Dos Conferencias sobre Israel*,[61] and *En los Mares de Ulises: Sicilia*.[62] Suffice it here to mention briefly the last work, for it reveals the breadth of Lombardo's interests and the depth of his knowledge. The work is a collection of six articles Lombardo wrote for the Mexican review *Siempre!* during his visit to Italy in 1956 to attend the Fourth Congress of the Italian General Confederation of Labor. Five of the articles deal with Sicily and one with the general problems of Italian development since the war. In the former, Lombardo briefly described the historical and classical background of Sicily, the Sicilian countryside and its development, the qualities of the remnants in Sicily of ancient Grecian architecture, the Sicilian agrarian reform, and popular Sicilian poetry.

In the course of the articles Lombardo revealed a rich knowledge of classical history and literature. From this knowledge and from his interpretation of Sicilian experiences, he drew inferences which he applied to Mexican problems. To give but one example: upon the basis of his analysis of the qualities of Grecian architecture Lombardo made a generalization which implied a warning against the denaturalizing influence of imperialism upon Mexican culture:

> The landscape [to which real architecture is functionally interrelated] is geography; but also it is history, especially in those countries in which architecture had an age of past splendor. To maintain one's own [character], one's national [character], in the form and to give it new content in accordance with the changes imposed by historical development, is to have one's own, unconfused architecture, and not

59. *Ibid.*, pp. 33-57, 59-73.
60. Mexico, 1936.
61. Mexico, 1951.
62. Mexico, 1956.

to break the spiritual thread of that supreme manifestation
of man—his culture. Because when there is discontinuity
in the art manifestations of a people, the latter constantly
has to rebegin its history and its infancy persists, with the
risk of never achieving maturity with personality and independence.[63]

Lombardo's attitudes toward the rise of fascism in the 1930's
and toward the beginnings of World War II are worthy of
separate consideration. Lombardo was an opponent of fascism from
its beginnings. In the January 15, 1934, issue of the review
Futuro (which he founded and directed), Lombardo noted the rise
to power of Hitler and forcefully attacked the fascist dictator for
his inhumane and anti-intellectual activities. He seemed, however, to underestimate Hitler's potentialities.[64]

Lombardo considered fascism but a form of capitalism; the
conflicts between fascist nations and other capitalist nations were
manifestations of interimperialist rivalries. He clearly recognized,
nevertheless, the superiority of democratic capitalism over its
diseased manifestation. "Between democratic capitalism and
fascist capitalism, the first is preferable: the exploited mass can
use its liberty to prepare its decisive historical action; under
fascism the preparation is very difficult."[65] In a speech delivered
in 1937, Lombardo made one of his most explicit explanations of
the nature and the consequences of fascism. He described fascism
as "the armed violence of the bourgeois regime which tries to
survive by destroying the positive works of civilization, throwing
the world into the bonfire of international war and into the
barbarity of the cruelest tyranny known to history."[66] To fight
against fascism, he then argued, is to fight for the Mexican Revolution.[67]

Lombardo was very critical of the policies of the western
capitalist nations toward the rise of fascism. He especially condemned the vacillation and hesitation expressed in the national

63. *Ibid.*, p. 30.
64. Vicente Lombardo Toledano, "Hitler, el Grotesco Dictador de Alemania," *Futuro*, IV (Jan. 15, 1934), 10.
65. Lombardo Toledano, *La Doctrina Socialista y su Interpretación en el Artículo 3°*, p. 27.
66. Vicente Lombardo Toledano, "El Veinte de Noviembre," *Futuro*, XXII (Dec., 1937), 5.
67. *Ibid.*

policies of England and France. Lombardo took advantage of his presence (as representative of the CTM) at the meeting of the Council of the International Labor Federation held in Oslo, Norway, in May 1938 to speak in criticism of the vacillating actions of the western European governments and to call upon the European workers to pressure their governments into action to impede the growth of fascism in Germany and Italy. He condemned the theory of the "lesser evil" which guided the rulers of France and Britain in the face of Hitler's threats as "not only a suicidal theory, but a theory contrary to the interests of humanity."[68] Lombardo repeated his criticisms at an International Labor Office reunion held in Geneva in June of the same year.[69]

The Munich betrayal gave rise to a special edition of *Futuro*. This edition together with the next regular issue of the review propounded the theme that war would come as a consequence of the Munich concessions.[70] Immediately after the German invasion of Poland, the Lombardo-influenced newspaper, *El Popular*, declared that "We cannot adopt an attitude of false, hypocritical, or cowardly neutrality...."[71]

The signing of the Soviet-German non-aggression pact brought a change in Lombardo's attitude in accordance with the new Soviet posture. His position remained antifascist and pro-Allied. Rather than urging common and forceful opposition to the Axis powers, however, he declared that neutrality was the proper course of action for those nations not involved directly in the combat. The Allies were responsible, according to Lombardo, for the Soviet Union's retreat to neutrality. By their vacillations, the reactionary governments of France and England had encouraged the German and Italian aggressions. Furthermore, Chamberlain and Daladier hoped to turn German and Japanese aggression against the Soviet Union. The Soviet Union, on the other hand, had staunchly and continuously attempted to create a system of collective security in Europe to oppose fascist expansionism. Confronted by the failure of its efforts and by the anti-Soviet maneuvers of the French and English representatives, the Soviet Union considered itself forced to sign the pact with Germany as a

68. Vicente Lombardo Toledano, "La Situación Actual," *Futuro*, LII (June, 1940), 39.
69. *Ibid.*, pp. 38-39.
70. *Futuro*, Oct. 10, 1938; *Futuro*, XXXIII (Nov., 1938).
71. *El Popular*, Sept. 2, 1939. Quoted in Kirk, p. 99.

measure of self-defense. France and England harvested what they had sown—disunity. The conflict was then but a bellicose manifestation of interimperialist rivalries for redivision of the world. As such it was similar in character to World War I—although World War II had "extraordinarily complex characteristics" which the former did not have.[72]

Throughout 1940 and the early part of 1941, Lombardo continued to treat the war as essentially an interimperialist rivalry—although always from a very anti-Axis, pro-Allied point of view. He insisted that Mexico, as a semicolonial country, must remain neutral in the fray. His attitude is summed up in statements made in an address of May 21, 1940, to a congress of the Partido Revolucionario Mexicano (PRM)—Mexico's official government political party at that time—held in Mexico City's Palace of Fine Arts:

> The labor movement of Mexico, adequately conscious of its historical destiny and sufficiently conscious of its responsibility as an integral part of the world proletariat, is and shall be always a fighting force against fascism. But also labor will be a force against the maintenance of the privileges of capitalist imperialism and of the false democracy of Western Europe which only in its formal aspects can be distinguished from Italian fascism or from German Nazism.
>
> Who are responsible for this hecatomb? Who? Both: the bourgeois regime, the capitalist regime, and those who associate with, embrace, and come to an understanding with this regime are responsible for the war. Two capitalist forces which once again are trying to divide the earth [share equal responsibility for the conflict]....[73]

He continued stating that the Mexican workers wanted a democratic order in Europe which would represent the people and not the bourgeoisie—an order which would guarantee peace, human rights, and human progress, and would put an end to colonialism.[74]

The following month, the first Executive Council meeting of

72. "La Nueva Guerra Imperialista," *Futuro*, XLIV (Oct., 1939), 3-4. Here and below several unsigned editorials in *Futuro* have been referred to in tracing Lombardo's thought. Lombardo has informed this writer that although he did not always write the editorials, they nevertheless accurately reflect his ideas.
73. Lombardo Toledano, "La Situación Actual," pp. 38-39.
74. *Ibid.*, p. 39.

the Confederación de Trabajadores de América Latina—Lombardo was its president—passed a resolution which declared, in part, that "the workers of Latin America consider the present war, like that of 1914, to be essentially a struggle between two major groups of capitalist countries, fighting for economic and political domination. This struggle is not the workers' concern. They have not provoked the crisis and are the only ones suffering from it."[75]

Lombardo realized fully that it was but a matter of time before Germany and the Soviet Union would go to war. To him Soviet actions in Finland, Poland, the Baltic nations, and Rumania were taken in preparation for the inevitable encounter.[76] He expressed hope, however, that popular uprisings would occur in the winter of 1940-1941 which would put an end to the war.

One thing, at least, was certain from the experiences of recent years: "Never before has the route to follow stood out with such clarity as at present: the route of the struggle of the working masses for the collectivization of the means of production and for the right to trace their own destinies, the route of socialism."[77]

Futuro editorials in the early part of 1941 praised Roosevelt for the firmness of his pro-Allied stand and expressed hope that the United States might enter the war. But concern was expressed over the imperialist interests within the Allied camp.[78] The editorials claimed that because the war was essentially merely an interimperialist struggle, Mexico's position must remain one of neutrality and defense of its national sovereignty.[79]

In a speech delivered before the National Council of the CTM shortly before the German attack upon the Soviet Union in June 1941, Lombardo suggested the organization of a continentwide antifascist, anti-imperialist, and democratic movement.[80] After the attack, Lombardo pursued the idea vigorously as he rushed to the support of the Soviet Union. Lombardo's position was summarized amply in an address he delivered on July 14, 1941, before

75. "Bajo la Sombra de Paraguas," *Futuro*, LIII (July, 1940), 13.
76. "Compas de Espera," *Futuro*, LIV (Aug., 1940), 13.
77. "Bajo la Sombra," p. 13.
78. "Donde y Como Terminará la Guerra?," *Futuro*, LX (Feb., 1941), 3-4; "La Trascendencia de la Ley de Plenos Poderes," *Futuro*, LXII (April, 1941), 3-4.
79. "Lucha Nacional contra el Fascismo," *Futuro*, LXV (July, 1941), 1-2.
80. *Ibid.*, p. 2.

a large meeting held at the call of the CTM in the Arena México in Mexico City.[81]

The present war, as World War I, Lombardo expounded, was the result of interimperialist rivalries. The aggressions of Nazi Germany were but a form of capitalist imperialist expansionism. The bourgeoisie of the world had been divided in the 1930's between those who sought to maintain the liberal institutions of nineteenth-century capitalism and those who sought to come to an understanding with Hitler and Mussolini in order to establish comparable dictatorships.[82] The attempts by several capitalist regimes to appease Hitler and to turn him solely against the Soviet Union failed.

The war, after the German invasion of the Soviet Union in 1941, was not an interimperialist struggle because the Soviet Union was a non-imperialist socialist nation. The popular forces of the world were given an opportunity to create a genuinely democratic world from the chaos of the war. The war, Lombardo maintained, was not a class war nor a war between socialism and capitalism. Rather, it was a "fight against the most ferocious of the historical tyrannies"—a struggle between civilization and barbarity. The Mexican people, consequently, should immediately join in the struggle against the Axis powers.[83]

Participation by Mexico in the struggle against fascism did not mean that the Mexican people should forget the development of the Mexican Revolution nor the realization of the immediate goals of the Mexican workers. Neither did it mean that Mexican national interests would be sacrificed to the imperialist designs of one of the Allies: "the result would be paradoxical if when all ally to fight against a common enemy one of the allies should fall in the hands of [another of the allies], perhaps even before the defeat of the common enemy. It is absurd to conceive such a possibility; similarly, it is impossible to admit that the fight against fascism should imply the growth of imperialism in a capitalist country against the sovereignty of the semicolonial countries."[84]

Lombardo's position on the war had changed. The war was a popular struggle against fascist barbarism; all help should be lent

81. "Barbarie contra Civilización, el Discurso de Lombardo Toledano," *Futuro*, LXVI (Aug., 1941), 1-2.
82. *Ibid.*, p. 1.
83. *Ibid.*, p. 2.
84. *Ibid.*

the Allied cause. His position in the summer of 1941 more closely resembled his pre-Moscow-Berlin pact attitude. It remained the same throughout the remainder of the war.

As president of the Confederación de Trabajadores de América Latina, Lombardo undertook a speaking tour of twelve Latin-American nations in order to rally support for an antifascist united front.[85] Neutrality was a thing of the past. In a speech delivered in January 1942, Lombardo stated: "There are only two fronts: against Hitler and his allies, or in favor of Hitler and his allies. Not only is it absurd to conceive of neutrality, but the neutral is nothing more than a fascist ambush, cynical and cowardly."[86] Shortly thereafter, he called upon Mexican President Ávila Camacho to declare war against Germany.[87]

In several speeches, Lombardo stated clearly his position on the Soviet Union. The Soviet regime and the Red army had saved humanity from fascism.[88] All must come to the defense of the Soviet Union—"To defend the only force capable of liquidating fascism is to defend oneself, and to guarantee the possibility of new and constant progresses in the future."[89] Again, "Think, comrades of Mexico, what a victory of Hitler over the Soviet Union would mean. For how many years more would the working class of the world have to await the moment to conquer its lost liberties and the possibility of attaining others even greater."[90]

The main theme of Lombardo's wartime speeches was that of unity within and among the Allied nations against the common Axis enemies. Consequently, Lombardo stressed solidarity between the United States and Latin-America. He did not, however, cease to criticize or warn against United States imperialism. This point is worthy of emphasis because some writers have given the impression that in stressing co-operation Lombardo suddenly and opportunistically abandoned prewar criticisms of American imperialism.[91]

In an address delivered in January 1942, Lombardo stated that Mexico must ally with the United States against fascism. All at-

85. Lombardo Toledano, *El Neonazismo*, pp. 52-53.
86. Lombardo Toledano, *Lenin, el Genio*, p. 20.
87. Hayes, p. 199.
88. Lombardo Toledano, *La Revolución Rusa—la Revolución Mexicana*, pp. 11-12.
89. Lombardo Toledano, *Lenin, el Genio*, p. 16.
90. *Ibid.*, p. 20.
91. Kirk, pp. 99-102; Alexander, pp. 340-341.

tempts by rightists to divide Latin-America from the United States over the issue of imperialism must be opposed. He went on to criticize United States imperialism as "the permanent enemy of our independence, of our internal liberty and of our progress"[92] but added that, nevertheless, the people of Latin-America must unite with those of the United States to oppose fascism, which is "the most ferocious of all imperialisms."[93]

In a report delivered in 1942 to the Second Inter-American Agricultural Conference, Lombardo proposed that Latin-America lend full economic support to the war effort. At the same time, he spoke of providing sound bases for Latin-American economic development by means of replacing the control of Latin-America's foreign commerce by a few large private corporations with a continental system of state control over foreign trade and prices.[94] He emphasized the general point that in the past Latin-American development has been conditioned by the needs of foreign (including American) imperialisms for food and raw materials. Future development, he felt, must be conditioned by Latin-America's own needs.[95]

In a work published in English in the same year, *The United States and Mexico; Two Nations—One Ideal*, Lombardo continued to emphasize inter-American unity and defeat of rightist attempts at division. He stressed common ideals and the positive aspects of hemisphere relationships. At the same time, though, he pointed to the negative aspects of past and present United States relations with Latin-America. The negative actions and policies were not the fault of the American people, however, but were the responsibility of a small number of imperialistic American monopolies. He expressed the wish that after the war the "American hemisphere economy" could free itself from United States imperialistic domination and develop on the basic of planning and co-operation between all the governments of the Americas. All must continue united for the promotion of liberty, progress, and the right of self-determination.[96]

One final example: in a speech delivered in El Paso's Liberty Hall on July 4, 1943, Lombardo continued to stress the theme of

92. Lombardo Toledano, *Lenin, el Genio*, pp. 18-19.
93. *Ibid.*, p. 20.
94. Lombardo Toledano, *Los Principales Problemas*, pp. 58-59.
95. *Ibid.*, pp. 70-79.
96. Lombardo Toledano, *The United States and Mexico*, pp. 9-21.

unity between the United States and Latin-America in the fight for liberty and democracy against fascist imperialism. But he criticized American imperialism, commenting that whereas the United States has developed rapidly economically, Latin America "has seen its development stagnated, its economic structure deformed and the fulfillment of its destiny impeded by the work of a small group of great financiers, industrialists and merchants of North America."[97] He pointed out, though, that "in Latin America, no people is an enemy of the United States nor of the North American people. On the other hand, all the peoples are enemies of imperialism."[98] Toward the end of his address, Lombardo predicted the postwar policies of the Latin-American proletariat: "if the Atlantic Charter is fulfilled faithfully, if the national liberation of our peoples is permitted and facilitated, Latin America will follow in peace exactly the same conduct as during war. And, on the contrary, if this compromise is not fulfilled the proletariat will fight for the national liberation of these peoples."[99]

As implied at the beginning of this chapter, Lombardo constantly and consistently has stressed the theme of world peace. "The great problem of our time is to avoid a new world war. [We must] fight for total disarmament, fight for peaceful coexistence of the different systems of social life and [fight for] respect for the right which every people has to give itself the form of government which it pleases."[100]

Mexico, says Lombardo, has a special interest in peace. In the event of future war, the United States would lose out in Europe, Asia, and Africa; consequently, it would increase its aggressiveness in Latin-America.[101] Mexico would be completely subjected to United States imperialism. National territory would be lost to serve as American military bases and part of the Mexican people would "serve as cannon fodder for a cause completely foreign to our history, to our present interests and to our future."[102]

The Soviet Union—together with the other socialist nations— is the greatest bulwark against war, Lombardo maintains. The Soviet Union requires peace in order to pursue its internal de-

97. *El Popular*, July 6, 1943, p. 6.
98. *Ibid.*
99. *Ibid.*
100. Lombardo Toledano, *Teoría y Prática*, pp. 154-155.
101. Lombardo Toledano, *En Torno al XX Congreso*, pp. 237-241.
102. Lombardo Toledano, *Por Vez Primera*, p. 13.

velopment. Socialism eliminates the harsh economic, social, and political contradictions which lead to war. By means of constant adjustments in social relationships, a controlled equilibrium is maintained in the Soviet Union between the developing forces of production and the social relations of production. Thereby the Soviet Union prevents the occurrence in her social structure of extreme, unreconciled contradictions which engender impulses toward foreign expansion as an alternative to genuine reconciliation of the contradictions. Such realistic solutions to its structural problems are possible because, he contends, there are no social classes in the Soviet Union with antagonistic interests and goals, and hence also with antagonistic solutions to major social problems. The planned, controlled development of society is possible.[103]

The capitalist-imperialist nations, Lombardo notes, on the other hand, are driven toward war and expansionism by the unresolved contradictions inherent within the capitalist mode of production. These contradictions arise from antagonisms between the developing forces of production and the capitalistic social relations of production; or, in other terms, from the antagonisms between social production and private appropriation of the product of social labor. Repercussions follow in social class conflicts and in political turmoil. War is sought as an escape from the inevitable solution to the contradictions—socialization of the means of production, exchange, and distribution. Thus, in preparation for war, the West is arming itself and is creating a variety of aggressive military blocs such as NATO and SEATO.[104]

Lombardo points out, however, that war is not inevitable. Lenin's dictum that war is inevitable as long as imperialism exists was justified at the time it was made. But conditions have changed. The correlation of world forces now favors socialism and peace.[105] Not only are the socialist nations for peace, but so are the vast majority of all the people of the world. It is the strength of these forces for peace which has so far prevented another world war. Peace can be maintained in the future. The popular forces of the world must seek it ardently.[106]

103. Lombardo Toledano, *La Revolución Rusa—la Revolución Mexicana,* pp. 12-14; *La Perspectiva de México,* pp. 18-19.
104. Lombardo Toledano, *La Perspectiva de México,* pp. 19-22; Lombardo Toledano, *La Rebelión del Mundo Colonial,* pp. 5-6, 23.
105. Lombardo Toledano, *Teoría y Práctica,* p. 154.
106. Lombardo Toledano, *La Perspectiva de México,* pp. 19-20; *En Torno al XX Congreso,* pp. 241-244.

VII. *Career as a Labor Leader,*
1933-1962

Lombardo's Marxist concepts have led him to place increased emphasis upon his activities within the labor movement. His objective has been to unify Mexican labor into a single labor confederation which would be independent of state control, democratic in its organizational procedures, revolutionary in its political orientation, and militant in its struggles with its class opponents. Further, Lombardo has sought to promote the international solidarity of the workers of the world. In common with other Marxist socialists, Lombardo sought to unify the labor movement because such unity together with the formation in Mexico of a common front of the working, petty bourgeois and elements of the national bourgeois classes was considered indispensable for the achievement of political power by the working class. Once in control of state power the working class will proceed to construct socialism.

The organization of the Confederación General de Obreros y Campesinos de México (CGOCM) in October 1933 was a major advance in labor unification and in the orientation of Mexican workers toward conscious class struggle. The CGOCM stressed three principal themes: class struggle, union democracy, and independence from state control. A majority of the nation's unions associated with the new national labor central.

The CGOCM, with Vicente Lombardo Toledano at its head, organized strikes, stoppages, protests, boycotts, and mass public meetings in pursuit of its objectives of unification, class struggle, and improved conditions for the workers. The workers' militancy was reinforced by their discontent over the generally poor economic conditions and the virtual cessation of revolutionary reform in the early 1930's. In 1933, 13 strikes occurred; in 1934, 202 involving 14,685 strikers and in 1935, 642 involving 145,212 strikers.[1] The strikes (both CGOCM and non-CGOCM directed) in the spring of 1935—the greatest wave of strikes in Mexican

1. López Aparicio, *El Movimiento Obrero en México*, p. 221; Dulles, p. 631; Weyl and Weyl, p. 240; J. H. Plenn, *Mexico Marches* (Indianapolis, 1939), pp. 271-272. Plenn puts the number of strikes in 1934 at 235.

history—affected a number of major concerns, such as Mexican Tramways Company, Ltd. (Canadian), Huasteca Petroleum Company (subsidiary of Standard Oil), Mexican Telephone and Telegraph (AT&T), and a number of mining companies.

Lázaro Cárdenas, elected president in 1934, early demonstrated a desire to renew with vigor the program of revolutionary reform. He faced opposition, however, from ex-president Plutarco Elías Calles, political strongman of Mexico since 1924. In a move to assert his control over Cárdenas and the Mexican nation, Calles (who owned shares in Mexican Telephone and Telegraph) in a statement made public on June 12, 1935, denounced the wave of strikes as subversive, attributed the strikes to the personal ambitions of Lombardo Toledano and other labor leaders, and threatened indirectly to overthrow Cárdenas as he had Pascual Ortíz Rubio in 1932.[2]

Cárdenas immediately delivered a speech in support of the workers, in which he declared: "I hereby declare that I have full confidence in the workers' and peasants' organizations, and I trust that they will know how to act with the temperance and patriotism that are required by the legitimate interests which they defend."[3]

Lombardo, as head of the CGOCM, rallied organized labor to the support of the President. In the name of his union, Lombardo issued a general call for a reunion of representatives of all the workers' organizations of Mexico to organize for the defense of the working class. As a result of the reunion, the National Committee for Proletarian Defense was created. Except for a few which were communist controlled, most of Mexico's unions adhered to the committee. The committee issued a joint pact which read:

> The organized labor and peasant movement of Mexico protests against the declarations of General Calles and declares that it will defend the rights of the workers, obtained by its efforts, such as strikes without restrictions, association in unions, and others; and that it will not cease fighting for the economic and social betterment of the wage earner.
>
> The strike movement assailed by Calles is due to a collective uneasiness and a state of social injustice. It is a phenomenon that can be ignored only by those who represent capitalist interests.

2. Dulles, pp. 634-639, discusses the background and summarizes and presents quotations from Calles's statement.
3. Quoted in Millan, p. 95.

Strikes will end only when a transformation of the bourgeois system under which we live has been achieved.

The organized labor and peasant movement of Mexico, being perfectly aware of the historical moment in which it lives, declares that it will oppose all transgressions of its rights, utilizing, if necessary, the general, nation-wide strike as the only means of defense against the possible implantation of a Fascist regime in Mexico. In the face of this threat, the Committee declares its intention of maintaining class unity.[4]

After a series of incidents which included the dynamite bombing of Lombardo's home, Calles was forced to leave the country in April 1936.

In the meantime, Lombardo had been pushing for the organization of a new national labor confederation. Against contrary opinion, Lombardo emphasized above all that the principal theme of the projected organization must be that of unity. Consequently, all unions should be members, regardless of their ideological or religious tendencies. Similarly, all political tendencies should be represented in the national direction.[5]

Between February 26 and 29, 1936, a constitutional convention organized the Confederación de Trabajadores de México (CTM); Lombardo was elected secretary-general for a five-year term. The CGOCM merged with the CTM and gave up its separate identity. The nature of the Lombardo-inspired CTM can be seen in the following quotations from its founding statutes:

> The Mexican proletariat will fight fundamentally for the total abolition of the capitalist regime. Nevertheless, taking into account that Mexico gravitates within the orbit of imperialism, it becomes indispensable in order to arrive at the first stated objective to attain first the political and economic liberation of the country.
>
> By means of the reaffirmation and the amplification of its solidarity with all the workers of the world, the Mexican proletariat will fight, organized and systematically, until it

---

4. Quoted in *ibid.*, p. 97.
5. The preceding account has been summarized from information presented in Lombardo Toledano, *Teoría y Práctica*, pp. 66-71; Millan, pp. 87-106; Dulles, pp. 625-649, 659-681; Harker, pp. 153-154, 195-198; Hayes, pp. 36-37; Plenn, pp. 124-126.

eliminates all the obstacles which hinder the attainment of its objectives.

The Mexican proletariat also will fight energetically for the attainment of all the immediate gains which are enumerated further on, without losing sight for a single moment that such gains should not turn it from its fundamental purposes....

The Mexican proletariat recognizes the international character of the worker and peasant movement and of the fight for socialism. By virtue of this, at the same time as it establishes the closest relations with the labor movement of the other countries of the earth and as it struggles for the development of the fullest and most effective international solidarity, it will do all it can on its part to achieve international unity of the organized proletarian movement....

The Mexican proletariat will fight at all cost to maintain its ideological and organizational independence and so that all its final objectives may be reached with entire class independence, by means of its own forces, free from foreign influences and tutelage....

The motto of the Confederation is:

"FOR A CLASSLESS SOCIETY."[6]

Most of Mexico's labor unions joined the new labor confederation, but two minor national confederations (the Confederación Regional Obrera Mexicana and the Confederación General de Trabajadores) and several regional federations remained unaffiliated.[7] At the peak of its strength the CTM claimed over one million members;[8] others, however, have put the figure at one-half million[9] or less.[10]

---

6. Confederación de Trabajadores de México, *C.T.M., 1936-1941* (Mexico, 1941), pp. 67, 69, 71.

7. Weyl and Weyl, pp. 237-240; López Aparicio, p. 224; Plenn, pp. 269-270. The CROM, of course, had been the largest labor confederation in Mexico during the 1920's, but its strength was greatly reduced by the split in its ranks which occurred in the early 1930's.

8. López Aparicio, p. 224.

9. "Mexican Labor in Hemisphere Politics," *The American Analyst*, Pilot Copy No. 4 (Oct. 15, 1946), p. 25. Weyl and Weyl, p. 238, estimated 600,000 members for the CTM at the end of 1938.

10. Rachel Newborn Hill, "A Sketch of the Mexican Labor Movement" (unpublished M.A. thesis, Columbia University, 1946), pp. 61-62.

Division threatened the CTM soon after its formation when the Mexican Communist party withdrew its member unions after it failed in its attempt to gain complete control of the confederation. With the assistance of Earl Browder and the American Communist party, the split was soon healed.[11] Lombardo claims that permanent damage had been done, however, as the Communists did not regain the three posts which they had previously held on the National Committee. Political moderates now held these positions, much to the future detriment of the socialist ideological orientation of the CTM.[12]

In accordance with the principles contained in the statutes of the CTM and in agreement with his personal Marxist convictions, Lombardo sought to guide the CTM along three paths: (1) Unity within labor in order that labor might struggle more effectively for its immediate and its long-range objectives; (2) unity of labor with the peasantry, the middle class, and other progressive forces in order to form a broad popular front to promote the Mexican Revolution; and (3) unity with the international forces opposed to fascism and imperialism and struggling for peace.[13] The CTM became a positive and principal force, along with the Cárdenas administration, in promoting the progress of the revolution. At the same time, it managed to remain independent of governmental domination.

The CTM won a number of victories for rural and urban labor. In general, the CTM received the support of the Cárdenas administration in its disputes with capitalists and landlords.[14] Some of the most important initial victories were won in agriculture. From 1934 to 1936 the CGOCM, under Lombardo's direction, made concentrated efforts to organize rural laborers, especially the sugar, cotton, and henequen workers. The CTM, under Lombardo's leadership, continued this policy. It organized hacienda workers and forced the owners to recognize and deal with the unions. Then it assisted the workers in preparing petitions to the government for a division of lands—preferably in the form of

11. Alexander, pp. 332-334.
12. Lombardo Toledano, *Teoría y Práctica*, pp. 80-82.
13. Ramírez y Ramírez, "Vicente Lombardo Toledano, Un Militante de la Clase Obrera de México," p. 41; *El Frente Único en México*, p. 25.
14. López Aparicio, p. 226. For a discussion of CTM tactics and Mexican labor law, see C. L. Jones, "If Lewis Sits Down in Mexico," *The American Scholar*, VI (Oct., 1937), 471-480.

large-scale co-operatives. After the land was partitioned, the CTM attempted to insure that the new users received financial credit, that democratic procedures prevailed in the functioning of the *ejidos*,[15] and that the bureaucratic control of the Ejidal Banks was restricted.[16]

The first major CTM-directed agrarian strike occurred in the La Laguna district centering around Torreón, Coahuila. The landowners of the region had refused to bargain collectively or to meet any of the workers' demands. Lombardo went to Torreón to direct negotiations. The owners were adamant, so a strike was called to begin on August 19, 1936. According to Lombardo, the owners not only had refused to discuss the demand for a collective labor contract but even had taunted the government to try to apply the Agrarian Code. If the lands were divided, the owners claimed, within a year the government would ask the former owners to repossess the lands because the agricultural workers (*peones*) would be incapable of working them. In brief, their attitude, according to Lombardo, was "provocative and aggressive." Lombardo reported the stand of the owners to President Cárdenas by telephone; Cárdenas asked Lombardo to come to Mexico City. In a personal meeting with Cárdenas, Lombardo stressed in response to the President's inquiries that the workers preferred a division of lands rather than a collective labor contract.[17]

President Cárdenas and the Labor Department lent their support to the strikers. When the owners attempted to bring in strike-breakers and created armed "white guard" groups to use force against the workers, the federal government heeded the CTM's request that federal troops be sent into the area to maintain order and to disarm the "white guards." In November 1936, the government began to expropriate and redistribute the lands of the La Laguna region. For the first time in Mexican history, the Agrarian Code—which previously had been applied solely to the benefit of village communities—was employed to the advantage of *peones*. Furthermore, Cárdenas, who had great faith in producers' and consumers' co-operatives as a means to ease Mexico's

15. Semicommunal or communal land-holding communities.
16. Hayes, pp. 71-72, Weyl and Weyl, pp. 181, 189, 191-192.
17. Information supplied personally to the author by Vicente Lombardo Toledano in Sept. 1962.

economic and social problems,[18] heeded Lombardo's and the CTM's wishes: Mexico's first agricultural co-operatives were organized. The pattern of many future expropriations and reorganizations was thus established.[19] "The division of *La Laguna* signifies, without any doubt, the most transcendental step and the step of greatest revolutionary breadth taken by the Government of President Cárdenas."[20]

A major labor crisis began in Monterrey, Nuevo León, in February 1936 (the same month the CTM was formed) as the workers of a glass factory, Vidriera de Monterrey, S.A., went on strike. Lombardo spoke in support of these strikers, and labor organizers and agitators were active in other of the city's manufacturing centers. The business owners of Monterrey responded with a general lockout. Disturbances reached such a point that President Cárdenas went to Monterrey to intervene personally in the dispute. He issued his famous "fourteen points" which supported the organizing, unification, and collective bargaining of labor and warned the business owners against actions which might lead to armed conflict.[21] "The employers' class all over the country felt the force of a united organization with capable and unquestionably honest leaders."[22]

In the summer of 1936, the CTM successfully directed a strike against the powerful Compañía Mexicana de Luz y Fuerza Motriz, S.A. (Mexican Light and Power Company). The workers demanded, among other things, bonus payments and worker representation on the company's board of directors. Business and other activity in the entire Mexico City area was paralyzed for eight days. Lombardo organized a campaign of national support for the Mexican workers against the foreign enterprise; he took the unusual step of explaining the character of the strike to a meeting

18. See Weyl and Weyl, pp. 80-83, 103-104, 129-133, 137, 198-227, 260-278.
19. Harker, pp. 242-251; Confederación de Trabajadores, pp. 118-149. For information on Mexico's agricultural co-operatives during the Cárdenas period, see Weyl and Weyl, pp. 198-227.
20. Confederación de Trabajadores, p. 119.
21. *Ibid.*, pp. 11-28; William Cameron Townsend, *Lázaro Cárdenas* (Mexico, 1952), pp. 129-132; Javier Ramos Malzarraga, "Los Grandes Huelgas Victoriosas de la C.T.M., *Futuro*, LXI (March, 1941), 32; Weyl and Weyl, pp. 253-254.
22. Ramos Malzarraga, p. 32.

of foreign residents in Mexico City. The government supported the workers and the victory of the strike was complete.[23]

The CTM was instrumental in achieving the total nationalization of the nation's railroads. The railroad workers went on strike in March 1936.[24] The workers immediately resumed their tasks, however, when the Federal Board of Conciliation and Arbitration declared the strike illegal. The government, in its turn, saw to it that the workers' economic demands were met. The following year the government nationalized most of the nation's railroads and subsequently turned their management over to the workers—until 1940, when the government resumed their direction.[25]

The CTM was victorious in a number of other strikes during the first five years of its history. Significant victories were achieved in the sugar, textile (especially in the Orizaba region), silk, and rubber industries, in the public services, and in the agricultural regions of Yucatán, Tabasco (Standard Fruit Company), the Mexicali Valley, and the Yaqui River Valley.[26] Hundreds of co-operative societies in which the workers managed the enterprises and shared the profits were organized in the transportation, mining, sugar milling, fishing, shipping, printing, and other industries.[27]

Major victories were achieved in labor organizing. With the assistance of Lombardo and the CTM, the nation's teachers were organized for the first time into a single, nationwide union. The program of the new union reflected the radicalism of its progenitors. In addition, Lombardo helped achieve the unionization of the federal government employees. Cárdenas prevented affiliation of the new union with the CTM; nevertheless, consultations on important decisions were common between the leaders of the two organizations.[28]

23. Confederación de Trabajadores, pp. 104-116; Harker, pp. 224-228.
24. The nation's railroads were partially nationalized in the first decade of the century.
25. Confederación de Trabajadores, pp. 273-277; Weyl and Weyl, pp. 269-276; Ramos Malzarraga, pp. 32-33; ''Steel Velvet,'' *The Literary Digest*, CXXI (May 30, 1936), 15.
26. Virginia Prewett, *Reportage on Mexico* (New York, 1941), p. 160; Ramos Malzarraga, pp. 33, 79. The collection, Confederación de Trabajadoes de México, *C.T.M., 1936-1941*, reprints a number of documents pertaining to the strikes of this period. Lombardo in his *Teoría y Práctica*, pp. 74-77, presents a general account of the major strikes.
27. Weyl and Weyl, pp. 253-278.
28. Hayes, pp. 69-70.

The greatest victory of Lombardo and the CTM occurred in the oil industry which was dominated by two foreign corporations, the Standard Oil Company and Royal Dutch Shell. The oil workers went on strike in May 1937, seeking a number of economic and organizational changes. Acting in accordance with previous plans, the workers lifted the strike and, in conformity with Mexican law, placed their complaint before the Federal Board of Conciliation and Arbitration. In December, the latter handed down a decision favorable to the demands of the oil workers. The oil companies appealed the decision to the Supreme Court of Mexico.[29] Lombardo foretold the future trend of events in a speech delivered to the CTM on February 22, 1938: "Comrades, it seems to be inevitable that the moment will come when the petroleum companies will have to be replaced by representatives of the State and the Mexican workers in order to maintain petroleum production. We are ready and willing to assume the technical, economic, legal, moral and historic responsibility that befits a nation of free men."[30]

Lombardo went on to predict with remarkable accuracy that once expropriated, the oil companies would cause Mexico serious economic difficulties by hindering the international sale of Mexican oil, and that internal foes, such as General Saturnino Cedillo, governor of San Luís Potosí, would attempt to take advantage of this situation to seek power and destroy the revolution.[31]

On March 1, 1938, the Supreme Court upheld the ruling of the Federal Board of Conciliation and Arbitration. The oil companies refused to accept the ruling and in so doing accused the court of being a tool of Lombardo.[32]

Lombardo's response was immediate. As secretary-general of the CTM he sent a request to all national federations, state federations, and national industrial unions to participate in a work stoppage and public demonstration in support of the oil workers and the Cárdenas government. The demonstration was to begin at 10:00 A.M., March 23.[33] In his official capacity, Lombardo dispatched three additional messages the same day. One was directed

29. Confederación de Trabajadores, pp. 286-293; Lombardo Toledano, *Teoría y Práctica*, pp. 75-77; Weyl and Weyl, pp. 293-296.
30. Quoted in Millan, p. 204.
31. *Ibid.*, pp. 204-205.
32. Weyl and Weyl, pp. 297-298.
33. *El Universal*, March 16, 1938, p. 16.

to the Oil Workers Union as a note of solidarity; another (signed by the members of the CTM's National Committee) was addressed to the newspapers of Mexico asking that ideological and political differences be forgotten and that all unite in support of the government and the nation "in defense of their nationality"; a third was dispatched in the form of a telegram to all the "labor centrals of the world" outlining the history of the dispute and requesting moral support for the Mexican people in their struggle "in defense of democracy and human liberties."[34]

On March 16, the National Committee of the CTM and the Executive Committee of the Oil Workers Union held an extensive meeting in which it was decided that on the following day they would present a written request to the Federal Board of Conciliation and Arbitration that the labor contracts in the oil industry be cancelled and that the oil companies be required to pay the indemnities which legally would be due the workers as a consequence of the cancellation.[35] The objective was to bring about the nationalization of the petroleum industry.[36] The CTM continued with its preparations for the demonstration on the twenty-third, and a number of unions sent telegrams of support to President Cárdenas as he faced the possibility of counteractions by the oil companies and by foreign governments.[37]

On March 17, the demand for cancellation of the labor contracts was presented to the federal board. The National Committee of the CTM sent messages of invitation to attend the demonstration of the twenty-third to President Cárdenas, to the secretaries of state, to the members of the National Congress and the Supreme Court, and to other members of the government. At the same time it issued similar invitations to a number of political and popular organizations, such as the National Peasant Confederation and the Mexican Communist party. Finally, the CTM requested that all business activity cease in Mexico City during the demonstration. The same day, a message of support was received from John L. Lewis, president of the CIO.[38]

On March 18, the federal board notified the petroleum workers that their contracts had been cancelled. The petroleum workers

34. *Ibid.*
35. *El Universal*, March 17, 1938, p. 1.
36. Lombardo Toledano, *Teoría y Práctica*, p. 77.
37. *El Universal*, March 17, 1938, p. 15.
38. *El Universal*, March 18, 1938, pp. 1, 4.

promptly sent a message to President Cárdenas announcing that work would stop at 12:01 A.M., March 19. During the same day, the national committee of the CTM sent a message to the various employers' associations in Mexico requesting their support in the forthcoming demonstration. At 7:00 P.M., Cárdenas held a conference with the chief members of his government. Shortly thereafter, President Cárdenas announced the expropriation and nationalization of the oil industry.[39]

Lombardo issued a statement the same evening which was printed in bold face type as an insert on page one of *El Universal* the following morning. It read:

> All those present at the transcendental act of the reading of the manifesto which the President of the Republic has directed to the Mexican people on the occasion of the expropriation of the petroleum industry have agreed in affirming that this document has the value of an act of national economic independence, in the same manner as that of 1821 has the significance of the act of the political independence of Mexico.
>
> The political Revolution, after more than a century, has produced, dialectically, the economic Revolution.
>
> Mexico begins to acquire today a profound sense of its great historic destiny.[40]

On March 19, the National Committee of the CTM issued a formal statement in support of the expropriation. It reviewed the dispute and demonstrated that the workers had acted legally at all times. It concluded by announcing that the demonstration set for March 23 would be one not only of support for the government but also of national rejoicing.[41]

The demonstration was held as planned on March 23, 1938. It was the greatest demonstration Mexico City had ever seen.[42]

Lombardo's prediction came true: as a consequence of expropriation Mexico suffered from economic difficulties as a consequence of the retaliatory tactics of the expropriated oil companies and from counterrevolutionary turmoil. In those difficult days,

39. *El Universal*, March 19, 1938, pp. 1, 8.
40. *Ibid.*, p. 1.
41. *El Universal*, March 20, 1938, p. 1.
42. *El Universal*, March 24, 1938, p. 1.

organized labor, directed by the National Committee of the CTM, was the primary bulwark of the Cárdenas government.[43]

Important to the support of the government was the reorganization of the government party, the Partido Nacional Revolucionario (PNR), into the popular front party, the *Partido de la Revolución Mexicano* (PRM). In accordance with a CTM resolution, Lombardo had issued a call in 1937 to the PNR, the Mexican Peasant Confederation, and the Mexican Communist party to constitute a popular front. All accepted the invitation, but the front was not formed. This failure was partly the consequence of reactions to public criticisms of Lombardo's leftism—the criticisms were aided and abetted by Trotsky (who arrived in Mexico in 1937) and his followers—and partly the consequence of steps taken by President Cárdenas. Although Cárdenas accepted the popular-front concept, he put an end to the possibility of the formation of a front under the CTM's initiative when, in December 1937, he issued a call for a new, official popular-front party to replace the PNR. In a long speech to the CTM, Lombardo vigorously and enthusiastically supported the proposal. A united front of Mexico's popular forces was necessary, he explained, in order to safeguard the revolution from both internal and external enemies which sought to hinder and destroy it. The new party, composed of labor, peasant, army, and "popular" (heterogeneous but predominantly middle-class) sectors was formed early in 1938. It served the Cárdenas administration well in the difficult times from 1938 to 1940.[44]

Lombardo and the CTM strongly protested the presence of Leon Trotsky in Mexico. A public campaign was conducted to counteract Trotsky's influence as he criticized the popular-front concept and attacked Lombardo as a paid agent of Moscow and betrayer of the interests of Mexican labor.[45] Such charges were common currency among Lombardo's rightist enemies also. They have never been substantiated, nor has Lombardo ever been proved to have

43. Weyl and Weyl, pp. 300-314; "Expropriation in Mexico," *The Economist*, CXXX (March 26, 1938), 678-679; Hudson Strode, *Timeless Mexico* (New York, 1944), pp. 333-344; Plenn, pp. 29-31, 44-50, 82-96.
44. *El Frente Único en México*, pp. 9-43; Weyl and Weyl, pp. 341-369; Prewett, pp. 162-166; López Aparicio, pp. 226-228.
45. Confederación de Trabajadores, pp. 268-272; Plenn, pp. 292-296; Prewett, pp. 164-166; Weyl and Weyl, p. 247.

been a member of the Mexican Communist party. (See Chapter II.)

As a contribution to the revolution, the CTM called an economic congress in order to present a plan for Mexican economic development on the basis of fulfilment of the agrarian reform and of industrialization of the nation independent from foreign domination.[46] The plan was never completely fulfilled.

Lombardo and the CTM took the lead in supporting the Spanish Republic in Spain's civil war. Speeches were made, demonstrations held, funds raised.[47] Lombardo recently stated that he had in his whole life never seen the Spanish flag carried publicly in Mexico, but that he carried one in a 1936 demonstration with the approval and applause of the Mexican people.[48] At the suggestion of President Cárdenas, the CTM sponsored the International Congress Against War and Fascism, "the first of its kind in the world."[49]

In keeping with its principle of promoting the international solidarity of the working-class movement, the CTM joined the International Federation of Trade Unions (Amsterdam) in July, 1936.[50] Lombardo, however, was not satisfied with this action alone. As early as 1933, Lombardo had proposed—in his capacity as secretary-general of the CGOCM—the calling of a congress to create a unified Latin-American labor organization.[51] In January 1936, he expressed a similar desire in a message to the First American Labor Conference meeting in Santiago, Chile. He claimed that whatever might result from the congress, "the most important problem for the working class is not that of social legislation, but that of its efficacious and urgent unification."[52] The congress which organized the CTM adopted a resolution instructing the National Committee to call a congress to unify Latin-American

46. Lombardo Toledano, *Teoría y Práctica*, p. 80.
47. Weyl and Weyl, pp. 245-247.
48. Statement made by Lombardo in an unpublished speech delivered in Mexico City's Universidad Obrera on April 25, 1962, on the occasion of the 25th anniversary of the defense of Madrid. Speech attended by the author.
49. Lombardo Toledano, *Teoría y Práctica*, p. 79; Confederación de Trabajadores, pp. 150-160; Weyl and Weyl, pp. 248-249; López Aparicio, p. 229. For information on the extent of Nazi and other fascist influences in Mexico, see Plenn, pp. 65-81 and Weyl and Weyl, pp. 359-369.
50. Confederación de Trabajadores, pp. 177-178; López Aparicio, p. 228.
51. Vicente Lombardo Toledano, *What Does the C.T.A.L. Mean?* (Mexico, 1944), pp. 11-12.
52. Lombardo Toledano, *Mensaje al Proletariado*, p. 4.

workers into a single organization. Lombardo called the congress for September 1938.[53]

Representatives of worker's syndicates from thirteen Latin-American nations attended the congress: Argentina, Bolivia, Chile, Colombia, Costa Rica, Cuba, Ecuador, Mexico, Nicaragua, Paraguay, Peru, Uruguay, and Venezuela. Observer delegates included among others, Leon Jouhaux, head of France's CGT, Ramón González Peña, Spanish labor leader and minister of justice and public education of the Spanish Republic, and John L. Lewis, president of the CIO. The congress organized the Confederación de Trabajadores de América Latina (CTAL). Lombardo was elected its president. The initial membership was broad and included both communist- and non-communist-controlled syndicates.[54]

The CTAL's "Declaration of Principles"[55] asserted that the social system which prevailed in the greater part of the world's nations had to be changed in the interests of social justice. A regime must be created which would end human exploitation and provide for political democracy, for national economic and political self-determination, and for the cessation of war as a means of settling disputes. The principal task of Latin-American workers was to promote the complete independence of their respective nations and to eliminate semifeudal survivals, so as to provide for the progress of the Latin-American masses. Minimum rights of Latin-American workers were specified which included, among others, the right to organize, to strike, and to bargain collectively. Fascism was denounced. The principal means of achieving these ends reflected the basic theme of Lombardo's tactical strategy, viz.:

> The intellectual and manual workers of Latin America... declare that in order to realize the ideal of social justice it is urgent to attain the unification of the working class in each country, [to achieve] the permanent and indestructible alliance of the workers... of every region and of every continent and [to gain a] clear and firm understanding between all the workers of the world, in order to realize true international unity.[56]

53. Lombardo Toledano, *What Does the C.T.A.L. Mean?*, p. 13.
54. *Ibid.*, pp. 13-18; Poblete Troncoso and Burnett, *The Rise of the Latin American Labor Movement*, pp. 134-135; *Time*, XXXII (Sept. 19, 1938), 22.
55. Confederación de Trabajadores, pp. 584-585.
56. *Ibid.*, p. 584.

In spite of the many achievements of Lombardo and his associates in promoting labor unity and the Marxist political orientation of the workers, powerful forces of opposition began to check the leftist movement in the latter 1930's and early 1940's. Continuing opposition to the Lombardo-led labor movement came from foreign and national capital interests, from elements in the army, from reactionary elements of the Catholic church, and from most of Mexico's newspapers.

The Mexican press, and especially the Nazi-sympathizing newspaper, *Excelsior*,[63] served as spokesman for the opponents of the Lombardo-led labor movement. Lombardo constantly was attacked and calumniated. His Marxist philosophy was criticized and his influence within the government was deplored. Lombardo, according to the press, was more interested in achieving personal political power than in promoting the interests of the working class. Further, Mexico would know no peace until the CTM abandoned its objective of achieving a classless society and instead co-operated with capital for the development of the nation. The attitude of the opposition press is exemplified in an editorial published in the weekly, *Hoy*: "We ask...that the Government of President Cárdenas...put a definitive and energetic stop to the demagogues who spread hatred. What our country needs is for the Mexican worker to become reconciled with Mexican capital, only in this way can the worker be fed and sustained."[64]

Mexican and foreign industrialists resisted concessions to the demands of organized labor; large land-owners resisted the claims of the peasants.[65] Mexican businessmen organized a national employers' association, the Confederación de Centros Patronales de la República Mexicana, which offered more powerful resistance to the labor movement than had any employers' association in the past. The Centros Patronales preached class collaboration and

63. Plenn, pp. 70-72, 74-75 and Weyl and Weyl, p. 361, indicate the pro-Nazi tendencies of *Excelsior*. Plenn (p. 70) characterized *Excelsior* as a "daily newspaper through which Nazism finds abundant expression." See also Plenn, pp. 334-336.

64. Quoted in Plenn, p. 279 and Hayes, p. 82. Translation revised by the author. For criticisms of the Cárdenas epoch from a conservative point of view, see Lic. Blas Urrea (pseud. of Luís Cabrera), *Veinte Años Después* (Mexico, 1937), pp. 205-375 and José Vasconcelos, *Breve Historia de México* (9th ed.; Mexico, 1963), pp. 517-526.

65. See Weyl and Weyl, pp. 180-188, 219-220. Roberto Hinojosa, *El Tren Olivo en Marcha* (Mexico, 1937), pp. 29-33, comments upon attempts to discredit and undermine the agrarian reform in the La Laguna district.

social reforms which would improve the workers' living conditions (and thereby blunt the class struggle).[66]

The CTM encountered some of its strongest opposition in the State of Nuevo León and especially in its capital, Monterrey. Officials of the state government co-operated with industrialists in efforts to prevent affiliation of local unions with the CTM. Industrialists organized a company union among Nuevo León workers in order to control the workers and at the same time thwart the organizing activities of the CTM. In addition, local politicians co-operated in the formation of company unions in the states of Sonora, Coahuila, and Durango. The atmosphere was especially repressive for the CTM in Sonora; Lombardo accused the governor, Ramón Yocupicio, of attempting to have him assassinated when he visited that state.

The Catholic church was critical of Lombardo's dialectical materialism and in general sided with his opponents. A few minor Catholic labor unions—none of which had been known to strike—had been organized in the 1920's, but the direct influence of the church upon the organized labor movement was negligible. Furthermore, the solidarity of the church on revolutionary issues was weakened by Cárdenas' moderate policies toward the church; the clergy was divided into conservative and moderately prorevolutionary segments. No major church-labor conflict occurred during the Cárdenas administration.[67]

The army was opposed to some of Lombardo's policies. The army especially was annoyed with Lombardo's newly organized worker's militia which it considered to be a rival to its authority. According to some conservatives, Lombardo was out to sovietize Mexico with his militia. Under pressure from the army, Cárdenas forbade the militiamen to bear arms.[68]

The attitude of President Cárdenas was of decisive influence in the development of the leftist labor movement. Cárdenas generally favored the workers in their disputes. His goal, however, was not the dictatorship of the proletariat. Cárdenas mistrusted the strong state at the service of the interests of a specific social class. Rather than state control, he favored either direct worker

66. López Aparicio, pp. 229-231.
67. Hayes, pp. 63-88; Plenn, pp. 204-211, 270, 274-283, 334-337; J. A. Magner, "Strong Men in Mexico," *The Commonweal*, XXIX (Nov. 18, 1938), 94-96. Weyl and Weyl, pp. 166-170, 239.
68. Hayes, pp. 76-80; Kirk, pp. 51, 84-92.

ownership of enterprises or more socially responsible private ownership.[69] In brief, he sought the strengthening of the working class but did not wish this class to dominate the state. Consequently, he promoted the organization of the Confederación Campesina Mexicana, thereby removing control over many rural workers from the CTM. He prevented the newly organized government workers from joining the CTM. Again, he generally sided with the army in its conflict with Lombardo over the creation of a worker's militia. Cárdenas' ideal, in short, was to maintain a balance between the workers, peasants, army, and middle class. Each sector was represented in a popular front (the PRM); democratic interplay between the groups would decide the future political course of the nation.[70] The ideal—which was both theoretically and practically impossible to achieve—was never realized. The interests of capital came to dominate Mexico in the 1940's and 1950's.

The specific Lombardo-Cárdenas relationship was complex. To consider the reforms of the period from 1934-1940 as essentially the work of one man, a progressive-minded president named Lázaro Cárdenas (or a Marxist labor leader named Vicente Lombardo Toledano) is to oversimplify greatly the complex processes at work in this epoch and to fall into the "great man" concept of history. Unquestionably, Cárdenas sought on his own initiative to introduce extensive land, labor, health, and educational reforms in Mexico. Nevertheless, the fundamental impetus to reform came from the struggle of the Mexican workers and peasants for improvements in their conditions of life. Without this popular

69. Weyl and Weyl, pp. 127-133 and Plenn, pp. 139-140 summarize Cárdenas' views on social reform and the role of the state in society upon the basis of the concepts Cárdenas expressed during his campaign for the presidency in 1934. In one of his campaign speeches, Cárdenas rejected the Soviet experiment in socialism because it substituted the "individual boss" with the "boss-state." Cárdenas defined his conception of the role of the Mexican state: "The function of the Mexican State is not limited to being a simple watchdog of public order...nor is the State recognized as a monopolist of the national economy, but our concept of the State is that of a regulator of the great economic phenomena which occur under our system of production and distribution of wealth." (Plenn, p. 140; translation by Plenn.) In another speech, Cárdenas stated that the future of Mexico lay in consumers' and producers' co-operatives (Plenn, p. 140). For a compilation of Cárdenas' speeches and messages, see Partido de la Revolución Mexicana, *Cárdenas Habla* (Mexico, 1940).

70. Hayes, pp. 31-35, 61-62, 91-93; Kirk, pp. 51, 84-92; Parkes, pp. 402-403, 406-407.

impetus, it is probable that pressures from domestic and foreign property interests would have thwarted any presidential program for reform.

Popular pressures had already led the Calles-dominated PNR to adopt a left-leaning Six-Year Plan in 1933 which, among other things, called for simplification of legal procedures in land reform, participation of *peones* in the distribution of land, granting of lands to all communities in need of them, enforcement of all the depositions of Article 123 of the Constitution of 1917 (the labor article), strengthening of the labor unions in their struggle with capital, promotion of the principle of collective bargaining, and construction of 12,000 new rural schools. The peasants were to possess their lands as small properties (although they could not sell their properties) and were to organize co-operatives to solicit credit and to market goods, among other things. Abelardo Rodríguez, Calles' man in the presidency from 1932-1934, began to put the plan into effect during the last year of his administration. For example, Rodríguez's regime continued efforts already begun to fix minimum wages by municipalities and, between February 20, 1934, and August 31, 1934, distributed 1,218,000 hectares among 97,000 heads of families.[71]

Thus, before Cárdenas took office, popular discontent had already led the party in power, the PNR, to adopt a left-leaning program of political action and to begin to put that program into practice. Cárdenas gave the general and in many respects rather vague plan a decidedly revolutionary interpretation. During his regime, Cárdenas went beyond the general features of this plan in two fundamental respects: in promoting the formation of agricultural and industrial workers' co-operatives, thereby superseding the more individualistic orientation of agrarian reform as conceived in the Six-Year Plan; and in nationalizing the railroads and the oil industry.

The CGOCM, organized in 1933 and led by Lombardo, was engaged in organizing the Mexican workers and peasants and in focusing their discontent upon the attainment of specific objectives.

71. Hubert Herring and Herbert Weinstock (eds.), *Renascent Mexico* (New York, 1935), pp. 88-139; Plenn, pp. 163-167, 232-235; Weyl and Weyl, pp. 111-121; Dulles, pp. 565-568, 598-602; Strode, pp. 292-294. Francisco Javier Gaxiola, Jr., President Abelardo Rodríguez's private secretary, discusses the formulation of the Six-Year Plan in his work, *El Presidente Rodríguez, 1932-1934* (Mexico, 1938), pp. 147-165.

It was this expression of popular discontent that helped push the PNR leftward. Organized labor's support for Cárdenas was invaluable in his power struggle with the Calles political machine. Cárdenas' victory over Calles paved the way for the realization of many of the progressive provisions of the Six-Year Plan, as well as other reforms.

Both Lombardo and Cárdenas sought to organize and strengthen the Mexican workers' and peasants' movement in order to achieve reforms. Lombardo's ultimate objective in organizing and unifying the Mexican working class was to achieve the socialization of Mexico. Cárdenas' objective was to realize a form of radical, petty bourgeois democracy in Mexico. When these differences in ultimate objectives led to conflicts in practice, e.g., over the unifying of the entire workers' and peasants' movement under Lombardo's leadership or the arming of the workers' militia, Cárdenas imposed his will. Lombardo, although careful not to push any issue to the point of breaking with Cárdenas, nevertheless had considerable freedom to maneuver within the bounds laid down by Cárdenas. This maneuverability was augmented by the fact that Cárdenas did not have a rigid blueprint of specific reforms which he wished to initiate. (The Six-Year Plan was more a general guide than a specific blueprint for reform.) Lombardo took advantage of this maneuverability to spread Marxist ideology among the workers and to focus popular discontent upon the attainment of certain specific objectives.

The nationalization of the oil industry is a case in point. There is general agreement that Cárdenas did not anticipate the expropriation of the oil industry.[72] The intelligence and care with which the oil workers proceeded in their prolonged conflict with the oil companies and the organization of nationwide support for the oil workers were vital elements in the final outcome of the dispute. Mexico's labor leaders took good advantage of the supercilious, overbearing, and myopic conduct of the representatives of the oil companies. As a consequence, Cárdenas was confronted with a situation in March 1938, in which he had to expropriate the oil companies in order to preserve his own and Mexico's dignity. Cárdenas, of course, had favored the workers all along in their struggle with the foreign companies. There is no indication that

72. Weyl and Weyl, p. 281; Howard F. Cline, *The United States and Mexico* (Cambridge, Mass., 1953), p. 237.

he was reluctant to fulfil his obligations on the evening of March 18, 1938!

In brief, the Cárdenas-Lombardo relationship was complex and reciprocal. In the last instance, Cárdenas, as president, dominated the relationship and saw to it that the labor movement served his and not Lombardo's ends. The basic motive force for reform during this period was not the personal desires of Cárdenas or Lombardo, but the struggle of Mexico's workers and peasants for improved conditions of life.[73]

During the 1940's and 1950's concerted attacks by opponents partially undid the successes which Lombardo had achieved in his struggle to unify Mexican and Latin-American labor and to organize a united front between labor, the peasantry, the petty bourgeoisie, and elements of the national bourgeoisie. Lombardo's opponents achieved moderate successes during the presidency of the politically moderate General Manuel Ávila Camacho. Lombardo supported the candidacy of Ávila Camacho in order to maintain the popular front unity of revolutionary forces against the serious threat of the rightists led by opposition candidate, General Juán Andreu Almazán. As Lombardo put it in a speech to the CTM: "We have defended with legitimate passion the interests which our organization represents, but at the same time we have fought with coolness, never forgetting that the worst that could occur is the rupture of the principal revolutionary forces of our country which in these moments, from the point of view of the electoral struggle, is represented by the Partido de la Revolución Mexicana."[74]

Important changes occurred in the leadership of organized labor during the administration of General Ávila Camacho. The anticommunist theme emphasized by Lombardo's opponents had been taken up within the CTM toward the end of the Cárdenas administration. Moderates began to favor Fidel Velázquez, a member of the CTM's National Committee, as Lombardo's suc-

---

73. Lombardo recognized this fact when he stated in response to Calles' public statement of June 12, 1935, which held Lombardo responsible for the recent labor conflicts: "Once again, I have the honor of being considered, by those ignorant of the real causes of these conflicts, responsible for the strike movements which have occurred recently in the country." Quoted in English in Dulles, p. 641.

74. Lombardo Toledano, *En Qué Consiste y a Cuánto Asciende la Fortuna de Vicente Lombardo Toledano*, no pagination.

cessor.[75] Reports were issued[76]—and denied[77]—that Lombardo had been forced from office; yet he completed his five-year term as secretary-general. At the CTM congress held in February 1941, he formally resigned as secretary-general "amid great ovations" of tribute. Fidel Velázquez was elected to succeed him.[78] Lombardo is reported to have said: "I leave office a rich man—rich in the hatred of the bourgeoisie."[79]

Under the leadership of Fidel Velázquez, the moderate elements gained increasing ascendency in the CTM during World War II. These elements used the wartime need for national unity and for restriction of strikes which might hinder the Allied war effort in order to justify their moderate policies and to consolidate their positions. Wartime prosperity caused by increases in investments and loans and purchases of Mexican goods by the United States enabled the moderate union leaders to concentrate the workers' attentions upon achieving immediate material benefits. The government reinforced this trend by enacting such laws as the social security act of 1944 and a 1943 law providing for periodic wage increases to compensate for price increases. Sentiments of class struggle and of internationalism were gradually disappearing from the labor movement.

The Ávila Camacho administration in general moderated the program of true revolutionary reforms and emphasized the formation of individual rather than of communal or semicommunal properties in agriculture. In brief, the Mexican bourgeoisie, and especially those of its elements which held positions of political power, was consolidating its position of dominance in Mexican society and government.[80]

During World War II Lombardo concentrated his efforts upon his duties as president of CTAL. Lombardo had been a staunch opponent of fascism since its origins. (He had seen fascism in practice as early as 1925 when he visited relatives in Italy.)[81] He

75. Hill, pp. 39-49.
76. "Lombardo Out," *Time*, XXXVI (Oct. 7, 1940), 30.
77. "The Trade Union Movement in Mexico," *International Labour Review*, XLII (Dec., 1940), 418.
78. "The Trade Union Movement in Mexico," *International Labour Review*, XLIII (April, 1941), 463-464.
79. "Man With a Mission," *Time*, XXXIX (April 13, 1942), 18.
80. López Aparicio, pp. 233-238; Hayes, pp. 110-114; Parkes, pp. 412-417.
81. Information supplied personally to the author by Vicente Lombardo Toledano in Sept. 1962.

advocated a hard line against the rise of fascism in the 1930's. Lombardo accepted the Russian-German non-aggression pact of 1939 as a measure taken by the Soviet Union in order to gain time to prepare for the inevitable German attack. He believed that the conclusion of the pact was forced upon the Soviet Union by the actions of Western governments in conciliating the Nazis and in attempting to turn Germany solely against the Soviet Union. Consequently, from the signing of the Russian-German non-aggression pact to the invasion of the Soviet Union in 1941, Lombardo had stressed the neutrality of Mexico and Latin-America in the conflict. From the summer of 1941, however, Lombardo became a vociferous supporter of total war against the Axis. (See Chapter VI for a complete discussion.) To Lombardo his duty lay in assisting the unifying of the Latin-American people in support of the Allied cause and against Axis propaganda and fifth-column activities. To this end, he used his official position as president of CTAL to make a successful speaking tour of twelve Latin-American republics. In emphasizing unity, Lombardo stressed effective economic co-operation in support of the war effort and called for the restriction of strikes which might damage that effort.[82]

In reference to the end of the war and the construction of the postwar world, Lombardo, as spokesman for the CTAL, called for the unconditional surrender of the Axis and the realization of the principles contained in the Atlantic Charter. He denied that the Latin-American labor movement sought the creation of proletarian dictatorships in Latin-America immediately after the war. Rather, it sought to promote national independence, economic development, higher material and cultural levels of living, and political democracy in Latin-America. These goals were to be achieved on the basis of the united action of the workers, peasants, and the anti-imperialist elements among the middle class and native capitalists. Accordingly, Lombardo promoted in Mexico the signing of a labor-industry pact in which labor and capital agreed to unite their efforts to promote national independence, economic development, and higher standards of living.[83] The Mexican

82. Poblete Troncoso and Burnett, pp. 135-138; Lombardo Toledano, *What Does the C.T.A.L. Mean?*, pp. 20-28.
83. Vicente Lombardo Toledano, *The C.T.A.L., The War and the Postwar* (Mexico, 1945), pp. 71-89, 115-128; *What Does the C.T.A.L. Mean?*, pp. 24-28. "Second General Congress of the Confederation of Latin American Workers," *International Labour Review*, LI (Feb., 1945), 236-243.

Pacto Obrero Industrial was accorded in April 1945 between the CTM and the Cámara Nacional de la Industria de Transformación. In addition to stipulating the above-mentioned objectives, the Pacto noted that both signatories retained the special interests of the social classes they represented together with the right to defend these interests.[84]

Continuing his policy of maintaining a united front of the revolutionary elements against the rightists, Lombardo ardently supported the candidacy of Miguel Alemán in the 1946 presidential elections. Alejandro Carrillo, a close associate of Lombardo and editor of *El Popular*, headed Alemán's publicity campaign. Opposition candidate Ezequiel Padilla, minister of foreign affairs under Ávila Camacho and Mexico's representative to the United Nations in San Francisco, was denounced by Lombardo as an enemy of the Mexican workers and as a servant of United States imperialism.[85] He charged that certain American companies were supporting Padilla and that the *sinarquistas*, a far right political group with close ties with the Catholic church, were importing arms from the United States.[86] The Mexican government denied the charges.[87]

The economic development of Mexico in terms of increments in gross national product continued through the 1940's and 1950's. This development occurred in spite of the fact that serious imbalances arose between the rates of growth of the various sectors of the economy; some sectors, such as that represented by Mexico's numerous small-scale agricultural producers, developed but little. Prosperity—although not shared by all—strengthened the hand of those elements of the bourgeoisie who controlled the state power. They felt emboldened to attack the revolutionary union movement. Thus, the Alemán administration (1946-1952) launched a concerted campaign against the unity, independence, and revolutionary consciousness of the Mexican labor movement. As a consequence, the labor movement declined drastically in unity and in militancy.

An initial serious division in CTM ranks had occurred in 1942 when the Bloque Nacional de Defensa Proletaria was formed claim-

84. López Aparicio, pp. 238-239.
85. Tomlinson, pp. 26, 75-76.
86. "Mexican Crisis," *The Economist*, CL (Feb. 23, 1946), 298-299.
87. New York *Times*, Jan. 6, 1946, p. 17.

ing 200,000 members.[88] A more serious division occurred in 1947. The reformist[89] leaders who dominated the CTM proposed Fernando Amilpa to succeed Velázquez as secretary-general. The radicals, primarily old Communist party leaders, supported the railroad worker, Luís Gómez Z. Realizing that they could not win, the radicals withdrew from the CTM before the elections were held and formed the Confederación Unitaria de Trabajadores (CUT), of which the railroad and sugar workers were the primary elements. The confederation was unsuccessful.[90] The CTM was now completely dominated by reformists who were amenable to government manipulations.

Lombardo, who at the time was organizing a new political party, the Partido Popular, remained in the CTM and supported the candidacy of Amilpa.[91] The CTM National Council initially had supported the idea of the new party. Their support was seconded by the National Congress of the CTM. Under pressure from the government, however, the National Council turned against the project and Lombardo and his followers were expelled from the CTM when they insisted upon continuing with the organizing. The CTM changed its declaration of principles and withdrew from the CTAL and the World Federation of Trade Unions (WFTU).[92] The new declaration of principles emphasized the pursuit of material and cultural improvements and the support of Mexico's bourgeois democratic revolution.[93]

Lombardo had organized a new labor central, the Alianza de Obreros y Campesinos de México (AOCM), within a few months after his expulsion from the CTM in January 1948. Affiliates included the oil workers, the mine and metallurgical workers, the railroad workers, and several organizations of farm workers. The central associated with the CTAL and the WFTU.

88. Hill, pp. 52-53.
89. By the term ''reformist'' the author refers to those labor leaders who sought only reforms within the capitalist system as contrasted to the ''radicals'' or ''revolutionaries'' who, while they might well seek reforms, had the transformation of the capitalist system as their fundamental purpose.
90. López Aparicio, pp. 241-242; Lombardo Toledano, *Teoría y Práctica*, pp. 82-83.
91. New York *Times*, Feb. 3, 1947, p. 5; New York *Times*, March 10, 1947, p. 3.
92. López Aparicio, pp. 242-243; Rosendo Salazar, pp. 117-120, 179-180; New York *Times*, Jan. 8, 1948, p. 32.
93. López Aparicio, pp. 242-243; New York *Times*, March 31, 1947, p. 3.

The AOCM was designed as a temporary expedient. In 1949 it gave way to a new and larger organization, the Unión General de Obreros y Campesinos de México (UGOCM). Although he was not its secretary-general, Lombardo's influence predominated in the UGOCM. Members included the mine and metallurgical workers, the oil workers, the sugar mill workers, the tramway workers of the Federal District, the dam and highway construction workers, and organizations representing a large number of *ejidatarios* and rural laborers. The UGOCM adopted the original principles and program of the CTM and affiliated with the CTAL and the WFTU. Over 500,000 members were claimed by the end of 1949.

Under the influence—and taking advantage—of Cold War propaganda and hostilities, the Alemán government followed the practice of intervening directly in internal union affairs, replacing democratically elected leaders with government pawns. The government intervened militarily to depose the leaders of the railroad workers union and to impose a government-selected secretary-general. The new government-imposed leadership caused the railroad union to separate from the Lombardo-led union movement. The wartime law of "social dissolution" was reformed so as to apply to leftist agitators and government critics. Several union leaders were imprisoned, including Luís Gómez Z. and Valentín Campa of the railroad workers. The government refused to recognize the UGOCM as a legal labor confederation and intervened to impose its own candidates as leaders of several of the major affiliates of the confederation. As a consequence, the sugar workers, the oil workers, and the mining and metallurgical workers withdrew from the UGOCM.[94]

Initiated in the 1940's, the "stage of pronounced decadence" in the labor movement (as one author has put it)[95] continued through most of the fifties. Divisions continued to multiply within the movement and the number of strikes declined. Attempts at reunification had limited success; such was the case with the Confederación Revolucionaria de Obreros y Campesinos (CROC) formed in 1952 and also with the CTM-dominated Bloque de Unidad Obrera (BUO) organized in 1955. In 1956 there were

94. Hayes, pp. 169-180; López Aparicio, pp. 243-244; Lombardo Toledano, *Teoría y Práctica*, pp. 83-88.
95. López Aparicio, p. 240.

eight major labor confederations, an independent government employees' federation, four important independent industrial unions, and several smaller independents. The government dominated all but the UGOCM.[96]

In 1958, there began a new wave of militancy and of attempts at achieving revolutionary orientation and unification within the labor movement. This increased militancy was the worker's response to the decline in real income suffered by a large portion of the Mexican people during the 1940's and 1950's. Also, the distribution of income became increasingly unequal during this period. The Mexican economist, Manuel Germán Parra, has calculated that whereas the wealthiest 1 per cent of the population received one-third of the national income in 1940, in 1955 it received two-thirds.[97]

Numerous strikes and demonstrations have occurred since 1958. Attempts to replace government pawns in the labor unions with democratically elected representatives were successful in two notable instances—in the railroad workers union and in Section IX of the national teachers' union. According to Lombardo, these gains were lost owing largely to improper tactics pursued by the new leaders. (See Chapter IV.)

The regime of President Adolfo López Mateos (1958-64) responded to the revived militancy in two ways: by suppression and by concessions. Thus, the railroad workers' strike of 1958-1959 was suppressed by the federal army with the arrest of thousands of workers. Some leading union and political party leaders such as Demetrio Vallejo, Filomeno Mata, and David Alfaro Siquieros have been jailed under the broad provisions of the "law of social dissolution." On the other hand, the López Mateos government gave new impulse to the revolution. Agrarian reform was extended and the irrigation works program pushed; the administration expects that the output of electric energy in 1964 will be double its 1958 level. The social security program was extended. The government nationalized, among others, the electric energy industry, most of the iron and steel industry, and part of civil aviation. The government insisted officially that

96. Poblete Troncoso and Burnett, pp. 104-106; Lombardo Toledano, *Teoría y Práctica*, pp. 88-89.
97. Parkes, pp. 436-437.

the right of national self-determination be respected in international affairs.[98]

Lombardo continued to have direct influence upon the Mexican labor movement through the UGOCM and the Partido Popular (Socialista). (The PP[S] is examined in Chapter VIII.) Lombardo's close associate and secretary for peasant affairs (asuntos campesinos) of the PP(S), Jacinto López, serves as secretary-general of the UGOCM. The other leaders of the confederation are also members of the PPS. The confederation claimed (1961) to represent 6 state and 77 regional federations with a total membership of approximately 300,000. Peasants and agricultural workers composed 70 per cent of the membership; the remainder consisted of "workers organized in local unions and cooperatives."[99] In 1960, the U.S. Department of Labor estimated that the UGOCM had a membership of from 5,000 to 10,000.[100]

The UGOCM has played an active role in the movement for agrarian reform. Its greatest strength, and consequently its most successful area of action, lies in Mexico's northwestern states from Baja California and Sonora to Michoacán. In March 1957 the UGOCM held a congress in Los Mochis, Sonora, in which it was agreed to undertake an invasion of latifundia lands the following year, if by then no lands had been granted the numerous (some 50,000) landless peasants in northwestern Mexico. Lombardo Toledano and Jacinto López were the authors of the plan.

In February 1958 Lázaro Rubio Felix and Joaquín Salgado Medrano, respectively the national secretary for agricultural affairs of the UGOCM and the director of UGOCM affairs in Culiacán, Sinaloa, led some 10,000 landless peasants in an invasion of latifundia lands in the Culiacán Valley. During the same month, Jacinto López led an invasion of lands in the State of Sonora. Directed almost exclusively against foreign land-owners (Greeks, Americans, Italians, Germans), the occupation of lands

---

98. I. A. Langnas, "Mexico Today; Aspects of Progress Since the Revolution," pp. 162-167; Howard T. Young, "Mexico; A Revolution Gone Bankrupt," *The New Republic*, CXLII (April 4, 1960), 14-15; Lombardo Toledano, *Teoría y Práctica*, pp. 92-95.

99. Lombardo Toledano, *Teoría y Práctica*, p. 89.

100. U.S. Department of Labor, *Directory of Labor Organizations: Western Hemisphere* (Washington, 1960), II, 26, 28. Howard Cline, *Mexico: Revolution to Evolution: 1940-1960* (London, 1962), p. 224, estimated 20,000 members for the UGOCM.

was symbolic only. The objective was to force government action against the foreign owners.

The tactics were successful. The Ruíz Cortines administration immediately expropriated 15,000 hectares of unirrigated lands on the fringes of the Culiacán Valley and organized the lands into *ejidos*—the first to be formed during that administration. Promises were given that an irrigation system would be constructed for the lands and that additional lands would be expropriated in the well-irrigated valley. The López Mateos government has expropriated 65,000 hectares of the irrigated valley lands. The dispute in Sonora concerned a 647,000-acre cattle ranch straddling the United States-Mexican border and owned by the American, William C. Greene, Jr. The Ruíz Cortines administration expropriated the lands of this huge ranch in August 1958, and the López Mateos administration organized them into a collective *ejido* in February 1959, the first collective ever to be formed in Mexican pastoral activities, and the first collective to be formed in the Mexican countryside since the days of President Cárdenas.[101]

The UGOCM presently is pressuring the government to examine land titles in the new irrigation districts of the nation where, contrary to the provisions of Mexico's Agrarian Code, individuals have monopolized large tracts of land. The UGOCM does this by means of presenting lawsuits before the government in individual cases where the illegal possession of lands could be proved. No further invasions of lands are contemplated for the present, because the López Mateos regime is pushing the agrarian reform to the extent that presidential orders for the expropriation of 10 million hectares of land were issued in the period from 1958-1962. Under such conditions, drastic action by the UGOCM could lead to government suppression and to alienation of the masses from the leaders of the UGOCM.[102]

Lombardo used the knowledge gained from years of experience with organized labor to assist the struggle for an independent and unified labor movement. His influence was especially helpful to

101. Information supplied to author by Lázaro Rubio Felix and Joaquín Salgado Medrano in separate interviews held in Sept. 1962; *Hispanic American Report*, XI (April, 1958), 192-193; XI (July, 1958), 364; XI (Aug., 1958), 425; *Time*, Latin American edition, Sept. 1, 1958, p. 26; Feb. 23, 1959, pp. 22-23.

102. Information supplied to author by Lázaro Rubio Felix and Joaquín Salgado Medrano in separate interviews held in Sept. 1962.

the struggle for unity and independence within the Sindicato Nacional de Trabajadores de la Educación (SNTE). The SNTE had been seriously divided in 1960 when newly elected leaders of Section IX of the federation, which was composed of some 19,000 pre-primary and primary school teachers of the Federal District, had attempted to usurp the direction of the entire federation. As a consequence, an Extraordinary National Council of the SNTE was called which deposed the leaders of Section IX. The rank and file of this section were left disgruntled and disillusioned. The PPS lent its co-operation to the newly elected National Executive Committee of the SNTE in a campaign to restore unity within Section IX. The PPS instituted a program for education and political orientation among the teachers of this section, the most notable features of which were a series of conferences given by Lombardo on the themes of the "Theory and Practice of the Mexican Union Movement"[103] and of the "Philosophy and the Proletariat."[104] Following a series of preliminary steps in which the will of the member teachers was consulted and respected at all times, a new Executive Committee was elected by strictly democratic procedures. Unity, militancy, and confidence of the rank and file in their leaders were restored. As a postscript it should be noted that SNTE is a member of an international confederation of teachers which in turn is affiliated with the WFTU. The SNTE sent delegates to the Latin-American labor congress held in Santiago, Chile, in September 1962.[105]

Lombardo's newspapers and periodicals, mentioned previously, ceased publication in the years after World War II. The newspaper *El Popular* continued to be issued until 1960, but Lombardo had not been associated with the paper since the early 1950's. Lombardo has been a frequent contributor of articles to the liberal, widely read magazine *Siempre!* since it was founded in 1953. Moreover, he directs the bimonthly review, *Avante*, which he founded in January 1961. The review serves as the organ of the Partido Popular Socialista. Averaging fifty to sixty pages each issue, *Avante* contains articles on political, economic, and social

103. Published under the title *Teoría y Práctica del Movimiento Sindical Mexicano* (Mexico, 1961).
104. Published under the title *La Filosofía y El Proletariado* (Mexico, 1962).
105. Jorge Cruickshank, "La Solución del Problema de la Sección IX del S.N.T.E.," *Avante*, XXVII (Sept., 1962), 47-57.

problems of Mexico, on current Mexican politics and problems of the political left, and on international affairs—including developments in Cuba, China, the U.S.S.R., and other socialist nations. Important documents and manifestos of the PPS are printed therein.

The Universidad Obrera, with Lombardo as its director, has continued to function as a center of Marxist political education for the Mexican workers. Its functions have expanded recently. Schools, in addition to the original one in Mexico City, have been founded in Tampico, Tamaulipas (1945), Morelia, Michoacán (1956), Culiacán, Sinaloa, Tepic, Nayarit (1961), and Ciudad Chihuahua, Chihuahua (1962). Schools were to be opened in Hermosillo, Sonora, and Guadalajara, Jalisco in 1962 and in Monterrey, Nuevo León, in 1963. The school in Mexico City has approximately two hundred enrolled students, the majority of whom are union leaders. The students of the other schools are primarily rank-and-file union members. The school in Tampico has approximately two hundred and fifty students, in Culiacán, one hundred and fifty, and in Tepic and Morelia, one hundred in each.

The Universidad claims that members from all labor union confederations and all political parties except for the rightist Partido Acción Nacional (PAN) are represented in the student body of the Mexico City school. Some 90 per cent of the students are either partyless or are members of the official government party, the Partido Revolucionario Institucional (PRI). The PPS has its own, separate system of political education.

The Universidad Obrera received a government subsidy from its founding date (1936) until the beginning of 1951. It has not received a subsidy since then. A patronage committee headed by General Lázaro Cárdenas attempts to alleviate the many economic problems which burden the school. The Universidad claims it cannot satisfy the demand for its courses—additional schools could be opened if more ample financial resources were available.[106]

In 1962, the Universidad in Mexico City was divided into several schools, including the School of Political Preparation, the School of Labor Law, and the School of Union Preparation. For

---

106. Information supplied to author by Adriana Lombardo Toledano (daughter of Vicente Lombardo Toledano), secretary of the Universidad Obrera.

a registration fee of ten pesos the student had his choice of courses offered. Current offerings included courses in economic geography, political economy, imperialism, history of Mexico, dialectical and historical materialism, history of the international labor movement, world history, history of political ideas in Mexico, history of philosophy, philosophy of dialectical materialism, elements of public and private law, wages, productivity and social security in Mexico, the collective labor contract, union constitution, statutes and bylaws, and labor tribunals: doctrine and tactics of the union struggle in Mexico. In addition, the Universidad had a miscellaneous section which offered courses in English, Spanish, speech, arithmetic and geometry, and union journalism. Students of the schools and of the miscellaneous section were offered a general course in "oral defense of the problems of the working class."[107]

Lombardo has continued to be prominent in the international labor movement. As president of the CTAL, he was one of the principal delegates to the conference held in London in February 1945, which laid the basis for the creation of the World Federation of Trade Unions (WFTU). Lombardo served on the Administration Committee and on the latter's Constitution Subcommittee designed to carry through the project of creating the world confederation. The WFTU was given definite form at a constituent congress held in Paris in September 1945. Lombardo was elected vice-president for Latin-American affairs.[108]

As a consequence of Cold War hostilities, the WFTU was divided in 1949 when representatives of the United States and British unions and of some of the French, Dutch, and Belgium unions demanded that either the WFTU accept the Marshall Plan or that it be dissolved as an organization. The Executive Bureau rejected the proposal and the dissident unions withdrew to organize the International Confederation of Free Trade Unions with headquarters in Brussels.[109]

Lombardo has continued as a vice-president of the WFTU, which has grown in size in recent years. He attends all major congresses of the organization. Shortly after the formation of

107. Information taken from curriculum posted in the Universidad Obrera, Morelos 91, Mexico, D.F.
108. Vicente Lombardo Toledano, "Cómo Surgió la Federación Sindical Mundial," *El Movimiento Sindical Mundial*, VI (June, 1960), 3-5; Alexander, pp. 342-343; López Aparicio, p. 267.
109. Lombardo Toledano, *Teoría y Práctica*, pp. 84-85.

the world labor confederation, its administrative board created a bureau of Spanish-language publications under Lombardo's chairmanship.[110] Lombardo became Spanish editor of the official organ of the WFTU, a monthly review published in Spanish under the title *El Movimiento Sindical Mundial.*

The Cold War maneuverings and hostilities following World War II together with the capture of many Latin-American governments by rightist elements led to a major weakening of the CTAL. According to Lombardo, the United States government directed a campaign to divide the Latin-American labor movement and to place control of the movement in the hands of "safe" reformist leaders.[111]

As part of this campaign, in 1947 the American Federation of Labor (AFL) took the lead in calling an inter-American labor congress to meet in Lima, Peru. There the Confederación Interamericana de Trabajadores (CIT) was organized. It had little success, however, and virtually ceased to exist as soon as it was formed. Nevertheless, when Lombardo resigned in 1948 (the end of his current term) as a member of the governing board of the International Labor Office (ILO), he was replaced by the president of the CIT, a Chilean.[112]

In 1951, the International Confederation of Free Trade Unions (ICFTU) held a Western Hemisphere conference in Mexico City. Divisions beset the congress from its inception as the CTM withdrew its representation and charges were hurled by many—including Fidel Velázquez, the politically moderate secretary-general of the CTM—that the congress was a tool of United States imperialism. Nevertheless, the Organización Regional Interamericana de Trabajadores (ORIT) was organized. It has continued to exist to date.[113]

The Latin-American labor movement was divided further when the Juán Perón regime in Argentina inspired in 1952 the creation of the Asociación de Trabajadores Latinoamericanos (ATLAS). ATLAS refused any co-operation with the CTAL.[114]

110. Information supplied to author by Vicente Lombardo Toledano in Sept. 1962; Alexander, p. 348.
111. Lombardo Toledano, *Teoría y Práctica,* pp. 85-86.
112. New York *Times,* July 4, 1948, p. 1; López Aparicio, p. 266.
113. *Hispanic American Report,* III (Feb., 1951), 5-6; López Aparicio, p. 268.
114. New York *Times,* Nov. 24, 1952, p. 11

CTAL affiliates in several countries broke away, including those in Colombia (CTG), Cuba (CTC), and Peru (CTP). In Mexico, only the UGOCM was represented.[115] The weakness of the CTAL has continued, although the Cuban Revolution has served as a revitalizing factor.

In October 1960, following his re-election as secretary-general of the PPS, Lombardo announced his resignation as president of the CTAL and as vice president of the WFTU.[116] The resignations, however, were not accepted and Lombardo continues to occupy these positions. Resurgent movements for national and international unity among Latin-American workers have progressed considerably in recent years. The mere presence of the movements reflected the rising tide of popular discontent in Latin-America. Several autonomous labor confederations arose in Latin-America during the 1950's which remained unaffiliated with any international labor organization, although friendly relations were maintained with all such organizations. Such unions arose, for example, in Chile, Bolivia, and Uruguay. The Chilean confederation (Confederación Único de Trabajadoes de Chile)—the first and perhaps still the strongest of the autonomous labor confederations —sponsored the Conferencia Sindical Latino Americana held in Santiago, Chile, on September 6-9, 1962. Representatives of labor unions from all Latin-America attended. Only Guatemala and Puerto Rico were not represented. The following Mexican unions were present: the UGOCM, the SNTE (Sindicato Nacional de Trabajadores de la Educación), and the FSTSE (Federación de Sindicatos de Trabajadores al Servicio del Estado).

In an address to the conference, Lombardo briefly outlined the history of the Latin-American labor movement since the end of World War II and hailed the attempt to create a new confederation of Latin-American workers. Unity of Latin-American labor through such a new organization, stated Lombardo, is indispensable to the complete success of the second general Latin-American revolution: the revolution for the economic liberation of the Latin-American people from imperialism.

Lombardo pointed out that fighting organizations of the working class are formed in certain historical periods in order to serve

115. Poblete Troncoso and Burnett, pp. 138-139.
116. U.S. Department of State, Telegram from U.S. Embassy, Mexico City to U.S. Secretary of State, Washington, D.C., Oct. 18, 1960.

the immediate needs of the working class in its long-term struggle to eliminate the exploitation of man by man. Such organizations are not intended to exist perpetually. The CTAL, created in 1938, served a useful function. Now a new and larger organization is needed. On the day that such a new Latin-American labor confederation is created, said Lombardo, "I will present myself before the Conference to declare that the Confederation of Latin American Workers has died because it has given life to a new and powerful organism of the proletariat and the peasants of our Hemisphere."[117]

Among others, the conference reached the following agreements:

(1) To approve a minimum program of action for all Latin-American workers.

(2) To call meetings of Latin-American labor unions by industrial branches (oil, mining, etc.).

(3) To reiterate support for Cuba.

(4) To issue a manifesto to the Latin-American working class explaining the present Latin-American panorama and calling for common action.

(5) To create an executive secretariat and a co-ordinating committee (composed of one representative from each country) to provide the groundwork for and to convoke (in September 1963) a Constituent Congress for a new Latin-American labor confederation.[118]

In summary, Lombardo's greatest successes in his efforts to unify the Mexican labor movement came in the 1930's, especially during the administration of General Lázaro Cárdenas. Lombardo organized and headed the largest and most militant labor confederation Mexico had known; he organized and served as president of a large Latin-American worker's confederation; he directed a Marxist worker's training school; and he founded and directed several widely read Marxist publications.

During World War II, Lombardo devoted his energies to promoting inter-American solidarity behind the war effort. During

---

117. Conferencia Sindical Latinoamericana de Trabajadores, *Intervención de Vicente Lombardo Toledano, Presidente de la Confederación de Trabajadores de América Latina* (Mexico, 1962), p. 4.

118. *Ibid.*, pp. 1-10 and information supplied personally to the author by Vicente Lombardo Toledano in Sept. 1962.

the same period the Mexican bourgeoisie, and in particular those in political power, took advantage of wartime prosperity and the voluntary restraint of class warfare on the part of labor to moderate the revolutionary tendencies of the Cárdenas period and to consolidate their control of the government.

Following World War II, the elements of the Mexican bourgeoisie which controlled the state power unleashed a concerted attack upon the unity, independence, and revolutionary consciousness of the labor movement. These elements in power took utmost advantage of Cold War propaganda and fears to divide, weaken, and control organized labor. The United States government, according to Lombardo, used the AFL and the ICFTU as tools in order to create the ORIT, whose purpose was to combat and divide the revolutionary class-conscious labor movement in Latin-America. As a consequence of this campaign, Lombardo was expelled from the CTM and the CTAL gradually disintegrated into a skeleton organization. Mexican labor unions lost their former independence as democratically elected union leaders were replaced —frequently forceably—by government pawns. The Lombardo-influenced UGOCM, organized in 1949, remained independent and militant. Lombardo's Marxist publications declined in number as the review *Futuro* ceased publication and Lombardo ended his association with the newspaper *El Popular*. In 1953, he began to contribute articles almost weekly to the new, widely read review *Siempre!*

The late 1950's and the early 1960's witnessed a revival of militant class consciousness within the labor movement in response to increased economic distress among the Mexican people. Forceful movements occurred within unions to replace government pawns with genuine representatives of the worker's class interests. In 1958, the Lombardo-influenced and militant UGOCM led invasions of lands in Sonora and Sinaloa which resulted in the expropriation of lands and the formation of *ejidos*. The UGOCM, which claimed some 300,000 members in 1961, has continued to give impetus to the agrarian reform movement under the López Mateos administration. In 1961, Lombardo founded the new Marxist journal, *Avante*. He was active in working for the unification of Mexican labor, making an important contribution to this end by assisting the successful movement for reunification of Section IX of SNTE. A Latin-American labor conference held recently in Santiago, Chile, laid the basis for the formation in 1963 of a new, large, and militant general confederation of Latin-American labor. Lombardo's Marxist training school for Mexican workers continued to function from its founding in 1936 to the present. Its activities were presently greater than ever; branches were opened in a number of cities.

The Mexican labor movement still faced formidable obstacles to its struggle for independence and unity. But progress had been made, and prospects were good. The firm Marxist orientation of Lombardo's thought as well as the knowledge he had gained from years of experience in the labor movement were and promised to remain vital assets to the development of Mexican and Latin-American labor.

VIII. The Partido Popular Socialista

The idea had long existed in the mind of Vicente Lombardo Toledano to organize a united-front political party. The party was to be composed of all the popular forces which supported the democratic, anti-imperialist, and antifeudal precepts of the Mexican Revolution. As secretary-general of the CTM, Lombardo had proposed the organization of such a party in 1937. President Lázaro Cárdenas, in his turn, in December 1937, proposed the creation of a united front to replace the official party, the Partido Nacional Revolucionario (PNR).

Early in 1938, speaking in support of the presidential initiative, Lombardo foreshadowed in some of his remarks the creation of the Partido Popular in 1948, "This is a popular Party which is to be created, a Party of the people of our country, and it will have more importance as such than if it were a Party exclusively of the proletariat. What is necessary now is to fight by uniting forces; we shall not tire of repeating it, and the proletariat is already organized."[1] Lombardo went on to state that although the proletariat was the social class with greatest revolutionary potential in Mexico, as a class it was not self-sufficient, for it could not alone successfully fight the reactionary forces and promote the revolution. To achieve these objectives, it should unite with the peasants, the artisans, the small merchants, and intellectuals and the other sectors of the middle class, and with the army. The object was not to sovietize the government—a revolution was a necessary precondition for that. "In Mexico," he exclaimed, "we are not going to sovietize the government; in Mexico we are going to make a simple popular alliance to defend the interests of the Mexican Revolution.... We will organize, then, a Popular Party within which the proletariat will have a place of importance, within which it will collaborate in a decisive manner and will orient national politics, looking after, in a preferential manner, the interests of the Mexican people."[2]

The party formed as a result of President Cárdenas's initiative, the Partido de la Revolución Mexicana (PRM), failed to

1. *El Frente Único en México*, p. 38.
2. *Ibid.*, pp. 39-40.

satisfy the Mexican Left as it was completely government dominated; moreover, from 1940 to 1946, it endorsed the moderate policies of the Ávila Camacho regime. In 1943, the short-lived Liga de Acción Política was formed by the leftist professional workers, Narciso Bassols, José Iturriaga, Victor Manuel Villaseñor, and others.³ In 1944, Lombardo attempted to unify the Mexican Left into the Liga Socialista Mexicana. Leading members, in addition to Lombardo, were Narciso Bassols, Mexican ambassador to the U.S.S.R., and Dionisio Encinas, secretary-general of the Mexican Communist party. Designed to bring Mexican Marxists together to study national and international problems, the league had little success and soon disappeared.⁴

In the same year, Lombardo presented a postwar program for Mexico to a general conference held in Mexico City. It called for national unity to promote the rapid industrialization of Mexico, which was considered a precondition for the achievement of complete national independence and of political democracy.⁵ Pursuing this theme, in 1945 Lombardo sponsored the signing of the Pacto Obrero Industrial (mentioned in Chapter II) between the CTM and the Cámara Nacional de la Industria de Transformación. Both signers agreed to co-operate in the industrialization of Mexico while at the same time retaining and defending their respective class interests.⁶ Also in 1944, another short-lived political party was created, the Partido Nacional Democrático Independiente. Its founders were two lawyers, Octavio Vejár Vásquez and Victoriano Anguiano, who later participated in the foundation of the Partido Popular.⁷

Further, during the war years a number of independent leftists talked of the necessity for creating new parties.⁸ The talk and rumors continued through 1945-1946.⁹ Finally, Lombardo issued a call for a round-table conference of Mexico's Marxists to dis-

3. Vicente Fuentes Díaz, *Los Partidos Políticos en México* (Mexico, 1956), II, 124.
4. "The Political Background in Mexico—I," *The Economist*, CXLIX (Nov. 24, 1945), 753; Hayes, pp. 153-154.
5. Vicente Lombardo Toledano, *El Nuevo Programa del Sector Revolucionario de México* (Mexico, 1944).
6. López Aparicio, pp. 232-234.
7. Fuentes Díaz, II, 125.
8. *Ibid.*, pp. 125-126.
9. "The Political Background in Mexico—II," *The Economist*, CXLIX (Dec. 1, 1945), 795; New York *Times*, Aug. 22, 1946, p. 6.

cuss the theme: "Objectives and Tactics of the Proletariat and of the Revolutionary Sector of Mexico in the Present Stage of the Historical Evolution of the Country." Held in Mexico City's Palacio de Bellas Artes, January 13-22, 1947, the conference was attended by representatives of the following groups: Grupo Marxista de la Universidad Obrera (of which Lombardo was the major representative), Partido Comunista de México, Grupo Marxista "El Insurgente," and Acción Socialista Unificada. In addition, several unaffiliated individuals were invited to participate in the discussion.[10]

Lombardo delivered the major talk of the conference. He emphasized the need for better theoretical understanding of contemporary Mexican problems. This could be achieved by applying Marxist principles to a study of contemporary social reality. Such a study of contemporary Mexico would reveal that the official political party, the Partido Revolucionario Institucional (PRI)—successor to the PRM—was deficient in promoting the revolution. The goals of the Mexican Revolution had been as yet but partially achieved; to assure the realization of these goals and to prevent the reactionary forces from gaining the upper hand, Mexico needed a new party. The new party, he reasoned, must be a genuine united-front party of the masses, independent from control by the state. It must be a popular party composed of workers, peasants, intellectuals, native industrialists, and other sectors of the middle class, and other popular elements. United under the direction of the proletariat, these social sectors would continue the movement of the Mexican Revolution toward attainment of its objectives of national independence, higher levels of living through sound economic development, and popular democracy. In international affairs, the party would fight for peace, for the eradication of fascism, for independence of the colonial and semicolonial countries, and for unity and realization of the principle of non-intervention in Latin-America. The party would not be Marxist, because Mexico already had a Marxist party—the Mexican Communist party; neither would it be Lombardo's personal party.[11]

In the extensive discussions that were held during the course of the conference, Lombardo succeeded in having accepted his basic concept that the proletariat was not self-sufficient but must unite

10. Lombardo Toledano, *Objectivos y Táctica*, p. 1.
11. *Ibid.*, pp. 51-56, 60-67, *passim*.

in a common party with other popular, anti-imperialist forces. His concepts, expressed publicly as early as 1937, were beginning to bear fruit.[12]

In May 1947, Lombardo clarified further his conception of the new party in a speech delivered at a banquet given him on the eve of his departure for Europe to attend a WFTU conference. The Mexican Revolution has a dual aspect, Lombardo claimed: it seeks to destroy the old semifeudal, semicolonial order and to create a new Mexico. The revolution is incomplete in both its positive and negative aspects. To build a new Mexico, above all, national autonomy must be attained and preserved. Further, the level of living of the Mexican people must be raised by means of a complete program of industrialization, the basic feature of which must be the mechanization of agricultural production. Finally, the progressive democratization of national political institutions and practices must be promoted.

Destruction of the revolution, he contended, is sought by the forces of the right, represented by the Partido Acción Nacional (PAN) and the Unión Nacional Sinarquista. United States' monopolies seek to dominate Mexico and the world. The creation of a new party, the Partido Popular, is necessary to promote the revolution, to bring its continuing objectives constantly to the awareness of the population, and to help oppose the maneuvers of the right to destroy the revolution—especially the attempts by PAN to win municipal elections which are alarmingly successful because in many municipalities there is no real organized opposition to PAN.

Lastly, Lombardo suggested a line of conduct which has guided the PP since its formation. The guiding interest of the party will be the promotion of the revolution. Consequently, the party will support those actions and policies of the PRI and the government which are positive in their revolutionary consequences, and it will oppose those which have negative implications. The party will be the constant, mortal enemy of the rightists and their parties.[13]

As discussions, speeches, and conferences progressed, groups and committees in favor of forming the new party sprang up

12. Alfonso Méndez Barraza, *Los Partidos Políticos en México* (Mexico, 1949), pp. 53-54.
13. Lombardo Toledano, *Un Nuevo Partido*, pp. 5-7, 12-14, 16-26, 28-30, 32, *passim*.

spontaneously in many of the states of Mexico. A National Coordinating Committee was created in Mexico City to aid the groups. The social composition of the committee as well as of the local groups was broad: workers, peasants, intellectuals, teachers, and students were represented.[14]

The CTM at first accepted the formation of the Partido Popular. Under pressure from the PRI and the government, however, the National Council of the CTM repudiated the embryonic party. Early in 1948, Lombardo and several of his companions were expelled from the labor central because they persisted in their efforts to organize the new party.[15]

After a year and one-half of nationwide discussions and preparations, the Partido Popular was founded by a constituent assembly held in Mexico City on June 20, 1948. The founders and early members represented a panorama of the Mexican Left. Included were many with long experience in the workers' and peasants' movements: Vicente Lombardo Toledano, Alejandro Carrillo, Jacinto López, Vidal Díaz Muñoz, Lázaro Rubio Félix, and Juán Manuel Elizondo. Others had participated for many years in Mexico's leftist organizations: Enrique Ramírez y Ramírez, Rafael Carrillo, Narciso Bassols, Diego Rivera, Leopoldo Méndez, Rodolfo Dorantes, José Alvarado, Luís Torres, José Revueltas, *et al.* Two of the above had been prominent members of the PRI: Díaz Muñoz (deputy) and Elizondo (senator). In addition, Deputy Victoriano Anguiano and Senator Alfonso Palacios—both of the PRI—were among the founders. These and other PRI members joined the new party.[16]

The Partido Popular was organized around a program rather than an explicit ideology. Neither the statement of "Historical Explanation and Principles" nor the program which were adopted in 1948 made mention of Marxism, socialism, or class struggle. Thus, the statement of principles adopted by the Constituent Assembly indicated merely that the PP was formed as an instrument to continue the struggle for realization of the goals of the Mexican Revolution. A new party was necessary because the Alemán regime and its party, the PRI, were abandoning the revolutionary objectives. These goals, antifeudal, anti-imperialist, and

14. Lombardo Toledano, *La Evolución de México*, p. 17.
15. Méndez Barraza, p. 54; Hayes, pp. 162, 165-169.
16. Fuentes Díaz, II, 123; Méndez Barraza, p. 54.

democratic in character, included the attainment of national economic independence, the raising of levels of living, the economic development of Mexico, and the democratization of national life.[17]

The foregoing theme—often repeated by Lombardo and the PP—is aptly summarized in the statutes of the PP:

> Article 4. The Partido Popular will base its public actions on the precepts of the Political Constitution of the United Mexican States and in respect for the national institutions which it establishes. It will organize the peaceful struggle of the Mexican people for the complete independence of the nation, for the economic development of the country, for the elevation of the level of living of its population, for the amplification of a democratic regime and for the friendship of Mexico with all the peoples of the earth, in a world of peace and justice.[18]

Vicente Fuentes Díaz, former functionary of the PP turned critic, has made an apt summary of the principal features of the lengthy program:

1st. Complete independence of the Nation and repulsion of all foreign intervention in the internal affairs of the country.

2nd. Fight against foreign monopolies which aspire to subordinate the national economy to the economic and political interests of other countries.

3rd. Regulation of foreign investments to prevent them from taking possession of the essential sources of national wealth. Nationalization of the electric industry and of others of public service.

4th. Assistance to industries sincerely disposed to the development of an independent economy with sufficient potentiality to satisfy the needs of the population.

5th. Development of a modern agriculture.

6th. Abundant and cheap land, water, credit and financing to the workers in agriculture and to the genuine small agriculturalists.

7th. Independence of the labor movement in respect to the government and to any other non-union force, and support for the worker's struggles for their legitimate demands.

17. Partido Popular, *Razón Histórica*, pp. 5-14.
18. *Ibid.*, p. 43.

8th. Protection for the small industrialists and the artisans, and modernization of their forms and means of labor.

9th. Economic, social and cultural improvement of the Army and of the youth, and respect for their political rights.

10th. Absolute political equality of women in respect to men and adequate and permanent attention to all their needs.

11th. Defense of the interests of the middle class.

12th. Scientific and democratic orientation in all grades of public instruction, and unification of the educational systems.

13th. Defense and increase of the natural resources of the country.

14th. Adoption, on the part of the state, of an economic and financial program oriented towards the independent and vigorous development of the economy.

15th. Establishment of a truly democratic regime on the basis of the intervention of permanent parties, of democratic character, in all aspects of the political and social life of the Nation.[19]

To this summary might be added the important point that the program called for the maintenance by means of state control of sound proportions between the rates of agricultural and industrial development.[20]

The program was rather moderate. In effect, it was a plan for the development of an advanced stage of state capitalism. That is to say, the program called for greater intervention by the state in the economy in order to promote economic development and to restrict foreign imperialist influences within the Mexican economy, but it did not demand the socialization of the economy; capitalism was to remain the predominant mode of production. Similarly, the plan called for democratic improvements in Mexico's political regime, but it did not seek the establishment of a People's Democracy in Mexico. It sought improvements in the educational system but did not demand that education be Marxist oriented. It sought to strengthen the labor movement and to improve the conditions of the working class, but it did not set the dictatorship of the proletariat as a goal.

The statutes adopted in 1948 provided that the integral parts

19. Fuentes Díaz, II, 128-129.
20. Partido Popular, *Razón Histórica*, p. 33.

of the party should consist of local, municipal, state, and national assemblies, each with its corresponding executive committee. National executive direction was provided in two bodies in addition to the National Executive Committee: a National Council composed of the members of the National Executive Committee and the heads of the executive committees of the states, territories, and the Federal District; and a National Political Directorate composed of the leading members of the National Executive Committee. The latter was designed to provide permanency to the direction of the party.

Party elections were indirect. The local assembly elected both the local committee and the delegates to the municipal assembly. The municipal assembly elected the municipal committee and the delegates to the state assembly. The state assembly elected the state committee and delegates to the National Assembly, and the National Assembly elected the members of the National Executive Committee. The latter in turn selected the members of the National Political Directorate.

Party candidates for political office were selected by the party organs which corresponded to the office sought. That is, the National Assembly designated the presidential candidates and approved the party's electoral platform. The party members of the various states nominated their respective senatorial candidates, the members of the various districts elected their respective deputorial candidates, and so forth down to the municipal level, where local party members nominated candidates for municipal offices. Gubernatorial, senatorial, and deputorial candidates had to be approved by either the National Council or the National Assembly; candidates for municipal posts had to be approved by the state committees.[21]

The PP was novel in several respects. It was not organized as a consequence of an agreement between a few leaders. Rather, it was formed with the free participation and accord of much of the Mexican Left after almost two years of preliminary discussions and exchanges of views on a nationwide basis. The PP was an independent leftist party of consequence, legally capable of participating in elections. This was in contrast with other important, durable national parties created since 1910 which either were

21. *Ibid.*, pp. 43-62.

formed by the government (PNR, PRM, PRI) or were rightist parties with strong financial backing (PAN).[22]

Immediately after its formation, the PP stimulated the ire of the government by criticizing the national financial policies which led to the devaluation of the peso in 1948. The PP was criticized from all sides. According to some it was communistic, "bought by Moscow gold"; in the opinion of others, it was subsidized by the Mexican government. In spite of criticism, the PP continued to propound its program to the Mexican people through speeches, conferences, and pamphlets.[23]

The PP entered candidates in a majority of the states' 1949 congressional elections.[24] Only one candidate, however, was declared elected by the Federal Electoral Board. (Four of the PAN candidates were elected.)[25] The PP claimed that extensive electoral frauds had occurred and protested attempts by public and PRI authorities at intimidation of its candidates and supporters.[26]

Several distinguished leftists withdrew from the PP after the 1949 elections. Included in their number were Diego Rivera, Narciso Bassols, and Victor Manuel Villaseñor. Diego Rivera claimed the poor electoral showing was due to Lombardo's failure to organize the party properly. In addition, he charged that Lombardo spent too much time participating in foreign conferences rather than in attending to domestic party problems.[27]

Lombardo, however, was not dismayed by the electoral results. He explained in an address delivered at a dinner held in commemoration of the second anniversary of the PP:

> we have said it a thousand times and we shall repeat it on the second anniversary of our Party, that we have not created a work for tomorrow, nor for the present period of the government, nor for the stage of the government which shall follow; rather we have constructed an institution for many and long years; we have proclaimed with pride, not with boastfulness, but with legitimate happiness, that we

22. Fuentes Díaz, II, 123-129; "El Partido Popular Socialista y El Movimiento de Liberación Nacional," *Avante; Documentos*, I (July, 1962), 3.
23. *Ibid.*; Fuentes Díaz, II, 129-130.
24. *El Popular*, May 3, 1949, p. 5; *El Popular*, May 19, 1949, p. 1; *Hispanic World Report*, II (April, 1949), p. 6.
25. *Hispanic World Report*, II (Sept., 1949), 6.
26. *El Popular*, July 4, 1949, p. 1; *El Popular*, July 6, 1949, p. 3.
27. *Hispanic World Report*, II (Nov., 1949), 9.

are the Party of the immortals because we serve a cause that cannot die—the cause of the people; we have affirmed that those who have gathered here have done so from profound conviction, and not from ambitions of a personal character, and that if someone should disappear from or leave our files, many others shall come to replace them, and that there never has been in the history of Mexico a party such as the Partido Popular which has consolidated as rapidly as ours. . . .

Because of this we are the Party of the future. And this affirmation is not made with the desire to arouse momentary enthusiasm; it is reality. We are constructing with great, enormous difficulties a permanent party in the life of Mexico for many, many years, until our Country is free, completely independent and its people can live happily. This is the goal and the declaration of our Party.[28]

In December 1951, the Partido Popular selected Lombardo as its candidate for president in the 1952 elections.[29] The electoral platform adopted was essentially a restatement of the party program adopted in 1948.[30]

Lombardo made an extensive speaking tour of Mexico. His expenses were financed partially by contributions from his audiences. The party estimates that, in all, 1,200,000 people heard him speak at one or another of the one hundred conferences and rallies he held during the campaign. An estimated 150,000 alone attended the address he gave from the center of the Zócalo, Mexico City's central plaza.[31]

During the campaign, an attempt was made to unify the parties of the Left in opposition to the candidates of the PRI and of the PAN. The Partido Popular and General Miguel Henríquez Guzmán's Federación de Partidos del Pueblo, however, could not come to an agreement. In a letter to the press, Dionisio Encina, secretary-general of the Mexican Communist party, blamed the failure upon the refusal of these parties to place national interests above their selfish concerns. The PP, on the other hand, claimed the breakdown in negotiations was the result of Guzmán's refusal to accept the proposal that both he and Lombardo step down in

28. *El Popular*, June 24, 1950, p. 4.
29. New York *Times*, Dec. 17, 1951, p. 3.
30. Lombardo Toledano, *Por Vez Primera*, p. 12.
31. Information supplied personally to the author by Vicente Lombardo Toledano in May 1962.

the interests of a third candidate (to be selected), and also to the FPPM's refusal to accept measures for nationalization of certain industries as part of a unified program.[32]

Ex-President Lázaro Cárdenas did not officially support any candidate. He did speak from the same platform as Lombardo, however, when the latter addressed a meeting in Cárdenas's home State of Michoacán. Cárdenas did not offer the same favor to any other candidate.[33]

Final official results of the July elections were as follows: Adolfo Ruíz Cortines (PRI), 2,713,419; General Miguel Henríquez Guzmán (FPPM), 579,745; Efrain González Luna (PAN), 285,555; Vicente Lombardo Toledano (PP), 72,482.[34] The PP (and the other defeated parties) claimed the elections were fraudulent. According to Lombardo, the most conservative estimate of the number of votes he actually received is one million.[35]

The Partido Popular has claimed that the greatest benefits it derived from the campaign were the opportunities it had to come into intimate contact with the Mexican people all over the nation and to define its character as a "defender of the working class" and thereby distinguish its position from that of the other political parties.[36]

Lombardo had a two-hour conference with President Ruíz Cortines less than three weeks after the latter took office. Afterward, Lombardo announced his support for Ruíz Cortines's program which, he said, now coincided with that of the Partido Popular.[37] Later, he explained that he had switched from opposition to support of the regime because "[Ruíz] Cortines had adopted the opposition program."[38] Lombardo, apparently, was continuing his policy of unity among the various revolutionary forces against the reaction. Thus, after his interview with Ruíz Cortines, he said: "My main purpose in running for the Presidency was to contribute to a change in the economic, social and political situation of Mexico. If this change takes place, as I expect, I

32. New York *Times*, Feb. 17, 1952, p. 27; New York *Times*, April 1, 1952, p. 14; New York *Times*, June 9, 1952, p. 8.
33. Rodman, p. 152.
34. New York *Times*, Sept. 13, 1952, p. 2.
35. Rodman, p. 152.
36. "El Partido Popular Socialista," *Avante; Documentos*, p. 4.
37. New York *Times*, Jan. 1, 1953, p. 5.
38. New York *Times*, Jan. 29, 1953, p. 12.

shall consider that my efforts were not in vain. Now that a new policy is being initiated in our country, the unity of the revolutionary family, destroyed in recent years, can be achieved.[39]

The PP continued active in the many fields in which it had participated since its formation: in electoral contests, in the study of national and international problems, in the drafting of national programs, and in the political education of the Mexican people. The party, however, was threatened by internal dissension and division.

According to former member of the PP, Vicente Fuentes Díaz, the party after the 1952 campaign entered into a period of "organic" and "political" decline which attained the dimensions of a genuine crisis. Lombardo has declared to the writer that the party's problems were not as great as Fuentes Díaz has implied. The party entered a period "of recess, of little activity, but not of crisis." This period of inactivity followed as a reaction to the enormous effort exerted by the party in the electoral campaign, an effort which was virtually beyond the strength of the recently created party.

The party's problems, said Fuentes Díaz, were due to a lack of cohesive organization and discipline within the party which were the consequences of the failure to give the party a definite, Marxist theoretical foundation around which party discipline could be organized and party members educated.

As it was, local party units were given too much discretion in doctrinal and tactical matters. Furthermore, Fuentes Díaz complained that whereas Lombardo allowed others within the party to express their opinions freely, Lombardo nevertheless dominated the party because the majority of the members unquestioningly accepted his opinions and decisions.

Some within the party, according to Fuentes Díaz, sought to maintain the loose organization formed around a program rather than around Marxist doctrine. He was especially critical of Vidal Díaz Muñoz, who argued that the peasantry should constitute the fundamental social basis of the party. (The peasantry, in fact, constituted over 60 per cent of party membership.) Fuentes Díaz, Enrique Ramírez y Ramírez, and Rodolfo Dorantes argued that the primary component of the party should be the proletariat. Lombardo, according to Fuentes Díaz, did not refute Díaz Muñoz's

39. New York *Times*, Jan. 1, 1953, p. 5.

position and thereby tacitly accepted it. The issue behind this dispute was vital: which social class was most fitted to gain control of the state power and socialize Mexico, the proletariat or the peasantry?

In 1955, the party adopted a proposal by Lombardo that scientific socialism be accepted as the theoretical foundation of the party and that party members be educated in accordance with its principles. Fuentes Díaz approved this step; he complained, however, that as a consequence of Lombardo's influence, the two persons whom he considered as the staunchest Marxists of the PP —Ramírez y Ramírez and Rodolfo Dorantes—were excluded from the new party leadership. The PP continued to sustain "an internal situation which impelled it more and more towards crisis and dissolution."[40]

Lombardo, for his part, has claimed that the PP would not have been legally registered as a political party if it had been organized originally as an avowedly Marxist-Leninist party. As it was, its formation around a program attracted a larger number of people to its ranks than would have been the case if it had been formed around an ideology. The internal dynamics of the party, influenced by practical political experience, impelled the party toward the acceptance in 1955 of the principles of scientific socialism (Marxism-Leninism) as its theoretical foundation and of the achievement of a Popular or People's Democracy and of socialism as its practical goals. In brief, according to Lombardo, the real experiences of the party members demonstrated to them the practical necessity of accepting Marxism as their guide to thought and action. As a consequence, the political orientation of the party and of its members was sounder than if the party formally—and rather superficially—had adopted Marxism when it was founded in 1948.

As a matter of principle Lombardo does not wish to base the party upon the peasantry. The predominance of peasants in party membership is merely a practical fact of party life. The party actively seeks to increase its working-class base. The only class capable of constructing socialism in Mexico is the proletariat.

According to Lombardo, members such as Ramírez y Ramírez did the party a great deal of harm by the opportunistic and di-

---

40. Fuentes Díaz, II, 144. The preceding account of Fuentes Díaz's criticisms is summarized from *ibid.*, pp. 131-138.

visive manner in which they pursued their criticisms. The extraordinarily ambitious Ramírez y Ramírez and others were expelled from the party because of their factionalism.[41]

Lombardo's position was made clear in the proposals which he offered in April 1955 and which the party accepted at its Second National Assembly held in November of the same year. Mexico had reached the stage in the development of its revolution where it was necessary for the party of the people, the Partido Popular, to declare its intention to establish a Popular Democracy as a step toward the eventual socialization of Mexico. Lombardo stated:

> It is necessary and urgent once again to put the Mexican Revolution in march.
>
> In face of the failure of the regime established by the parasitic bourgeoisie which has governed Mexico in recent years, we praise a different regime. The regime which we postulated in the 1952 campaign. The system of government which we conceived in our speeches of the electoral tour, whose constant, central and essential idea was this: the need in Mexico for a democratic and antiimperialist government, based fundamentally on the workers, the peasants, the middle class and the patriotic industrialists....
>
> What type of government do we postulate?
>
> A people's democracy![42]

The working class was to direct the revolution and the construction of the new regime. Lombardo defined a People's Democracy as "A government composed of the workers, the bourgeoisie and the petty-bourgeoisie of the city and the country who are insubornable by the reaction and by imperialism, *under the direction of the working class.*"[43]

The party needed firmer organization and stricter party discipline. The PP was originally organized as a coalition party of diverse ideological views. Now, the party must be consolidated and its position defined more clearly. Scientific socialism (Marxism-Leninism), he reiterated, should be adopted as the party guide in ideology and tactics. The education of the Mexican people

---

41. Ideas expressed personally to the writer by Vicente Lombardo Toledano in May 1962.
42. Lombardo Toledano, *La Perspectiva de México*, p. 78.
43. *Ibid.*, p. 79 (italics mine).

should be undertaken in accordance with its principles. The fight against imperialism should continue to be the *raison d'être* of the party.

A People's Democracy must be achieved peacefully in Mexico. The use of violence to change the social order would cause American imperialism to intervene to establish a repressive, reactionary regime in the nation. Consequently, electoral contests—although still not free—are of great importance in Mexico. The PP was urged especially to participate in elections for municipal councils (*ayuntamientos*) because these political bodies had direct and immediate contact with the masses.[44]

The following year Lombardo used the themes of the report of the Twentieth Congress of the Communist party of the Soviet Union to reinforce his previously expressed views on the nature of the transition to socialism. The report supported his views that the transition to socialism may be peaceful as well as violent (the "many roads to socialism" theme), that the transition must result from a national, popular movement, and that the real transition to socialism can occur only when the state is under the control of the working class.[45] Lombardo recognized weaknesses in the party which, he said, were due principally to the lack of political education among its members and among the Mexican population in general. This shortcoming had to be overcome.[46]

In 1957, the party did away with its system of indirect party elections in favor of a system whereby the basic *unidades* or local party groups directly elected delegates to all the major party assemblies—municipal, state, and national. As a consequence, party organization was made both stronger and more democratic.[47]

In the same year, the PP formulated its *Thesis on Mexico*[48] which contained an extended discussion of all the issues facing the Mexican nation. The issues considered ranged from the concerns of international peace to the national problems of economic development, foreign investments, agrarian reform, industrializa-

44. *Ibid.*, pp. 80-85, 103-111.
45. Lombardo Toledano, *En Torno al XX Congreso*, pp. 171-176, *passim*. See Chap. VII above for a discussion of Lombardo's views on the nature of the transition to socialism in Mexico.
46. *Ibid.*, p. 252.
47. Partido Popular, *Estatutos del Partido Popular* (Mexico, 1960), pp. 8-9.
48. *Tesis sobre México* (Mexico, 1958).

tion, education, and political democracy. A total of 250 general and specific proposals for reform were made.

The program did not call for the socialization of Mexico. It provided, rather, for the development of a very advanced form of state capitalism in which the state was to direct national development and was to own many basic resources and industries, but in which private native and foreign investments (the latter under strict controls) were to be permitted. Thus, the program did not go far beyond the one offered by the party in 1948. The 1957 *Thesis*, however, was much more fully elaborated and called for greater nationalization of resources and industries.

Important changes in the declaration of principles and in the structure of the PP were adopted by the party's Third Ordinary National Assembly which met in October 1960. The Partido Popular—renamed the Partido Popular Socialista—became more firmly and avowedly a Marxist-Leninist party (e.g., it formally adopted dialectical materialism as its philosophical guide) which sought the construction of a Popular Democracy and of socialism. The organizational structure was made at the same time stronger and more democratic. Provisions were made for the thorough political education of party members.

The National Directorate of the PP declared that the changes were necessary in order to make the party more agile, disciplined, and capable ideologically, and to give it a program which looked at the present more realistically and at the future more optimistically than in the past.[49]

Respecting the change in the name of the party, the National Directorate declared, "When we propose that the Partido Popular be called the Partido Popular Socialista, we affirm only that we want to constitute an army of citizens who, prepared in the doctrine of scientific socialism, can convert themselves into the vanguard of the working class of our country, to educate it in order that its class consciousness should be robust and firm, so that the proletariat fulfills the historic tasks which it should accomplish."[50]

The new fundamental principles and goals of the party included the following: adoption of dialectical materialism as a guide to the study of national and international problems; pursuit of

49. Partido Popular, *III Asamblea*, p. 8.
50. *Ibid.*, p. 10.

proletarian internationalism while preserving the complete independence of the party; acceptance of democratic centralism in party structure; support—in order to achieve national independence from imperialism—of steps taken by the government in the direction of nationalization of the basic industries, the public services, and the essential manufacturing industries; increased political democracy on the basis of freedom of action of political parties in conducting campaigns and in overseeing the honesty of elections; complete independence of municipal governments (*ayuntamientos*); more equitable distribution of wealth by means of revisions in the taxation and other economic policies of the government; the alliance of the free and united working, peasant, petty bourgeoisie, and national bourgeoisie classes into a democratic popular front which seeks the independence of Mexico; unification into a single party of all the Marxist-Leninist parties of Mexico; support for the positive, and criticism of the negative, acts of the government; the establishment of a People's Democracy in Mexico; and the continuous amplification of democracy in Mexico from its present basis to the establishment of socialism.[51]

The new party program embodied most features of the May 1957 *Tesis sobre México*. The new proposals, however, were more concisely and clearly stated and the demands for nationalization were more extensive and categorical. The program, in brief, made proposals for the realization of the immediate objectives of the PPS: the complete economic and political independence of Mexico from imperialism; the nationalization of the principal natural resources, the basic industries, and the public services of Mexico; the broadening of political democracy, including the adoption of a system of proportional representation in all elected bodies; respect for individual and social rights; progressive increases in the material and cultural levels of living of the Mexican masses; and more equitable distribution of wealth.[52]

The new party statutes maintained and amplified the principles of democratic centralism incorporated into the party structure in 1957. The party organs are the local unit (*unidad*), the assembly of units in each municipality, the assembly of units in each state and territory and in the Federal District, and the assembly of units in the nation. (Thus, members of the local party units

51. *Ibid.*, pp. 19-20.
52. *Ibid.*, pp. 23-32.

directly elect representatives to all party assemblies from the local to the national level.) Every unit and each assembly elects its corresponding executive committee. The National Assembly—the supreme legislative authority of the party—elects the Central Committee of the party (which replaces the old National Committee). The Central Committee—the executive organ of the party—in turn elects the National Executive Directorate (which replaces the old National Directorate). The old National Council is abolished. The National Executive Directorate is composed of nine secretaries: the secretary-general and the secretaries of organization, union affairs, peasant affairs, foreign affairs (*relaciones*), political education, information, electoral affairs, and finances.

In accordance with the principles of democratic centralism, the statutes called for free discussion and criticism within the party and at the same time tightened party discipline. The minority must accept the democratically expressed will of the majority in the party; divisive factionalism had to be avoided. In addition, party membership dues were modified and simplified. Each member must pay a quota amounting to 1 per cent of his monthly income. Members who cannot afford to meet this quota as well as unemployed housewives must pay a minimum of 3 pesos monthly. Peasants may delay meeting their dues until the harvest season. Finally, the study of Marxism-Leninism was made obligatory for all members. Special "Schools of the Masses" and "Schools of Cadres" were to be created by the Central Committee for the purpose of political education.[53]

In a report to the Central Committee of the PPS published in April 1961, Lombardo stipulated the qualities required in party candidates for political office:

> The selection of candidates should be more rigorous today than in the past.
>
> The minimum qualities which Party candidates should possess are: (a) Ideological loyalty; (b) Proved militancy; (c) Capacity to defend in the tribune of congress the principles, the program and the initiatives of the PPS and to refute the ideas and proposals of the deputies which are opposed to those of the Party; (d) Absolute discipline to the instructions of the National Executive Directorate of

---

53. *Ibid.*, pp. 35-36, 43-44.

the Party; (e) Punctual payment of the quotas which the Party sets for its deputies.[54]

The PPS continued to participate in local, state, and national elections. Some PPS candidates have been elected to municipal and state offices. The PPS has never controlled a municipal council or a state legislature, nor has it ever elected one of its members as governor. In the 1955 congressional elections, the party had put up 66 candidates for the 162 seats contested in the Chamber of Deputies. One of its candidates was declared elected by the Federal Electoral Commission. As a measure of protest against controlled elections, the party refused to allow its successful candidate to take his seat. The candidate insisted on entering congress, however, and consequently was expelled from the party. The PRI won all but nine seats in the Chamber.[55]

In the 1958 elections, the PP named 69 candidates for the 162 seats in the Chamber of Deputies and 21 candidates for the 60 seats in the Senate. Rather than nominate a candidate for the presidency, the party instructed its members to vote for the PRI candidate, Adolfo López Mateos. This was done, according to Lombardo, in order to maintain united support of the revolutionary forces behind López Mateos who, the PP expected, would be a moderately progressive president.[56] The PP refused the request of the Mexican Communist party for support of its candidate for the presidency, Miguel Mendoza López, a seventy-four-year-old, non-party lawyer.

The results of the elections were similar to those in 1955. One PP candidate was declared elected; the party refused to permit the candidate to take her seat and expelled her from the party when she insisted. The PRI won all the seats in the Senate and 153 of those in the Chamber. (PAN won six seats and two minor parties took one each.)[57]

In the 1961 congressional elections, the PPS entered 88 candidates for the 178 Chamber seats. The PPS campaign was con-

54. Vicente Lombardo Toledano, ''Primera Reunión del Comité Central del Partido Popular Socialista: Informe al Comité Central,'' *Avante*, VI (April, 1961), 10.
55. *Hispanic American Report*, VIII (Oct., 1955), 405; Robert E. Scott, *Mexican Government in Transition* (Urbana, Ill., 1959), pp. 147, 243.
56. Statement made to the writer by Vicente Lombardo Toledano in April 1962.
57. Scott, pp. 147, 191, 242-243.

ducted most actively in the states of Baja California, Durango, Guerrero, Jalisco, Michoacán, Nayarit, and in the Federal District. The Federal Electoral Commission accredited the PPS with one victorious candidate and with 1.9 per cent of the total vote. (PAN was accorded 11 per cent of the vote.) Both the PPS and PAN charged the elections were fraudulent.[58]

PPS membership, according to Lombardo, increased steadily from the founding of the party in 1948 until shortly after the 1952 elections, when it reached 200,000. Membership has since remained approximately the same quantitatively. Qualitatively, however, there have been changes. The peasantry still represents some 56 to 58 per cent of the membership, but larger numbers of workers and youths have entered the party. The latter are organized into the Juventud Popular Socialista. The ideological maturity of the members is firmer. The great internal problem of the party, however, consists in the political education of its members which is a very difficult task and proceeds slowly.[59]

The party has grown since the Third National Assembly adopted changes in the principles and structure of the party. New local units have arisen where previously none existed and new state committees have been formed. Many of the original founders and other old members who had withdrawn from the party rejoined its ranks.[60]

58. *Hispanic American Report*, XIV (May, 1961), 292; XIV (Sept., 1961), 586; XIV (Oct., 1961), 675.
In the 1964 elections, the PPS supported Gustavo Díaz Ordaz, the PRI candidate for the presidency. It put up 167 candidates for the 178 seats in the Chamber and 11 candidates for the 60 Senate seats (according to data of the Federal Electoral Commission published in the newspaper, *El Día*, April 29, 1964, pp. 6-7). A constitutional amendment adopted in 1962 provided for the election of "party deputies" (*diputados del partido*) on the basis of one deputy for each 0.5 per cent of the total popular vote received by the party. These deputies represented their parties rather than congressional districts and served in addition to the deputies elected by majority vote. A maximum of 20 party deputies was permitted. On the basis of this new electoral system, the PPS had 1 deputy elected by majority vote (Joaquín Salgado Medrano from the Culiacán, Sinaloa district) and 9 elected as party deputies (among whom was Vicente Lombardo Toledano). The PAN won 2 Chamber seats by majority vote and had 18 elected as party deputies. Consequently, according to the Federal Electoral Commission, the PPS received 5 per cent of the total national vote, and the PAN, 10 per cent.
59. Information supplied personally to the author by Vicente Lombardo Toledano in May 1962.
60. Lombardo Toledano, "Primera Reunión del Comité Central," pp. 9-10.

Since 1958, there have been increased manifestations of unrest and criticism in Mexico. Labor union and peasant militancy has revived, the latter to the point of outbreaks of armed violence on occasions.[61] Strikes have been more numerous; serious student demonstrations have occurred.

The Mexican government has responded to the strikes and agitation by repressions and concessions. The 1958-1959 railroad strike was suppressed by the army, a number of leftist union and political party leaders were jailed, militant union leaders were replaced with government pawns, and peasant leaders were assassinated. At the same time, the López Mateos regime has given new stimulus to the Mexican Revolution. Land distributions have increased, irrigation and hydroelectric projects have been extended, a number of important industries have been nationalized, the social security program has been extended, and the principle of national self-determination has been upheld in international affairs (with important positive consequences for the Cuban Revolution).[62]

The PPS, for its part, has both encouraged the increased militancy and criticized some of the tactics employed. According to the PPS, the primary objective to be sought is revolutionary unity within the working class and between the working class and other popular, anti-imperialist classes and groups. Frequently though—as in the railroad strike and in the maneuvers of Section IX of the national teachers union (SNTE)—the tactics employed are anarchistic and opportunistic. As explained previously, the railroad worker's union was smashed by the government when the leaders of the union insisted upon striking even though the government had declared the strike illegal. The radical leaders of Section IX of SNTE were removed from their union positions by the national officers of the SNTE when these section heads attempted to usurp the leadership of the entire organization. In both cases the rank-and-file union members were left disgruntled and disillusioned. Thus, according to Lombardo and the PPS, the

61. *Hispanic American Report*, XIV (Nov., 1961), 775.
62. Accounts of unrest and of government repressions and reforms in Mexico are found in I. A. Langnas, "Mexico Today; Aspects of Progress Since the Revolution," pp. 162-167; Howard T. Young, "Mexico; A Revolution Gone Bankrupt," pp. 14-15; *The Economist*, CLXXXVIII (Sept. 6, 1958), 739; "A Mexican Tightrope," *The Economist*, CXCVI (July 30, 1960), 484-485.

tactics employed by these leaders lent themselves to the division rather than to the unification of the working class.[63]

Responding to its own convictions and to the considerable sympathy with the Cuban Revolution which has been expressed among the Mexican masses, the PPS has staunchly defended the Cuban Revolution. At the time of the April 1961 invasions sponsored by the United States, the party requested (and was denied) permission from the Mexican government to send volunteers to the defense of Cuba.[64]

On September 7, 1962, the National Executive Directorate of the PPS issued a declaration on the Cuban situation. The United States, stated the declaration, is preparing a new aggression against Cuba. Bellicose statements by United States politicians were noted. It was pointed out that President Kennedy's statement that the United States will not invade Cuba "at this time" implied that the United States would invade Cuba at the opportune moment. The declaration further called attention to the aggressive actions of Cuban counterrevolutionaries which were being undertaken with the aid and support of the United States and of some Central American governments.

In light of these events, the National Executive Directorate declared:

(1) That any direct or indirect aggression by imperialism upon the heroic people and the government of Cuba will be considered by all the people of Latin America as an aggression upon all of them.

(2) That the Cuban people, as the President of Mexico, Adolfo López Mateos, affirmed on the first of September in his fourth governmental report, is alone capable to choose its road and to construct its own destiny.

(3) That Cuba is the aggressed and not the aggressor, as the government of the United States of North America would like it to appear.

63. Lombardo Toledano, *Teoría y Práctica*, pp. 91-95, 125-131, *passim*; Partido Popular, *La Situación Política*, pp. 31-52. The PPS's influence upon the agrarian reform movement through the UGOCM as well as its role in reunifying Section IX of SNTE were discussed in the previous chapter.

64. *Hispanic American Report*, XIII (July, 1960), 298; XIII (Aug., 1960), 366-367; XIV (June, 1961), 292-294; Lombardo Toledano, *Al Pueblo Mexicano*, pp. 5-11.

(4) That an aggression upon Cuba would signify the beginning of the third world war, initiated by imperialism in its desperation.[65]

The declaration went on to call for the formation of a national democratic front for solidarity with the Cuban people. It called upon President López Mateos to use his influence to avoid a new aggression upon Cuba and to prevent Cuban counterrevolutionaries living in Mexico from engaging in subversive activities.

The declaration concluded with the following paragraph: "The imperialist states have declared that they can be pushed too far in the Cuban situation, and we say that the peace loving peoples can be pushed too far by imperialism."[66]

In addition, the National Executive Directorate directed an "Urgent Circular" to all the organs and members of the PPS. The circular (to which the declaration quoted above was attached) called for concrete action by PPS members in support of the Cuban Revolution. Declarations by the National Executive Directorate on the Cuban situation were to be diffused by all available means. Steps were to be taken toward unification of all democratic political, social, and cultural organizations in Mexico in support of the Cuban Revolution. A campaign of letters, telegrams, and meetings was to be started urging the petitioning of President López Mateos to continue supporting the principle of non-intervention in Cuba. Meetings and conferences were to be held to explain the Cuban situation. Finally, the party organs and members were to keep the National Executive Directorate informed of their activities and were to remain vigilant to detect all pro-imperialist and counterrevolutionary activities in respect to Cuba.[67]

In search of its goal of revolutionary, anti-imperialist unity, the PPS has attempted to achieve unity among Mexico's leftist political parties. In 1960, Mexico had three major leftist parties: the PPS, the Mexican Communist party (PCM), and the Partido Obrero Campesino (POC, Worker-Peasant party). The latter party was formed in the early 1940's as the result of a split within the PCM. An alliance between these three parties had been

65. Partido Popular Socialista, "Declaración del Partido Popular Socialista," *Política*, XLVIII (Sept. 15, 1962), 9.
66. *Ibid.*
67. Partido Popular Socialista, "Circular Urgente," *Política*, XLVIII (Sept. 15, 1962), 9.

sought through the years; serious talks were resumed in 1960.⁶⁸ An agreement for the early integral unification of the PPS and the POC was achieved finally in the spring of 1962.⁶⁹ The PPS and the PCM, though, still remain at odds. Periodically exchanging recriminations, the PPS has charged that the PCM has ignored proposals for joint study and discussion of national and international issues, while the PCM, on its part, has attacked the PPS members as opportunists and revisionists. The PCM, says the PPS, has continued to use—to the detriment of revolutionary unity—the extreme, Trotskyist, and divisive tactics it has employed through most of its history. The PPS, nevertheless, states that, in the interests of revolutionary unity, it still seeks agreement with the PCM.⁷⁰

In 1961, there arose a new element of disunity within the Mexican Left. In March of that year, the Latin American Conference for Economic Emancipation, National Sovereignty and Peace was held in Mexico City. The conference organized the Movimiento de Liberación Nacional (MLN) as a permanent Mexican body to diffuse the conference's resolutions and to stimulate the activities of all anti-imperialist persons and organizations in Mexico.

The PPS wished the MLN to be a co-ordinating committee for the entire Left—that is, a popular-front organization composed of representatives from the major leftist political parties and popular organizations in Mexico. The PPS has charged, though, that instead of accepting this form of organic, functional representation, the MLN has constituted itself as an organization "with individual affiliations and with a centralized direction." The MLN, therefore, is in reality but another Mexican political party; it does not really represent the united Mexican Left. It is, Lombardo stated to the writer, a party "without any prospect" composed of intellectuals resident in Mexico City who lack any real contact with the masses. The PPS has refused to participate in the MLN and

68. New York *Times*, March 13, 1960, p. 31; *Hispanic American Report*, XIII (Jan., 1961), 771-772.
69. Information supplied personally to the author by Vicente Lombardo Toledano in April 1962, and "El Partido Popular Socialista," *Avante; Documentos*, p. 5.
70. "El Partido Popular Socialista," *Avante; Documentos*, pp. 5-6; Lombardo Toledano, "Primera Reunión del Comité Central," pp. 5-8.

has denied its members the right of parallel membership in the movement.[71]

The PPS continues to fight for revolutionary popular unity and for the implementation of its program. The best summary statement of this program was made by Lombardo in 1957. In a sharp, hitting manner, he outlined future plans and tactics, reasoning that in order to promote complete national independence, higher levels of living and political democracy, Mexico must

1. Impede the concentration of land. Destroy the latifundios, no matter to what activities they are dedicated. Pursue the agrarian reform in all its aspects at an accelerated pace. Organize financially and technically the *ejidatarios*, colonists, small and medium agriculturalists. Open new zones to cultivation in order to settle the rural population which lacks employment. Elevate by these and other means, such as the defense of the prices of agricultural products, the level of living of the rural population, not only as an elemental principle of justice, but because the industrialization of the country depends upon the growth of the internal market, constituted by the country people who represent the majority of the active population.

2. Orient agriculture and live stock raising toward the satisfaction of the necessities of the people and of national industry, and not preferentially toward the gaining of profits, because this desire converts agricultural and livestock production into a complement of foreign markets, especially to that of our northern neighbor.

3. Nationalize basic industry—electricity,[72] coal, iron and steel, and the chemical industry—(with that of petroleum already accounted for), in order that its orientation and its development obey exclusively the ends of the nation's economy. While this objective is being achieved, the state should foment the Federal Electricity Commission and surround it with facilities. The Commission should establish its own distribution networks and cease selling energy which it produces to private enterprises. It should require private enterprises to fulfill the duties indicated in the concessions by which they were established and the obligations of the respective laws. Consider as public utilities the coal, basic chemical and iron and steel industries, programming and

71. "El Partido Popular Socialista," *Avante; Documentos*, pp. 6-11.
72. Nationalized under the López Mateos administration.

controlling their development and impeding the intervention of foreign capital in these branches.

4. Expedite a law which shall set the basic conditions for foreign investments, as much for private loans as for loans from institutions of an international character and for direct investments. These [foreign investments and loans] should be permitted by previous authorization only. Those which increase the national income should be accepted. They should not compete with national establishments with the capacity or the possibility to satisfy the national demand. Those should be prevented which seek to exploit unrenewable resources or to dedicate themselves to the key industries of the national economy.

5. Protect national industry against internal and external competition from foreign industries and facilitate the credit necessary for its development.

6. Nationalize credit, in the sense of obligatorily channelizing the credit of the state and of the national banking system towards agriculture and industry and mobilize the inactive capitals in the official and private credit institutions.

7. Establish exchange controls.

8. Expropriate and nationalize the public service monopolies.

9. Formulate a tax policy which stimulates productive investments and places obstacles upon unnecessary or superfluous investments and expenditures.

10. Set limits to the profits of all enterprises and set the percentage of profits which obligatorily must be reinvested in their own activities or in others which the government authorizes.

11. Organize a national system of price controls which will stimulate production, avoid abuses by intermediaries and protect the consuming masses.

12. Reform the existing procedures for determining minimum wages to the end that it may be a true, vital wage which is adequate for the principal necessities of a worker's family, in accordance with the spirit of Article 123 of the Constitution.[73]

[73] Art. 123 contains the advanced labor provisions of the Mexican Consti-

13. Establish a moving scale system for wages and pensions to the end that they augment automatically with each increase of five per cent in the prices of the necessary articles of consumption.

14. Diffuse foreign commerce, carrying our products to the markets which pay best for them and buying in those which represent the greatest advantages to our country.

15. Reform the Constitution to establish an electoral system which facilitates the creation and guarantees the rights of permanent political parties. Make the requirements for the participation of political parties in elections uniform throughout the Republic, within democratic and equitable principles. Form a permanent and unfalsifiable poll of the citizens. Create organisms in which the parties effectively participate to watch over the electoral process. Install a system of proportional representation for the integration of the municipal councils (*ayuntamientos*), the State legislatures and the houses of the Congress of the Union.[74]

Although not his latest statement, Lombardo's fifteen points are a valuable political legacy. The Mexican nation must decide whether it wishes to be guided by these points in the future; the alternative, according to Lombardo, is drastic:

Without these principles and methods to guide the economic, political and social life of Mexico, the only future, of our country is to become converted into a satellite of the United States, with a forever hungry people who will continue slowly to lose their personality, governed by a minority more and more insensitive to the exigencies of the nation, servants of the foreigner, and whose only industry will consist in politics, reduced to taking possession of state revenues in order to enrich those who direct it, at the expense of the well being of the majority and of national independence.[75]

tution of 1917. Among other things, the article grants the workers the right to organize unions, to bargain collectively, and to strike. Compulsory arbitration of labor disputes is provided for as well as the setting of minimum wages. Child labor and peonage are prohibited and provisions are made for profit-sharing, for the construction of houses and schools by employers, and for compensation to the workers for injuries.

74. Lombardo Toledano, *La Sucesión*, pp. 18-21.
75. *Ibid.*, p. 21.

IX. Summary and Conclusions

Vicente Lombardo Toledano has devoted his life to struggle for the advancement of the Mexican Revolution. As a young man in the 1910's and 1920's, Lombardo first was a supporter of the system of state capitalism which Mexico was developing as a consequence of the revolution which began in 1910. After participating as a leader in the labor movement of the 1920's, Lombardo changed his views and became initially an evolutionary socialist in the tradition of the Second International, and then a Marxist socialist. Lombardo became a Marxist in the latter 1920's at a time when the process of revolutionary reform had reached its lowest ebb since the purely military phases of the revolution had ended. The principal goals, he decided, of the revolution—economic independence, higher levels of living for all Mexicans through economic development, and equitable distribution of wealth, and political democracy—could be achieved only if Mexico socialized the ownership of the means of production, exchange, and distribution and planned its economic development. Only a socialist society would provide Mexicans with the opportunity to develop all their potential as human beings.

As a Marxist socialist, Lombardo has analyzed the Mexican Revolution extensively in both its positive and its negative aspects. The Mexican Revolution, says Lombardo, was a bourgeois-democratic revolution. It was not entirely similar to nineteenth-century bourgeois revolutions, however, because in addition to possessing democratic and antifeudal characteristics, it was also anti-imperialist in nature.

The Mexican Revolution has accomplished much, according to Lombardo. Mexico no longer is the backward agricultural country of former days. The semifeudal hacienda system was destroyed and extensive redistributions of lands were undertaken. Government irrigation and hydroelectric projects have stimulated agricultural development, especially of commercial crops such as cotton and coffee. Rural purchasing power has increased in comparison with its 1910 level and as a consequence has stimulated industrial production. Industrialization has so progressed that in 1950 the value of industrial production was greater than that of agricultural and mineral production combined. Nationally owned telephone, telegraph, and highway networks were constructed.

The Constitution of 1917 delimited liberal economic and financial doctrines by providing for considerable state intervention into the fields of agrarian reform and of reclamation of national subsoil rights. In addition, the constitution declared that private property was not an inherent right but rather was subject to modifications in accordance with social needs.

Upon these bases the state has expanded its functions to the extent that today the structure of Mexican society properly may be designated as state capitalistic. The Mexican state intervenes in the economy to stimulate production and to supply capital where private capital is unavailable. The state now owns a number of industries: electricity, petroleum, petrochemicals, coal deposits, iron mines, most of the iron and steel industry, the railroads, part of civil aviation, most of the nation's telecommunications, and a number of factories in various industries—sugar, textiles, newsprint, fertilizers, and others. The state has moved into the field of banking with the creation of a national central bank, a bank for industrial investment, and banks for loans to the various categories of farmers and to town and state governments.

In education, the rural and secondary schools were created and extended and, in 1937, the National Polytechnic Institute was founded. The constitution prohibited religious corporations from establishing or directing primary schools. The state stepped into the field of social insurance with the formation, in 1925, of the Civil Pensions Administration for government employees and with the creation in 1944 of the Mexican Social Security Institute.

In spite of progress made, states Lombardo, the revolution is not complete since all its original goals have not been achieved. The short-comings of the revolution are many. The growth of the Mexican population threatens in the future to outstrip the rate of economic development. Economically, according to Lombardo, Mexico is an occupied country. Her invaders are primarily United States capitalists and their associates. Welcomed and applauded by the press and the government, these foreign interests have taken control of some of the most valuable of Mexican resources—especially the mineral deposits. They dominate the nation's foreign commerce and they are extending themselves more and more in the manufacturing industry. A larger share of total American investments in Mexico is in manufacturing rather than in the traditionally predominant field of mining. Making use of their great resources, these foreign monopolies are in mortal competition with native Mexican industries for control of the domestic market.

The process of national capital formation is obstructed. Unrestricted by national legislation, Lombardo claims, the foreign corporations send 80 per cent of their huge profits out of the country. In order to acquire the exchange necessary for foreign purchases—especially of capital goods—Mexico has developed the production of commercial crops for export—to the detriment of the needs of the agriculture which produces for the domestic market. Fluctuations in the prices of export commodities—the prices are set by international monopolies and foreign governments, he argues—lead to balance-of-payments crises and to devaluations of the peso, with consequences which are detrimental to national levels of living and to national economic development. Mexico presently is saved from even greater balance-of-payments crises owing to two fortuitous additions to expenditures within the country: those of American tourists and those of Mexican farm laborers returning from the United States. Derived in this manner, these expenditures—which are beyond Mexican control and are subject to fluctuations and reductions—increase Mexico's dependence and subject her to a crude "yankeefication" and to a humiliating loss—if only temporary in most cases—of her lifeblood. Mexico's balance-of-payments problems have led to the monopolization by the United States of more than three-quarters of Mexico's foreign trade.

Lombardo regrets that the agrarian reform is but partially completed. The supplies of land, water, credit, and machinery and the dissemination of scientific procedures are insufficient for the needs of the majority of Mexican farmers. The best of the newly irrigated lands are given to political favorites who exploit the properties as absentee capitalist landlords. Local and state political bosses, in his opinion, have corrupted and controlled *ejido* government. Most of the rural population suffers from a dreadful poverty with little immediate hope for improvement. The rural market for industrial products is small and stagnant. This is the situation in spite of the fact that a modern, progressive agriculture is the *sine qua non* for the effective industrialization of the nation.

Mexican industry operates under severe handicaps, which include the lack of an extensively developed heavy industry and the consequent necessity to import capital goods, the flooding of the market with foreign produced goods, and the limited, inelastic purchasing capacity of the domestic market. There is none of the co-ordination between the development of agricultural and industrial production which is so essential to sound economic growth.

Credit facilities are inadequate—especially for the needs of *ejidatarios* and small farmers—and to a great extent are devoted to commerce and usury.

The national distribution of wealth, Lombardo warns, is becoming increasingly more inequitable. Real wages are declining steadily while huge fortunes are being made by a minority of individuals who either are associated with North American enterprises or are in political positions which give them control over the financial and administrative resources of the nation.

The government, complains Lombardo, has intervened in the labor movement to replace militant union leaders with government puppets, although the Lombardo-influenced UGOCM has remained independent. The result has been seriously to divide the labor movement and to encourage corruption, reformism, and opportunism in union leadership. The reformist leaders thwart efforts by the workers to achieve genuine economic gains and to organize a unified, militant labor movement.

Education in Mexico suffers from many disabilities. Acting contrary to constitutional provision, the clergy has regained a position of influence in education. Mexican education, he claims, lacks the orientation of a scientific pedagogy adapted to Mexican needs. United States methods and institutions (such as the high school) have been copied without regard to Mexican needs or to the shortcomings and confusion in American education. The various levels of Mexican education (primary, secondary, preparatory, and university) lack integration in programs and in objectives. Teachers generally are poorly trained and inadequately compensated. Because of the unattractiveness of the profession, many capable persons either avoid teaching or look upon it merely as a stepping stone to positions of greater prestige. Educational facilities are woefully inadequate, especially in rural areas. In imitation of the United States, a number of universities have been established throughout the nation; most of these institutions, however, have insufficient facilities and personnel to be considered genuine universities. Almost one-half the population is illiterate and much of the rest is poorly educated.

Further, he is convinced that politics are thoroughly corrupt. *Caciquismo* and *caudillismo* abound. All elections are controlled by the official party, the PRI. Municipal councils, state legislatures, governorships, and the national congress all are appointed rather than elected organs. Thus, the president (who fulfils the function of national *cacique*) and the Secretariat of Gobernación appoint all major office-holders in the Republic; lesser *caciques* (such as governors) appoint the holders of minor positions. As elections are fraudulent and office-holders do not represent the people, the Mexican masses have lost interest in elections. Justice is bought and sold. Corruption extends throughout the government, reaching even into the Supreme Court of the nation.

Mexican youth lacks horizons. Few, Lombardo laments, can aspire to land ownership. Jobs in factories are scarce and are expanding slowly in number; unemployment and underemployment abound. Educational facilities are inadequate. Consequently, Mexican youth is bored and restless.

In order to give Mexico an effective organ of struggle to surmount its problems, Lombardo took the lead in organizing the Partido Popular (PP). Founded in 1948, the party originally was organized rather loosely around a program rather than around an ideology. Successive measures have since clarified the ideological orientation and tightened the structure of the party. In 1955, the party accepted as its goal the establishment of a People's Democracy which was to serve as the basis for the construction of socialism in Mexico. The principles of democratic centralism were incorporated into the party structure in 1957. Several important measures were taken by the party in 1960, including the formal adoption of the principles of Marxism-Leninism as the ideological guide to the practical actions of the party, the elaboration of the principles of democratic centralism in the party structure, and the change of the party's name to that of the Partido Popular Socialista (PPS).

Claiming 200,000 members, the PPS is the major leftist party in Mexico. Other parties on the left include the Partido Comunista Mexicano (PCM), the Partido Obrero Campesino (POC), and the recently organized Movimiento de Liberación Nacional (MLN). Recent attempts at unification among these parties have been largely unsuccessful. The MLN was created in 1961 to act as a co-ordinating committee for the Left but instead it converted itself into another political party. One notable success has been achieved, however: during 1963 the POC unified itself organically with the PPS.

With anti-imperialism as its principal theme, the PPS aspires to realize the traditional goals of the Mexican Revolution: national independence, higher levels of living, and political democracy. As a long-term project to achieve these ends, the PPS seeks to establish a Popular Democracy in Mexico which, in turn, will serve as a means to the construction of socialism. The essential feature of the Popular Democracy is a government composed of representatives of the workers, peasants, middle classes, and national bourgeoisie under the leadership of the representatives of the working class. The Popular Democracy will seek rapidly to develop the productive forces of the nation so as to provide the material basis for socialism. Socialism will be achieved when the means of production, distribution, and exchange have become public property, when the last vestiges have disappeared of the class system of exploitation of man by man, and when, in practice, the primary purpose of society is to permit and to provide the conditions necessary for the full development of the capacities of every individual.

Two questions assert themselves as most important in interpreting Lombardo's thought and political career. Does Mexico in fact need to socialize its economy (at some indefinite but not too remote time in the future) in order to continue its economic and human development? Are the strategy and tactics pursued by Lombardo adequate to attain this goal of socialism?

If the answer to the first question is negative, the only matter which remains of interest is why such aberrant thought as Lombardo's arose in Mexico and why Lombardo was able to form an entire political movement around his aberration. If the answer is affirmative, we must move to the second question to see if Lombardo is genuinely and effectively seeking the goal of socialism in Mexico. If he is not, he emerges as merely a farcical opportunist.

If he is, he becomes unquestionably an outstanding personage of recent Mexican history.

If the subject of this study was, say, an eighteenth-century French Jacobin or a nineteenth-century Russian anarchist, it would be relatively easy to answer similar questions about him. In the case of Lombardo, however, events have not proved either whether socialism is necessary in Mexico or if Lombardo's tactics are the most effective. In order even to attempt to provide an adequate answer to these questions, it would be necessary to write another volume or two.

Consequently, in these conclusions I shall merely note briefly my opinion that Mexico will have to socialize its economy sometime in the future in order to continue its economic and human development. Several social and technical elements have interacted to place severe obstacles to Mexico's economic and human development. These elements include the characteristics of the capitalist mode of production, which contains an inherent contradiction between social production and private appropriation of the product; the advanced and complex nature of twentieth-century technology which demands that a nation which undertakes a modern program of industrialization either has available or rapidly acquires huge investment resources, extensive markets, and a large, skilled labor supply; internal institutional obstacles to economic development in Mexico in the form of minifundia and latifundia; and the domination of international trade and investment by a few capitalist imperialist nations who themselves have serious domestic economic, social, and political problems which they attempt to resolve at least in part at the expense of the dependent, underdeveloped economies. The interaction of these elements has resulted in an unbalanced growth of Mexico's economy, which is most evident in the uneven development of agriculture and industry, an extremely unequal distribution of wealth, and increased foreign capitalist influences within the national economy.

The Mexican government has counteracted these economic tendencies in a number of ways which include increased state control and regulation of economic activities, nationalization of some key industries, the distribution of land, the construction of irrigation works, the extension of credit to small producers and other measures in the countryside, and introduction of social reforms, such as social security. Nevertheless, these fundamental tendencies toward unbalanced growth, unequal distribution of wealth, and increased dependence upon foreign capital continue to assert themselves.

In time, Mexico will have to choose either to nationalize the major means of production, distribution, and exchange and plan its economic development free from foreign control, or to increase its dependence upon capitalist imperialism as a means to maintain its economic solvency and to repress popular discontent. Hence, I believe that the strategy which Lombardo proposes is most adequate for the Mexican working class to follow to achieve control of the state in order to construct a socialist regime in Mexico. This strategy, it will be remembered, consists of the formation of a national, anti-imperialist front composed of workers, peasants, urban petty bourgeoisie, and elements of the national bourgeoisie and of the bourgeoisie in control of the state power. A basic prerequisite to the creation of this front is the achievement of revolutionary unity within the working class. These statements, I repeat, are offered here merely as personal opinions with which the reader may or may not agree. I hope to develop at length my reasons for holding these opinions in a future work.

It might be noted here—as a bit of information, not as proof that such a front is in order in Mexico—that national, anti-imperialist fronts similar to that proposed by Lombardo for Mexico have been formed in other nations. Indeed, it is the strategy which generally is followed by national liberation movements in colonial and semicolonial countries throughout the world. The world presently is witnessing the brilliant success of such a front in South Viet-Nam.[1] I don't mean to imply by calling attention to these facts that the Mexican front would necessarily have to pursue the guerrilla warfare tactics employed in Viet-Nam and elsewhere. Mexico's road to socialism must be adapted to the special circumstances of Mexico's national life.

If we accept as given that Mexico must socialize its economy and that the formation of an anti-imperialist front is the proper strategy to achieve that end, then it is possible to evaluate in some detail the adequacy of the tactics which the PPS employs.

One of the principal tactics of the PPS is to support the posi-

---

1. For information on the South Viet-Nam front, see Wilfred G. Burchett, *Vietnam: Inside Story of the Guerrilla War* (New York, 1965).

tive actions and to criticize the negative measures of the government. This tactic appears valid. In order to remain in control of the state power, the PRI takes measures which promote economic development and which head off popular discontent. Some of these measures, such as the nationalization of vital industries, help to create the bases for a transformation to socialism in Mexico. Others, such as the encouragement of foreign investments in Mexico and the obtaining of foreign loans to maintain Mexico's financial stability in the face of balance-of-payments problems, increase Mexico's dependence upon foreign imperialism.

How do some government policies create the bases for a transition to socialism in Mexico? Nationalization of sources of wealth in the hands of foreign or national capitalists and increased state control of the economy weaken the economic and hence also the political power of these capitalists within the Mexican nation; division of lands among peasants weakens the economic and political power of the large land-owners; increased state controls and measures of social reform undermine traditional bourgeois concepts of private property and of the roles of the individual and the state in society; and improved democratic processes permit leftist political parties to operate with greater freedom in all spheres—within labor unions, in the congress, and so forth. The weakening of the traditional economic, political, and ideological power of the bourgeoisie correspondingly strengthens Mexico's forces for socialism.

It is important to note that the PRI takes reform measures such as these because they are necessary to sustain Mexico's economic development and social stability and therefore also to maintain the PRI's control of the state power. The PRI prolongs its control of the state power and extends the life of Mexico's system of state capitalism only at the expense of partially transforming that system and thereby laying the bases for a future transition to socialism.

In supporting the positive and criticizing the negative measures of the government, the PPS does more than encourage reforms which strengthen the position of the Left within Mexican society. It also encourages those elements within the PRI most favorable to these reform measures and correspondingly discourages those PRI elements who wish to rely more upon foreign investments and foreign loans to ease Mexico's economic and social problems.

Summary and Conclusions

The PPS feels that the anti-imperialist orientation of many elements within the reformist left wing of the PRI makes these elements potential allies of the national, anti-imperialist front.

We arrive at the conclusion, consequently, that the strategy and tactics advocated by Lombardo and the PPS are the most adequate for the Mexican proletariat to employ in its struggle to gain control of the state power.

In regard to Lombardo's ideas, then, perhaps the only criticism of real importance we can make is that Lombardo has demonstrated a lack of complete intellectual independence in his uncritical acceptance of the foreign and domestic policies as well as the doctrinal line of the Communist party of the Soviet Union. Such uncritical acceptance of the practices and policies of the CPSU probably grates sharply upon the sensibilities of Mexicans who might be ready to accept a sympathetic yet more balanced interpretation of Soviet realities.

Lombardo, in his speeches and writings, has interpreted life in the Soviet Union in terms of Marx's and Engel's theoretical conceptions of the characteristics of life in an advanced industrial-socialist society which has arisen upon the basis of an industrial-capitalist society. He has not interpreted the concrete realities of life in the U.S.S.R., which was an underdeveloped, largely agrarian nation when the Bolsheviks took control of the state power and which has not yet equaled the degree of industrial development of the most advanced capitalist nation in the world. That Lombardo in fact does have a more realistic appraisal of life in the socialistic and popular democratic nations is evident from some of the comments he made when discussing the Hungarian Revolution and from his praise of the self-criticisms made within the Soviet Union (and in other socialist nations) since 1956. The important point to Lombardo evidently is his belief that the Soviet Union is developing directly and rapidly toward realization in practice of the type of society envisioned in socialist theory. Perhaps he feels that too forceful criticisms might harm the unity of the socialist forces.

The Soviet Union probably is developing in the direction indicated by Lombardo. It would seem, however, that this development would be helped rather than hindered by a thoroughly realistic appraisal of life in the Soviet Union since it was created in 1917. Lombardo's uncritical acceptance of the Soviet line probably has contributed to the fact that he has not made an original theoretical contribution to social science. It is difficult to be both orthodox and seminal in one's theoretical propositions. It must be noted, though, that Lombardo has devoted his attention to the practical problems of achieving socialism in Mexico rather than, say, to theoretical problems of Marxian economics.

When we turn from Lombardo's concept of the strategy and tactics which the PPS should follow to the tactics which that party employs in practice, however, we find that Lombardo and the PPS do not fully carry out the tactics which they advocate. As we have seen, Lombardo has indicated the positive and negative aspects of governmental policy on a number of occasions and has analyzed the characteristics of the PRI as a political party. Lombardo, nevertheless, has mitigated the import of his criticisms by limiting the frequency with which he makes them. In addition, as we noted, the PPS places its greatest emphasis upon realizing a program of concrete reforms in alliance with the progressive elements of the PRI. These tactics make Lombardo and the PPS appear moderate and cautious to many Mexicans.

Furthermore, Lombardo, except in the case of Miguel Alemán, rarely criticizes Mexican presidents directly in public. Also, although Lombardo has made extensive general criticisms of agricultural practices in Mexico, he has never made public specific information on the exact location or size of latifundia in given states or regions, even though the UGOCM (as several PPS members admitted to me) possesses abundant information of this sort. (Instead of making this information public, the PPS uses it in private to pressure public officials into action in specific cases.) Finally, the PPS is restrained in its promotion of public demonstrations although, of course, it has promoted and participated in many such demonstrations.

Why does not the PPS live up to the tactics it advocates? Essentially, I think, because if the PPS did fulfil its tactics to the letter it would encounter severe government harassment and repression. The game of Mexican politics demands a degree of conformism from its players. An essay in Mexican sociology will help explain my point.

Social relationships in Mexico are characterized by the importance of personalism or *caudillismo*. Individuals with the slightest authority in the social hierarchy demand and receive almost total submission and unconditional support from those subject to their authority. In return, these individuals or *caudillos* grant their followers such favors and protection as are at their disposal. Lesser *caudillos* are as subservient to greater *caudillos* as are the followers of these lesser *caudillos* to them. In the last instance, all *caudillos* are subservient to the president of the republic. In order then to play the game of politics in Mexico one must abide by the rules. You can never call a spade a spade to a *caudillo*, especially not if he is president.

What does the PPS gain by moderating its tactics? The PPS can participate freely in elections and has a voice in the congress; thus, the PPS can spread its doctrines among the Mexican people. It can maintain a Worker's University with branches in various parts of the Republic which instructs workers in the elements of dialectical and historical materialism. It can control a labor confederation which allegedly possesses some 300,000 members; it can work relatively freely among the Mexican peasants through this confederation and it can achieve the division of lands and other reforms in practice. It can place its members in strategic positions in reformist-controlled labor unions. It can infiltrate government offices. It can talk freely and frequently with members of the PRI and thereby influence these individuals and prepare some of them psychologically for the formation in the future of a national, anti-imperialist front.

Perhaps more important than the above is the fact that the PPS's tactics permit that party to retain intact a large membership which is being trained constantly in the principles of Marxism-Leninism. (In personal conversations and in indoctrination of party members, the PPS, of course, does not have to pull its punches as it does sometimes in public statements for national consumption.) Thus the PPS is forming a core of revolutionary leaders important to Mexico's future.

Also, the PPS's moderation tends to set the PRI against the PAN and other rightists as its principal enemies. The PRI, in attacking the PAN, also coerces the rightists within its own party (some of whom differ from members of the PAN only over the issue of clericalism) and encourages the leftists within it. It is these PRI leftists who are potential candidates for the national, anti-imperialist front which the PPS seeks to form.

Finally, and most important, the PPS's moderation tends to

influence its potential allies in the national, anti-imperialist front more favorably than does the intransigent, extremist, and dogmatic posture of the PCM. The ultimate success of the PPS as a revolutionary party of the Mexican proletariat depends upon the PPS's ability to attract allies from other social classes because the Mexican proletariat is too small to gain control of the state power by its own efforts alone. It is this desire to gain allies which is probably the principal motive behind Lombardo's decision to moderate the PPS's tactics in accordance with the rules of Mexican politics. It would be quite deleterious to the interests of the PPS to break with elements of the revolutionary petty bourgeoisie and national bourgeoisie who either are members of the PRI or who feel their interests leagued with those of the PRI, because many of these elements are potential members of the national, anti-imperialist front.

What are the negative consequences of the PPS's failure to carry out the tactics which it advocates? As a consequence of playing the game of Mexican politics, Lombardo at least in part has confused the Mexican public as to the nature of the regime in power, the distinctions which exist between the left wing of the PRI and the PPS, and the motivations behind the PPS's moderation in practice.

Lombardo does not usually explain the motivations which impel the PRI to take progressive measures. He does not indicate clearly and constantly that the primary interest of the PRI is to retain control of the state power in order that a group of politicians may retain their privileges; in order to retain power the PRI must take measures which promote economic development and head off popular discontent. Nor does Lombardo indicate constantly why it is that regardless of the motives for which the PRI takes progressive measures, it is in the interests of the Mexican people that they be taken. Lombardo, directly or indirectly, has indicated all of these things at various times but the point I am making is that he has not done so often and directly enough to make these matters absolutely clear to all who hear him or other members of the PPS (all of whom tend to follow the Lombardo style).

Specific examples of cases in which Lombardo seemingly confused the public as to the nature of the regime in power are numerous. We shall note two. It seems that Lombardo hardly could have caused greater confusion among the public as to the nature of the PRI and the PP and the distinction between the two parties than by declaring his support for the program of the president, Ruíz Cortines, in 1952, because the latter "had adopted the opposition program." Many might have asked themselves, since Lombardo did not offer a precise and detailed clarification of his position, why then had Lombardo run for the presidency against Ruíz Cortines a few months previously?

As another example, we may note Lombardo's characterization of the PRI as differing only in degree from the PPS, while the difference between the PP and the PAN, he claimed, was absolute. Lombardo was referring, of course, to the fact that the PRI takes many progressive measures which the PP can support, while the PP and the PAN oppose each other on every issue. Also, some members of the PRI may participate in the national, anti-imperialist front to be formed in the future, while the opposition of the PAN to such a front is likely to be absolute. However, Lombardo would seem to have confused public opinion as to the nature of the PRI and the PP with this statement because he did not go on to point out the motivations behind the PRI's progressive policies nor to indicate that in the last instance, the PRI as a bourgeois party and the PPS as a Marxist-Leninist party of the proletariat, have mutually antagonistic interests.

In both these cases, Lombardo was pursuing his tactic of uniting all the progressive forces in Mexico in order to promote concrete reforms and his ideas and his behavior probably were fundamentally correct. Nevertheless, by refraining from clarifying these issues to the Mexican workers and peasants, Lombardo confused public opinion as to the nature of the regimes in power, the nature of his motives, and the character of the PP.

These negative consequences of the PPS's tactics are rather serious. It would seem that a primary objective of a Marxist political party should be to sharpen the revolutionary consciousness of the workers and peasants. The PPS tactics at least partially—to the degree that they deviate from the tactics which it advocates in theory—thwart the realization of this objective. To fail to criticize the negative policies of the government frequently and frankly and to praise the positive actions of the PRI without directly, thoroughly, and frequently explaining the motives which compel the PRI to take such measures confuse the Mexican people as to the true character of the PRI. This confusion would seem to ill prepare Mexico's popular elements for the decisive revolutionary role which they must play in the future.

These criticisms must be qualified with the following remark. PPS members claim that on a local level—in dealing with the peasants in the UGOCM, in some local elections—the PPS pulls no punches in criticizing the negative aspects of the PRI and of government policy. Unfortunately, I have not had the opportunity to verify this claim. If it is true, then my criticisms are mitigated in part.

Finally, some Mexicans, I have found, consider the PPS opportunistic as a consequence of that party's failure to carry out fully its tactic of criticizing the negative and supporting the positive policies of the government. This image of the PPS in the minds of some Mexicans would seem to raise an obstacle to the revolutionary effectiveness of that party. This conception of the PPS is widespread among middle-class intellectuals who reside in Mexico City. Just how generalized this opinion is among workers and peasants and among petty bourgeois intellectuals in other parts of the republic is difficult for me to say. The considerable support which the PPS has achieved among the peasantry, especially in northwestern Mexico, would seem to indicate that this opinion of the PPS is not too widespread. The members of the POCM, which merged with the PPS in 1963, were largely of working-class origin. Also, the PPS has gained more intellectuals and professionals as members than has the PCM. Finally, the potential adherents to the national, anti-imperialist front among the non-intellectual urban petty bourgeoisie, the national bourgeoisie, and the bourgeoisie in control of the state power, in general regard Lombardo in particular, and the PPS in general, with more respect than they do the PCM, which these elements largely disregard or deride for its ineffectualness and its extremism.

This opinion among leftist opponents that the PPS is opportunistic arises in part from the still prevalent influences of anarchistic concepts in Mexican thought which lead many to consider that the only true revolutionary position is one of complete hostility to the government. As we have seen, this is not true. Nevertheless, the failure of the PPS to live up fully to its quite valid tactic of supporting the positive and criticizing the negative policies of the government has given arms to its enemies and spread confusion and doubt among some of its potential allies.

The PPS's lack of appeal to some middle-class intellectuals of leftist tendencies may offer an explanation for the origin of the MLN, whose membership consists largely of middle-class intellectuals and professionals. The MLN, therefore, fulfils the function of giving these individuals an organization through which they can exert some influence upon Mexico's national life. The MLN and, especially, the PCM, possess the virtue of criticizing the negative policies of the government directly and frankly. (The PCM has the defect that its conception of Mexican reality is sketchy and stereotyped, its concepts dogmatic, and its attitude so sectarian as to cause profound distrust among its potential allies in the national, anti-imperialist front.) Thus, the MLN and the PCM possess merits which complement those of the PPS and make up for the deficiencies in the latter's tactics. Therefore, although no Mexican party is the ideal prototype of a party on the Left, the positive characteristics of each of the three parties on the Mexican Left sum up the qualities of such a party. The ideal party would be one which would carry out in practice the strategy and tactics which the PPS advocates but feels itself unable to realize in full because of the peculiar character of Mexican politics.

How does the PPS come out on balance? In general, the PPS gains much more than it loses by moderating its tactics in accordance with the rules of Mexican politics. As noted previously, the principal objective of the PPS's tactics is to gain allies in the national, anti-imperialist front to be formed sometime in Mexico's future. In spite of the opinion of many of its leftist opponents that the PPS is opportunistic (an opinion of which rightists take good advantage), the PPS nevertheless appears in general to be regarded with more respect by the potential components of the anti-imperialist front than any other party on the Left. The PPS managed to effect a merger with the POCM in 1963, even though that party had over a period of years sought to merge with the PCM. The PPS has a large membership, whereas the PCM has only three or four thousand members. In practical achievements, such as the attainment of land reforms and the infiltration of labor unions and government offices, the PPS far outdistances the PCM.

Thus, in spite of the negative consequences of its tactics, the PPS is preparing the ground much more effectively than any other leftist party in Mexico for the attainment of the principal goal of Mexico's revolutionaries: the formation of a national, anti-imperialist front which is controlled by the representatives of the working class and which is composed of the workers, the peasantry, the urban petty bourgeoisie, and elements of the national bourgeoisie and the bourgeoisie in control of the state power. At this moment in Mexico's history, less moderate tactics might be more attractive to some middle-class intellectuals, but might well also be detrimental to the gaining of allies in the anti-imperialist front to be formed sometime in Mexico's future.

The *sine qua non* of a political party which pretends to lead the proletariat into control of the state power is that the party act in a decisive and revolutionary fashion at a moment of revolutionary crisis in its nation's history. If the PPS does so, then it is most likely that the negative aspects of its present tactics will not serve as an insurmountable obstacle to the effective action of that party. The mass base which it has achieved to date (especially in northwestern Mexico), the training in Marxism-Leninism which its numerous members receive, and the influence which it has among Mexico's various social classes will be invaluable to it at that time. If the PPS does not act decisively, however, another party (new or old) is likely to surge forward into revolutionary leadership.

History will pass the final verdict on Lombardo. If the PPS fails to fulfil the role assigned it as a Marxist-Leninist party, history is likely to judge Lombardo rather severely. If the PPS does manage to assume the leadership of the Mexican socialist movement and lead the Mexican proletariat into control of the state power, then history will measure Lombardo as one of Mexico's greatest men.

APPENDIX A
VICENTE LOMBARDO TOLEDANO:
BIOGRAPHICAL DATA

Place and Date of Birth

Teziutlán, State of Puebla, Mexico, July 16, 1894.

Academic Degrees

Bachillerato. National Preparatory School of the University of Mexico (June 1, 1914).
Bachelor of Laws. Faculty of Jurisprudence of the National University of Mexico (March 15, 1919).
Academic Professor. Faculty of Higher Studies of the National University of Mexico (June 13, 1920).
Doctor of Philosophy. National University of Mexico (August 18, 1933).

Honorary Academic Degrees

Honorary Member of the College of Lawyers of the Republic of Costa Rica (May 13, 1933).
Doctor Honoris Causa. University of Guadalajara (January 18, 1943).
Doctor Honoris Causa. Michoacán University of San Nicolás de Hidalgo (May 8, 1943).

Educational Services

Secretary of the Popular Mexican University, created by the Ateneo de México (September 1917).
Secretary of the Faculty of Jurisprudence of the National University (April 1919).
Chief of the Department of Libraries of the Secretariat of Public Education (October 1921).
Director of the National Preparatory School of the National University (March 1922).
Founder and Director of the Night School of the National Preparatory School (April 1923).
Director of the Summer School for Foreigners of the National University (May 1922).
Director of the Central School of Plastic Arts of the National University (May 1930).
Director of the National Preparatory School of the National University for the second time (January 1933).
Director of the Gabino Barreda Preparatory School created

on the initiative of Vicente Lombardo Toledano (February 1934).

Director of the Gabino Barreda University created on the initiative of Vicente Lombardo Toledano (February 1934).

Director of the Worker's University of Mexico created on the initiative of Vicente Lombardo Toledano (from 1936 to date).

Professor of the following subjects from 1918 to 1933 in the National Preparatory School, in the Faculty of Jurisprudence, in the Summer School and in the Faculty of Business Administration of the National University; and from 1933 to 1950 in the Gabino Barreda Preparatory School, in the Gabino Barreda University and in the Worker's University of Mexico: History of Philosophical Doctrines, Dialectical Materialism, Logic, Ethics, Elements of Public Law, Sociology, Public Law, Political Economy, Labor Law, History of Imperialism, History of Mexico, History of the Mexican Revolution.

Occasional speaker in universities and institutions of science and political education in Mexico and other nations.

Public Offices

Chief Clerk of the Federal District Government (February 1921).

Governor of the State of Puebla (December 1923).

Alderman of the municipal government of Mexico City. (Elected in January of 1924. He filled the office again in 1925, after holding that of governor.)

Deputy to the Congress of the Union (September 1924). (He occupied the post at the end of 1925, resigning that of alderman of the municipal government of Mexico City.)

Deputy to the Congress of the Union for a second time (1926-1928).

Labor Union Activities

Secretary-General of the League of Professors of the Federal District (August 1920).

Secretary-General of the Solidary Group of the Labor Movement (February 1922).

Member of the Central Committee of the Regional Confederation of Mexican Workers (CROM) from 1923 to 1932.

Secretary-General of the National Federation of Teachers (January 1927).

Secretary-General of the Federation of Labor Unions of the Federal District (April 1932).

Organizer and leader of the General Confederation of Workers and Peasants of Mexico (October 1933).
Organizer of the National Committee of Proletarian Defense (June 12, 1935).
Organizer and Secretary-General of the Confederation of the Workers of Mexico (CTM) from 1936 to 1940.
Organizer and President of the Confederation of Latin American Workers (CTAL) from 1938 until present.
Member of the Administrative Council of the International Labor Office (1944).
Member of the Administrative Committee of the World Trade Union Conference of London (February 1945).
Vice-President of the World Federation of Trade Unions from September 1945 until present.
Member and collaborator of the General Union of Workers and Peasants of Mexico (UGOCM) created on June 20, 1949.

Political Activities

Member of the Mexican Labor Party (1921-1932).
Organizer—in conjunction with others—and one of the leaders of the Party of the Mexican Revolution (PRM) (March 1938).
Organizer and Secretary-General of the Mexican Socialist League (September 1944).
Promoter and leader of the Partido Popular (from June 1948 until present) which was reorganized with the name of the Partido Popular Socialista by its Third National Assembly held in the month of October 1960.
Member of the World Council of the Partisans of Peace (April 1949).
Candidate for the presidency of the Republic of Mexico (1952).

Journalistic Activities

Editorialist of the daily *El Heraldo de México* (1919).
Collaborator of the daily *Excelsior* for several years, starting from 1923.
Collaborator of the daily *El Universal* for several years, starting from 1917 when he was a student.
Collaborator of the review *C.R.O.M.* (1925-1932).
Founder of the bibliographical review *El Libro y el Pueblo* (1921) of the Secretariat of Public Education.
Founder and director of the *Revista de la Escuela Nacional Preparatoria* (1922).
Collaborator of the *Revista de la Universidad Nacional de México*, starting from 1917.

Founder of the review *Puebla* (1923).
Founder and Director of the review *Futuro* (1933).
Founder of the review *U.G.B.*, theoretical organ of the Gabino Barreda University (October 1935).
Founder of the review *U.O.*, theoretical organ of the Worker's University of Mexico (February 1936).
Founder of the bulletin "Mexican Labor News" of the Worker's University of Mexico (1937).
Founder of the review *América Latina*, organ of the CTAL (March 1939).
Founder and Director of the daily *El Popular* in its first epoch, starting from the first of June 1938.
Founder of the review *Noticiero de la C.T.A.L.* (July 1945).
Founder of the review *DOCUMENTOS* dedicated to questions of philosophy, economics, and politics from the Marxist-Leninist point of view (May 1946).
Collaborator of the review *Democratie Nouvelle*, Jacques Duclos Director, Paris (from 1947).
Collaborator of the review *HOY* (1952).
Collaborator of the review *Siempre!* since its first number (July 27, 1953).
Occasional contributor to important reviews of Europe, Asia, and America.

Honors Received as a Political Militant

Knight Commandery (*Encomienda*) of the Order of Isabela the Catholic granted by the Council of Ministers of the government of the Spanish Republic (February 9, 1938).
Decoration "Emiliano Zapata" awarded before the tomb of Zapata by the Union of Veterans of the South (April 10, 1939).
Decoration of the Combatant subscribed by the most prominent writers, artists, men of science, and labor leaders of Mexico (February 28, 1946).

APPENDIX B
LIST OF ABBREVIATIONS

Political Parties
MLN—Movimiento de Liberación Nacional
PAN—Partido Acción Nacional
PCM—Partido Communista Mexicano
PLM—Partido Laborista Mexicano
PNR—Partido Nacional Revolucionario

POC—Partido Obrero Campesino
PP—Partido Popular
PPS—Partido Popular Socialista
PRI—Partido Revolucionario Institucional
PRM—Partido de la Revolución Mexicana

Labor Organizations

AFL—American Federation of Labor
AOCM—Alianza de Obreros y Campesinos de México
ATLAS—Asociación de Trabajadores Latinoamericanos
BUO—Bloque de Unidad Obrera
CGOCM—Confederación General de Obreros y Campesinos de México
CGT—Confederación General de Trabajadoes
CIT—Confederación Interamericana de Trabajadores
CROC—Confederación Revolucionaria de Obreros y Campesinos
CROM—Confederación Regional Obrera Mexicana
CTAL—Confederación de Trabajadores de América Latina
CTM—Confederación de Trabajadores de México
CUT—Confederación Unitaria de Trabajadores
FSTSE—Federación de Sindicatos de Trabajodores al Servicio del Estado
ICFTU—International Confederation of Free Trade Unions
ILO—International Labor Office
ORIT—Organización Regional Interamericana de Trabajadores
SNTE—Sindicato Nacional de Trabajadores de la Educación
UGOCM—Unión General de Obreros y Campesinos de México
WFTU—World Federation of Trade Unions

LIST OF WORKS CITED

Archival and Manuscript Material

Harker, Mary Margaret. "Organization of Labor in Mexico Since 1910." Unpublished Ph.D. dissertation, University of Southern California, 1937.

Hayes, James Riley. "The Mexican Labor Movement, 1931-51." Unpublished M.A. thesis, University of California, 1951.

Hill, Rachel Newborn. "A Sketch of the Mexican Labor Movement." Unpublished M.A. thesis, Columbia University, 1946.

United States Department of State. Correspondence from U.S. Embassy, Mexico City to U.S. State Department, Washington, D.C., December 11, 1928. National Archives.

———. Correspondence from U.S. Embassy, Mexico City to U.S. State Department, Washington, D.C., December 27, 1927.

———. Dispatch from W. O. Jenkins, U.S. Consular Agent, Puebla to George T. Summerlin, Chargé d'Affairs, American Consular Service, Mexico City, December 8, 1923.

———. Telegram from U.S. Embassy, Mexico City to U.S. Secretary of State, Washington, D.C., October 18, 1960.

Books and Pamphlets

Alba, Victor (pseud.). *Historia del Frente Popular.* Mexico, 1959.

Alexander, Robert J. *Communism in Latin America.* New Brunswick, N.J.: Rutgers University Press, 1957.

Bergson, Henri. *Creative Evolution.* New York: The Modern Library, 1944.

Bulnes, Francisco. *Las Grandes Mentiras de Nuestra Historia.* Mexico, 1904.

———. *El Porvenir de las Naciones Hispano-Americanas ante las Conquistas Recientes de Europa y los Estados Unidos.* Mexico, 1899.

Burchett, Wilfred G. *Vietnam: Inside Story of the Guerrilla War.* New York: International Publishers, 1965.

Caso, Antonio. *El Acto Ideatorio: las Esencias y los Valores.* Mexico, 1934.

———. *Discursos a la Nación Mexicana.* Mexico, 1922.

———. *Doctrinas e Ideas.* Mexico, 1924.

———. *Filósofos y Doctrinas Morales.* Mexico, 1915.

———. *Problemas Filosóficos.* Mexico, 1915.

Clark, Marjorie. *Organized Labor in Mexico.* Chapel Hill, N.C., 1934.

Cline, Howard F. *Mexico: Revolution to Evolution: 1940-1960.*
London: Oxford University Press, 1962.
———. *The United States and Mexico.* Cambridge, Mass.:
Harvard University Press, 1953.
Confederación de Trabajadores de México. *C.T.M., 1936-1941.*
Mexico, 1941.
Conferencia Sindical Latinoamericana de Trabajadores. *Intervención de Vicente Lombardo Toledano, Presidente de la Confederación de Trabajadores de América Latina.* Mexico, 1962.
Crawford, William Rex. *A Century of Latin-American Thought.*
Rev. ed. Cambridge, Mass.: Harvard University Press, 1961.
Current Biography, 1940. New York, 1940.
Dulles, John W. F. *Yesterday in Mexico: A Chronicle of the Revolution, 1919-1936.* Austin, Texas: University of Texas Press, 1961.
El Frente Único en México. Ed. Marcos Díaz. Havana, 1938.
Fuentes Díaz, Vicente. *Los Partidos Políticos en México.* 2 vols.
Mexico, 1954 and 1956.
Gaxiola, Jr., Francisco Javier. *El Presidente Rodríguez, 1932-1934.* Mexico, 1938.
Gruening, Ernest. *Mexico and Its Heritage.* New York, 1928.
Herring, Hubert, and Weinstock, Herbert (eds.). *Renascent Mexico.* New York, 1935.
Hinojosa, Roberto. *El Tren Olivo en Marcha.* Mexico, 1937.
The International Who's Who. London, 1952.
Kawage Ramia, Alfredo. *Con Lombardo Toledano: Un Hombre, una Nación, un Continente.* Mexico, 1943.
Kirk, Betty. *Covering the Mexican Front.* Norman, Okla.: University of Oklahoma Press, 1942.
Lombardo Toledano, Vicente. *La Batalla de las Ideas en Nuestro Tiempo.* Mexico, 1949.
———. *Carta a la Juventud.* Mexico, 1960.
———. *Causas de la Elevación del Espíritu Humano.* Mexico, 1960.
———. *La Constitución de los Cristeros.* Mexico, 1963.
———. *Las Corrientes Filosóficas en la Vida de Mexico.* Mexico, 1963.
———. *Ante la Crisis de Hungria.* Mexico, 1956.
———. *Cristianos y Socialistas Unidos contra la Regresión.* El Paso, Texas, 1943.
———. *The C.T.A.L., The War and the Postwar.* Mexico, 1945.
———. *Definiciones sobre Derecho Público.* Mexico, 1922.
———. *Democracia y Partidos Políticos.* Mexico, 1957.

———. *El Derecho Público y las Nuevas Corrientes Filosóficas.* Mexico, 1919.
———. *Diario de un Viaje a la China Nueva.* Mexico, 1950.
———. *Discurso Pronunciado por el Lic. Vicente Lombardo Toledano en Representación del Gobierno del Distrito Federal, al Clausurarse el Primer Congreso Agrarista Celebrado en Ixtapalapa, D.F.* Mexico, 1921.
———. *La Doctrina Monroe y el Movimiento Obrero.* Mexico, 1927.
———. *La Doctrina Socialista y su Interpretación en el Artículo 3º.* Mexico, 1935.
———. *Dos Conferencias sobre Israel.* Mexico, 1951.
———. *El Drama de México: Nuestros Grandes Problemas Económicos.* Mexico, 1954.
———. *Escritos Filosóficos.* Mexico, 1937.
———. *El Estado y la Iglesia: La Revolución y la Religión: Progreso y Retroceso.* Mexico, 1943.
———. *Ética.* Mexico, 1922.
———. *La Evolución de México durante la Primera Mitad del Siglo XX.* Mexico, 1956.
———. *50 Verdades sobre la U.R.S.S.* Mexico, 1935.
———. *La Filosofía y El Proletariado.* Mexico, 1962.
———. *El Fracaso Actual de la Industria Azucarera y las Estupendas Perspectivas para su Triunfo.* Mexico, 1952.
———. *El Frente Nacional Democrático.* Mexico, 1964.
———. *Geografía de las Lenguas de la Sierra de Puebla.* Mexico, 1931.
———. *La Influencia de los Héroes en el Progreso Social.* Mexico, 1919.
———. *La Izquierda en la Historia de México.* Mexico, 1963.
———. *Judíos y Mexicanos ¿Razas Inferiores?* Mexico, 1944.
———. *Lenin, el Genio.* Mexico, 1942.
———. *La Libertad Sindical en México.* Mexico, 1926.
———. *El Llanto del Sureste.* Mexico, 1934.
———. *En los Mares de Ulises: Sicilia.* Mexico, 1956.
———. *Menoscabar la Libertad de Creencia Religiosa es Conspirar contra el Progreso Democrático de México.* Mexico, 1952.
———. *Mensaje al Proletariado de la América Latina.* Mexico, 1936.
———. *¿Moscú o Pekín? La Via Mexicana hacia el Socialismo.* Mexico, 1963.
———. *El Neonazismo: Sus Características y Peligros.* Mexico, 1960.

———. *Un Nuevo Partido para la Defensa de México y de su Pueblo.* Mexico, 1947.
———. *El Nuevo Programa del Sector Revolucionario de México.* Mexico, 1944.
———. *Objetivos y Táctica del Proletariado y del Sector Revolucionario de México en la Actual Etapa de la Evolución Histórica del País.* Mexico, 1947.
———. *Una Ojeada a la Crisis de la Educación en México.* Mexico, 1958.
———. *La Perspectiva de México: Una Democracia del Pueblo.* Mexico, 1956.
———. *Presente y Futuro.* Mexico, 1952.
———. *Los Principales Problemas de la Agricultura y de la Economía del Continente Americano.* Mexico, 1942.
———. *El Problema de la Educación en México.* Mexico, 1924.
———. *Al Pueblo Mexicano: Defender a Cuba es Defender a México y a la América Latina.* Mexico, 1961.
———. *En Qué Consiste y a Cuánto Asciende la Fortuna de Vicente Lombardo Toledano.* Mexico, 1940.
———. *Qué Ha Sido la Reforma Agraria Ayer y Qué es Durante el Régimen Actual.* Mexico, 1952.
———. *La Rebelión del Mundo Colonial Contra el Imperialismo.* Mexico, 1950.
———. *La Reforma Agraria en China y en México: Semejanzas y Diferencias.* Mexico, 1954.
———. *El Régimen Actual Ha Hecho de Matamoros un Gran Monumento contra el Agrarismo.* Mexico, 1952.
———. *La Revolución del Brasil.* Mexico, 1936.
———. *La Revolución Rusa—la Revolución Mexicana: Pasado, Presente y Porvenir.* Mexico, 1943.
———. *La Sucesión Presidencial de 1958.* Mexico, 1957.
———. *Summa.* Mexico, 1964.
———. *Teoría y Práctica del Movimiento Sindical Mexicano.* Mexico, 1961.
———. *La Tercera Devaluación del Peso Mexicano en los Ultimos 15 Años.* Mexico, 1954.
———. *En Torno al XX Congreso del Partido Comunista de la Unión Soviética.* Mexico, 1956.
———. *The United States and Mexico: Two Nations—One Ideal.* New York, 1942.
———. *La Universidad Obrera de México y la Educación Política del Proletariado.* Mexico, 1943.
———. *Por Vez Primera en la Historia Contemporanea de*

Nuestro País la Revolución está en la Oposición al Gobierno. Mexico, 1952.
——. *Un Viaje al Mundo del Porvenir.* Mexico, 1936.
——. *Vicente Lombardo Toledano en Nicaragua.* Managua, 1943.
——. *Victoria de la Revolución China.* Mexico, 1950.
——. *What Does the C.T.A.L. Mean?* Mexico, 1944.
——, and Caso, Antonio. *Idealismo vs Materialismo Dialéctico: Caso—Lombardo.* Mexico, 1963.
——, and Icaza, Xavier, et al. *Marxismo y Anti-Marxismo.* Mexico, 1934.
López Aparicio, Alfonso. *El Movimiento Obrero en México: Antecedentes Desarrollo y Tendencias.* 2nd ed. Mexico, 1958.
Martin, Michael Rheta, and Lovett, Gabriel H. *An Encyclopedia of Latin American History.* New York: Abelard-Schuman Co., 1956.
Méndez Barraza, Alfonso. *Los Partidos Políticos en México.* Mexico, 1949.
Millan, Verna Carleton. *Mexico Reborn.* Boston, 1939.
Parkes, Henry Bamford. *A History of Mexico.* 2nd ed. Boston: Houghton Mifflin Co., 1950.
Partido Popular. *Estatutos del Partido Popular.* Mexico, 1960.
——. *Razón Histórica, Programa y Estatutos del Partido Popular.* Mexico, 1948.
——. *La Situación Política de México con Motivo del Conflicto Ferrocarrilero.* Mexico, 1959.
——. *Tesis sobre México.* Mexico, 1958.
——. *III Asamblea Nacional Ordinaria del Partido Popular: Materiales de Estudio.* Mexico, 1960.
Partido de la Revolución Mexicana. *Cárdenas Habla.* Mexico, 1940.
Peral, Miguel Angel. *Diccionario Biográfico Mexicano.* 3 vols. Mexico, [1944].
Plenn, J. H. *Mexico Marches.* Indianapolis, 1939.
Poblete Troncoso, Moises, and Burnett, Ben G. *The Rise of the Latin American Labor Movement.* New York: Bookman Associates, 1960.
Prewett, Virginia. *Reportage on Mexico.* New York, 1941.
Puig Casauranc, J. M. *El Sentido Social del Proceso Histórico de México.* Mexico, 1936.
Ramírez y Ramírez, Enrique. *La Obra y La Lucha de Vicente Lombardo Toledano.* Mexico, 1952.
Ramos, Samuel. *Profile of Man and Culture in Mexico.* Austin, Texas: University of Texas Press, 1962.

Rodman, Selden. *Mexican Journal: The Conquerors Conquered.* New York: Devin-Adair Co., 1958.
Romanell, Patrick. *Making of the Mexican Mind: A Study in Recent Mexican Thought.* Lincoln, Neb.: University of Nebraska Press, 1952.
Salazar, Rosendo. *Líderes y Sindicatos.* Mexico, 1953.
Scott, Robert E. *Mexican Government in Transition.* Urbana, Ill.: University of Illinois Press, 1959.
Strode, Hudson. *Timeless Mexico.* New York, 1944.
Tannenbaum, Frank. *Mexico: The Struggle for Peace and Bread.* New York: Alfred A. Knopf Co., 1950.
Townsend, William Cameron. *Lázaro Cárdenas.* Mexico: George Wahr Co., 1952.
United States Department of Labor. *Directory of Labor Organizations: Western Hemisphere.* 2 vols. Washington, D.C.: Government Printing Office, 1960.
Universidad Obrera de México. *Vicente Lombardo Toledano: Curriculum Vitae.* Mexico, 1961.
Urrea, Lic. Blas (pseud. of Luís Cabrera). *Veinte Años Después.* Mexico, 1937.
Vasconcelos, José. *Breve Historia de México.* 9th ed. Mexico, 1963.
Weyl, Nathaniel, and Weyl, Sylvia. *The Reconquest of Mexico: The Years of Lázaro Cárdenas.* London, 1939.
Who's Who in Latin America. 2nd ed. Stanford, 1940.
World Biography. 2 vols. New York, 1948.
Zea, Leopoldo. *Apogeo y Decadencia del Positivismo en México.* Mexico, 1944.
———. *El Positivismo en México.* Mexico, 1943.

Periodicals

"Bajo la Sombre de Paraguas," *Futuro*, LIII (July, 1940), 13.
"Barbarie contra Civilización, el Discurso de Lombardo Toledano," *Futuro*, LXVI (August, 1941), 1-2.
"Communications" section, *The Commonweal*, XXVIII (August 5, 1938), 389-390.
"Communications" section, *The Commonweal*, XXVIII (August 19, 1938), 429-430.
"Compas de Espera," *Futuro*, LIV (August, 1940), 13.
"Conferencia de Prensa del Secretario General del P.P.S.," *Avante*, XXV (May, 1962), 9-24.
Cruickshank, Jorge. "La Solución del Problema de la Sección IX del S.N.T.E.," *Avante*, XXVII (September, 1962), 47-57.

"¿Donde y Como Terminará la Guerra?," *Futuro*, LX (February, 1941), 3-4.
The Economist, CLXXXVIII (September 6, 1958), 739.
"Expropriation in Mexico," *The Economist*, CXXX (March 26, 1938), 678-679.
Futuro, Special ed. (October 10, 1938).
Futuro, XXXIII (November, 1938).
Hispanic American Report, III (February, 1951), 5-6; VIII (October 1955), 405; XI (April, 1958), 192-193; XI (July, 1958), 364; XI (August, 1958), 425; XIII (July, 1960), 298; XIII (August, 1960), 366-367; XIII (January, 1961), 771-772; XIV (May, 1961), 292; XIV (June, 1961), 292-294; XIV (September, 1961), 586; XIV (October, 1961), 675; XIV (November, 1961), 775.
Hispanic World Report, II (April, 1949), 6; II (September, 1949), 6; II (November, 1949), 9.
Jones, C. L. "If Lewis Sits Down in Mexico," *The American Scholar*, VI (October, 1937), 471-480.
Langnas, I. A. "Mexico Today: Aspects of Progress Since the Revolution," *World Today*, XVII (April, 1961), 158-167.
"Lombardo Out," *Time*, XXXVI (October 7, 1940), 30.
"Lombardo Toledano, Líder de los Trabajadores de México, es Entrevistado por la 'Revista del Trabajo,'" *Revista del Trabajo*, XI (January, 1941), 8-12.
Lombardo Toledano, Vicente. "Alegato en Favor de Siquieros," *Siempre!*, CDLXVII (May 30, 1962), 20-21.
——. "La Bandera Mexicana y el Proletariado," *Futuro*, III (February, 1936), 22-24, 31.
——. "Cómo Surgió la Federación Sindical Mundial," *El Movimiento Sindical Mundial*, VI (June, 1960), 3-5.
——. "El Derecho Internacional Americano y El Movimiento Obrero," *Derecho Obrero*, II, xiv (1928), 4-7.
——. "La Evolución del Movimiento Obrero," *Futuro*, XLVIII (February, 1940), 14-15, 43-44.
——. "Las Grandes Lecciones de 1962," *Siempre!*, CDXCV (December 12, 1962), 18-19.
——. "Hitler, el Grotesco Dictador de Alemania," *Futuro*, IV (January 15, 1934), 10.
——. "No es la Hora de Buscar Culpables," *Siempre!*, CDLXV (May 16, 1962), 18-19.
——. "Primera Reunión del Comité Central del Partido Popular Socialista: Informe al Comité Central," *Avante*, VI (April, 1961), 1-12.

———. "Reforma Agraria," *Siempre!*, CDLXVI (May 23, 1962), 22-23.

———. "El Sentido Humanista de la Revolución Mexicana," *Universidad de México*, I (December, 1930), 91-109.

———. "La Situación Actual," *Futuro*, LII (June, 1940), 7-9, 37-39.

———. "El Veinte de Noviembre," *Futuro*, XXII (December, 1937), 5.

"Lucha Nacional contra el Fascismo," *Futuro*, LXV (July, 1941), 1-2.

Magner, J. A. "Strong Men in Mexico," *The Commonweal*, XXIX (November 18, 1938), 94-96.

"Man with a Mission," *Time*, XXXIX (April 13, 1942), 18.

"Mexican Crisis," *The Economist*, CL (February 23, 1946), 298-299.

"Mexican Labor in Hemisphere Politics," *The American Analyst*, Pilot Copy No. 4 (October 15, 1946), 24-34.

"A Mexican Tightrope," *The Economist*, CXCVI (July 30, 1960), 484-485.

"La Nueva Guerra Imperialista," *Futuro*, XLIV (October, 1939), 3-4.

Partido Popular Socialista. "Circular Urgente," *Política*, LVIII (September 15, 1962), 9.

———. "Declaración del Partido Popular Socialista," *Política*, LVIII (September 15, 1962), 9.

"El Partido Popular Socialista y El Movimiento de Liberación Nacional," *Avante; Documentos*, I (July, 1962), 2-11.

"The Political Background in Mexico—I," *The Economist*, CXLIX (November 24, 1945), 753-754.

"The Political Background in Mexico—II," *The Economist*, CXLIX (December 1, 1945), 795.

Pond, Randall. "Toledano and Mexico," *The Commonweal*, XXIV (June 12, 1936), 173-174.

Ramírez y Ramírez, Enrique. "Vicente Lombardo Toledano, Un Militante de la Clase Obrera de México," *Futuro*, LXI (March, 1941), 35-42.

Ramos Malzarraga, Javier. "Los Grandes Huelgas Victoriosas de la C.T.M.," *Futuro*, LXI (March, 1941), 31-33, 79.

"Second General Congress of the Confederation of Latin American Workers," *International Labour Review*, LI (February, 1945), 236-243.

"Steel Velvet," *The Literary Digest*, CXXI (May 30, 1936), 15.

Sylvester, Harry. "A Revolution Doesn't Come Off," *The Commonweal*, XXVIII (June 24, 1938), 232.

"The Trade Union Movement in Mexico," *International Labour Review*, XLII (December, 1940), 418.
"The Trade Union Movement in Mexico," *International Labour Review*, XLIII (April, 1941), 463-464.
"La Trascendencia de la Ley de Plenos Poderes," *Futuro*, LXII (April, 1941), 3-4.
Time, XXXII (September 19, 1938), 22.
Time, Latin American edition, (September 1, 1958), 26; (February 23, 1959), 22-23.
"Toledano Faces Labor Revolt," *World Report*, I (December 31, 1946), 30.
Tomlinson, Edward. "Mexican Choice," *Colliers*, CXVIII (July 6, 1946), 26.
Young, Howard T. "Mexico: A Revolution Gone Bankrupt," *The New Republic*, CXLII (April 4, 1960), 13-15.
Newspapers
New York *Times*.
El Popular.
El Universal.

Note: Use was made of additional sources which were not cited in the text, such as the *Christian Science Monitor* and the London *Times*. On various dates between April and October, 1962, this writer held personal interviews with Vicente Lombardo Toledano, Lázaro Rubio Félix, and Joaquín Salgado Medrano. Conversations with Alejandro Gascón, member of the Partido Popular Socialista and Lombardo's personal assistant, aided this writer in understanding the program and tactics of the PPS.

INDEX

Agriculture, criticisms of, 45-46, 49-53, 82, 182, 184-85, 188, 192; solution to problems of, 53-54; PPS on, 160-61, 179-80. *See also* Braceros, Land reform, Unbalanced development

Alemán, Miguel, land policies of, 50; labor policies of, 62-63, 141, 143; corrupt regime of, 74; Lombardo supports for presidency, 141; abandons revolution, 159; mentioned, 192

Alianza de Obreros y Campesinos de México (AOCM), 142-43

Alliance for Progress, 42

Almazán, Juán Andreu, 138

American Federation of Labor, and Pan American Federation of Labor, 23; and ORIT, 83, 150, 153

American Smelting and Refining Co., 73

Amilpa, Fernando, 142

Anguiano, Victoriano, 156, 159

Army, 134, 135, 137

Asociación de Trabajadores Latinoamericanos (ATLAS), 150

Asociación Pro-Cultura Nacional, 132

Ateneo de la Juventud. *See* Generation of 1910

Atlantic Charter, 115, 140

Avante, 147-48, 153

Ávila Camacho, Manuel, attends school with Lombardo, 4; criticized, 50, 73, 74; presidency of, 138-39; mentioned, 113, 141, 156. *See also* Confederación de Trabajadores de México

Barreda, Gabino, 6

Bassols, Narciso, 156, 159, 163

Bergson, Henri, thought of, 6; influences Lombardo, 8

Bloque de Unidad Obrera (BUO), 63, 143

Bloque Nacional de Defensa Proletaria, 141-42

Bolsheviks, 191

Bourgeoisie in power, definition of, 59-60; and national front, 65, 72-73, 84, 87; corruption of, 74; strengthened, 141; and labor, 153; criticized, 168. *See also* Partido Revolucionario Institucional

Braceros, 51, 184

Browder, Earl, 121

Bulnes, Francisco, 5

Cabrera, Luís, 11

Calles, Plutarco Elías, and revolutionary reform, 26; conflict with Cárdenas, 37, 118-19, 137; evaluated, 73; and Six-Year Plan, 136, 137; mentioned, 15

Cámara Nacional de la Industria de Transformación, 141, 156

Campa, Valentín, 143

Capital and capitalism, young Lombardo defends, 9-11; internal contradictions of, 29-30, 43, 93-94, 97, 116, 118; and Mexican Revolution, 84; anachronistic, 85-86; crisis of, 89; CTM criticizes, 119-20; and Cárdenas era, 133-34, 135; consolidates position, 139, 141, 153. *See also* Imperialism, Fascism, State capitalism

Cárdenas, Lázaro, distributes lands, 26, 48, 122-23; and conflict with Calles, 37, 118-19, 137; CTM supports, 62; Lombardo praises regime of, 73-74; presidency of, 118-38; and Monterrey strikes, 123; and petroleum strike, 125-28, 136, 137-38; social philosophy of, 134-35; and Lombardo, 135-38; and Universidad Obrera, 148; and 1952 elections, 165; mentioned, 146, 152, 153. *See also* Nationalization, Partido de la Revolución Mexicana

Carranza, Venustiano, 73

Carrillo, Alejandro, 141, 159

Casas, Bartolomé de las, 36

Caso, Antonio, and Generation of 1910, 4; thought of, 7; influences Lombardo, 7-8, 13, 33; debates with Lombardo, 31-33

Castro, Fidel, 44, 86

Catholic church, and Obregón-Calles reforms, 25; and education, 67-71, 78-79, 183, 185; and primitive Christianity, 77-78; and politics, 78-79;

and the Revolution, 78-80; and freedom of conscience, 79-80; and socialism, 90; opposes Lombardo, 134; and Cárdenas regime, 134; and *sinarquistas*, 141
Cattle industry, 51
Caudillismo, criticized, 75-76, 186; defined, 192-93
Cedillo, Saturnino, 125
China, People's Republic of, Mexico lacks relations with, 98; development of, 103-4; disputes with U.S.S.R., 104-5; mentioned, 148
Científicos, 5
Civil Pensions Administration, 183
Clay, Henry, 95
Comintern, 39
Communist party of the Soviet Union, Lombardo accepts concepts of, 29, 40, 42, 93, 100-1, 191-92; Lombardo denies is agent of, 39-40; and many roads to socialism thesis, 87, 169
Compañía Mexicana de Luz y Fuerza Motriz, S.A., 123-24
Confederación de Centros Patronales de la República Mexicana, 133-34
Confederación de Trabajadores de América Latina (CTAL), and labor unity, 62; and World War II, 111, 113, 139-40; CTM calls for formation of, 129-30; principles of, 130-31; organization of, 131; and Universidad Obrera, 132; CTM withdraws from, 142; AOCM affiliates with, 142; UGOCM joins, 143; participates in organizing WFTU, 149; division and decline of, 150-51, 152, 153; mentioned, 103. *See also* Conferencia Sindical Latino Americana
Confederación de Trabajadores de México (CTM), and PCM, 37-38, on freedom of conscience, 79-80; and invasion of U.S.S.R., 111; organization and statutes of, 119-20; membership, 120; goals, 121; organizing and strikes, 121-28; supports popular front, 128, 155; plan for economic development of, 129; opposition to, 133-34; relations with Cárdenas, 135; and Ávila Camacho, 138-39; Lombardo resigns as secretary general of, 139; Velázquez and moderates control, 139; signs pact, 141, 156; division within, 141-42; expels Lombardo, 142, 153, 159; organizes BUO, 143; and ORIT, 150. *See also* Confederación de Trabajadores de America Latina; Spanish Civil War; Trotsky, Leon
Confederación General de Obreros y Campesinos de México (CGOCM), Lombardo organizes, 27; objectives, 117; organizing and strikes, 117-18, 121; and Cárdenas-Calles conflict, 118-19; merges with CTM, 119; calls for Latin-American labor organization, 129; supports Marxist education of workers, 132; role of, 136-37
Confederación Interamericana de Trabajadores (CIT), 150
Confederación Regional Obrera Mexicana (CROM), founded, 12; Lombardo member central committee of, 15, 25; corruption within, 15; and gains for labor, 15-16; Lombardo's role within, 16; role of in educating workers, 19; principles and tactics of, 20-21; dissension and division within, 26-27; Lombardo resigns from, 26-28; aloof from CTM, 120. *See also* Partido Laborista Mexicano
Confederación Revolucionaria de Obreros y Campesinos (CROC), 143
Confederación Único de Trabajadores de Chile, 151
Confederación Unitaria de Trabajadores (CUT), 142
Conferencia Sindical Latino Americana, 151-52, 153-54
Constitution of 1917, Lombardo's original concept of, 9, 12; Art. 3 of, 9, 37, 67-68, 70, 183, 185; Art. 27 of, 9, 12, 48, 49, 53, 183; Art. 123 of, 9, 12, 136, 180; precepts of abandoned, 26; precepts of must be realized, 53; major achievement of the Revolution, 81; PNR amends, 132; and Six-Year Plan, 136; PPS upholds, 160; PPS on reform of, 181; and state capitalism, 183
Credit system, inadequate for agriculture, 51; positive and negative aspects of, 54-55, 56, 183, 185; PPS on reforms in, 180
C.T.A.L. News, 131

Index

Cuban Revolution, example for Latin America, 43-44, 86, 105; and the United States, 105; PPS defends, 176-77; mentioned, 148, 175

Democracy, in *ejidos*, 52-53, 74-75, 76, 82, 122, 184; in labor unions, 61-64, 74, 76, 82, 143-44, 153; in politics, 73-77, 82, 85, 186; bourgeois variety of, 75, 85, 95; PPS on, 76-77, 158, 160, 162, 163, 165, 168, 171, 181; in U.S.S.R., 99-100; mentioned, 85, 110, 126, 171, 190. *See also* Democratic centralism; Mexican Revolution, goals of; Popular Democracy
Democratic centralism, PPS adopts, 169, 171-72, 186
Devaluation of peso, consequences of, 46, 56, 184; PPS criticizes, 163
Dialectical materialism, seeds of in Lombardo's thought, 13-14; and Lombardo's career, 28; basic concepts of, 30-31; contrasted with idealism, 31-33, 40-41; and modern irrational philosophies, 33-35; Universidad Obrera utilizes as guide, 132, 193; church criticizes, 134; PPS accepts as guide, 170; mentioned, 7. *See also* Marxism
Díaz, Porfirio, 4, 5, 44, 52, 73
Díaz Muñoz, Vidal, 159, 166
Dilthey, Wilhelm, 34
Dorantes, Rodolfo, 159, 166, 167

Education, and ethics, 13; report to CROM on, 17-19; and workers, 18-19, 131-32; socialist orientation of, 37, 132; and Indians, 66; criticisms of Mexico's system of, 67-71, 183, 185-86; solution to problems of, 71-72. *See also* Universidad Obrera
Ejidos, character of, 48; lands distributed to, 48; insufficient lands of, 49-50; undermined, 50, 52; organized as collectives, 122-23, 136, 146, 153. *See also* Democracy
Elections, 1940, 138; 1946, 141; 1949, 163; 1952, 164-66, 195; 1955, 173; 1958, 173; 1961, 173-74; 1964, 174n
Electric energy industry, nationalized, 47, 144, 179n; PPS urges nationalization of, 160, 179

Elizondo, Juan Manuel, 159
Encinas, Dionisio, 156, 164
Engels, Frederick, 3, 191
Excelsior, 133
Existentialism, 34-35

Fascism, origins of in Germany, 106, 108; rebirth of in West Germany, 106-7; rise of in 1930's, 108-9; and Calles, 119; Lombardo on, 139-40, 157; mentioned, 100, 102. *See also* Union of Soviet Socialist Republics, World War II
Federación de Partidos del Pueblo, 164, 165
Federación de Sindicatos de Trabajadores al Servicio del Estado (FSTSE), 151
Federación de Sindicatos Obreros del Distrito Federal, 131
Federal Bureau of Investigation (FBI), 83, 98
First American Labor Conference, 129
Foreign investments, PPS on regulation of, 47, 160, 180. *See also* Imperialism
Fuentes Díaz, Vicente, 160, 166, 167
Futuro, 108, 111, 131, 153

Gabino Barreda University, 132
Garibaldi, Giuseppe, 13
General Confederation of Workers (CGT), Lombardo criticizes, 21; aloof from CTM, 120
Generation of 1910, influences university, 4, 6; rejects positivism, 4-6; influenced by "spiritualism" and humanism, 6; praised by Lombardo, 33
Gómez Z., Luís, 142, 143
González Luna, Efrain, 165
González Peña, Ramón, 130
Good Neighbor Policy, 95
Greene, Jr., William C., 146
Grupo Acción, nature of, 15; attitude toward Lombardo, 16; and book by Lombardo, 21
Gutiérrez Zamora, Veracruz, 3

Havana Charter, 42
Heidegger, Martin, 34
Henríquez Guzmán, Miguel, 164, 165
Hidalgo, Miguel, 79

Historical materialism, Lombardo criticizes, 10, 13; Lombardo increasingly accepts, 13-14, 22; Lombardo defines, 29, 30; and anti-rational philosophies, 35; Universidad Obrera utilizes as guide, 132, 193. *See also* Marxism
Hitler, Adolph, 102, 106, 108, 109, 112, 113
Hoy, 133
Humanism, influences young Lombardo, 7, 11, 24, 26; Marxist interpretation of contrasted with anti-rational philosophies, 35; and early Christianity, 78; and socialism, 88-92, 104, 182, 187; and art, 107-8. *See also* Generation of 1910
Hungarian Revolution, 102-3, 191

Idealism, and positivism, 4-6; influences Lombardo, 8-11, 13, 18; contrasted with dialectical materialism, 31-33, 40-41. *See also* Caso, Antonio; Dialectical materialism; Idealism, non-philosophic
Idealism, non-philosophic, Lombardo's youthful expressions of, 7-8, 26, 33; Lombardo's mature expressions of, 88-90
Imperialism, Lombardo's youthful tolerance of, 9; Lombardo's youthful criticisms of, 22-23, 24; and Latin America, 22, 43-44, 94-97; internal contradictions of, 30, 43, 93; major obstacles to Mexico's independence and development, 36, 45-48, 83, 96-98, 107-8, 158, 183-84, 188, 189; distinctive feature of, 42; history of in Mexico, 44-45; hinders industrialization, 44, 45-46, 56, 83, 184; agents of in Mexico, 60, 83-84; hostility of Mexicans toward, 60; attacks revolutionary unity workers, 62-63; and PAN, 72, 73, 84; and ORIT, 83; opposes socialism, 93-95; threatens peace, 93-94. *See also* Confederación de Trabajadores de México, Cuban Revolution, Fascism, National Anti-Imperialist Front, United States
Income, Lombardo on unequal distribution of, 46, 55-56, 82-83, 85, 182, 184, 185; PPS calls for equitable distribution of, 171; and Mexico's development, 188, 189
Indian communities, protection of, 65-66
Industry and industrialization, prerequisite for true independence, 54; positive and negative aspects of, 55-56, 82-83, 182-85; obstacles to, 57-58, 85-86, 188; solution to problems of, 58; Lombardo encourages, 156, 158, 161, 171. *See also* Imperialism, Unbalanced development, *and* individual industries
Inés de la Cruz, Sor Juana, 36
Instituto Politécnico Nacional, 67, 70, 183
Intellectuals, Lombardo on instability of, 60-61
International Confederation of Free Trade Unions, 149, 150, 153
International Congress Against War and Fascism, 129
International Federation of Trade Unions, 129
Internationalism, Lombardo's youthful conception of, 23, 24, 27; and proletariat, 40, 117, 120, 121, 129; and PPS, 40, 160, 170-71. *See also* Confederación de Trabajadores de América Latina, World Federation of Trade Unions
International Labor Office, requests book by Lombardo, 19; Lombardo attacks fascism at reunions of, 109; Lombardo resigns from governing board of, 150
Irrationalism, in philosophy, 33-35
Iturbide, Agustín, 73
Iturriaga, José, 156

Jaspers, Karl, 34
Jouhaux, Leon, 130
Juárez, Benito, 3, 36, 69, 73, 79, 95, Justice, corruption of, 75, 82, 186
Juventud Popular Socialista, 174

Kant, Immanuel, 33
Kennedy, John F., 176
Kierkegaard, Soren, 34

Labor movement, influences young Lombardo, 3, 11-12, 25; Lombardo's youthful concepts of, 19-20, 22-23,

Index

24; Lombardo on unity and independence of, 23, 24, 27-28, 61, 64, 84, 86, 94, 117, 119, 121, 130, 146-47, 151, 153-54, 155, 160, 171, 175, 185; goals and tactics of, 61-64, 94, 140; role of in Cárdenas regime, 135-38; division and decline of, 143-44, 153, 185; revived militancy of, 144, 151, 153-54, 175. *See also* National Anti-Imperialist Front *and* individual unions

La Laguna, shortage of lands in, 49; CTM strike in, 122; land distributed, 122-23

Land Reform, Lombardo's early participation in, 12; in Obregón-Calles epoch, 25-26; history of, 48-49; benefits of, 49, 81-82, 182; negative aspects of, 49-53, 82, 184-85; and Rodríguez regime, 136; PPS foments, 160, 179, 193, 197; undermines power of landlords, 190. *See also Ejidos*, La Laguna, Latifundism, Unión General de Obreros y Campesinos de México

Latifundism, new form of, 50, 82, 184; obstacle to development, 188. *See also* Land Reform, Unión General de Obreros y Campesinos de México

Latin American Conference for Economic Emancipation, National Sovereignty and Peace, 178

Law, new currents within, 8-11; social origins of, 14-15

League of Professors of the Federal District, Lombardo organizes, 25

Lenin, Vladimir Ilich, Lombardo studies ideas of, 3; translation work of unintelligible, 8; Lombardo accepts concepts of, 29; and revolutionary spirit, 89; conceived as great man, 101; and war, 116. *See also* Marxism

Lewis, John L., 126, 130

Liberalism, Lombardo supports, 9-11; Lombardo rejects, 13, 14, 24; and Constitution of 1917, 183

Liga de Acción Política, 156

Liga Socialista Mexicana, 156

Lincoln, Abraham, 95

López, Jacinto, 145, 159

López Mateos, Adolfo, nationalizes electric energy industry, 47, 144; promotes land reform, 50, 144, 146, 153, 175; labor policies of, 63-64, 144, 175; presidency of, 144-45, 175; PPS supports candidacy of, 173; and Cuban Revolution, 176-77

Manifest Destiny, 96

Mao Tse-tung, 101

Marshall Plan, 42, 149

Marx, Karl, Lombardo studies works of, 3, 21; Lombardo criticizes, 10; Lombardo partially accepts concepts of, 23; and CROM constitution, 27; Lombardo accepts concepts of, 21, 27, 29; meeting in honor of, 38; and Lombardo's interpretation of U.S.S.R., 191. *See also* Marxism

Marxism, and Lombardo's early environment, 3; Lombardo criticizes, 9-11; Lombardo's changing attitude toward, 13-14, 16, 17, 20, 23, 24-25, 27-28, 182; Lombardo accepts principles of, 21, 27, 29; Lombardo's mature concepts of, 29-31, 182; and religion, 80; and transition to socialism, 87; and labor unity, 117, 154; attacks upon, 133; and objectives of proletariat, 156-58; and original principles and program of PPS, 159, 161; and disputes within PPS, 166-67; PPS accepts as guide, 167, 168-69, 170, 172, 186; and tactics of PPS, 188-98. *See also* Dialectical materialism, Historical materialism, Partido Popular Socialista, Universidad Obrera

Mata, Filomena, 144

Maximilian, Archduke, 73

Mendoza López, Miguel, 173

Mexican Labor News, 131

Mexican Revolution, young Lombardo on salient characteristic of, 21; Marxism answer to problems of, 26; goals of, 26, 53, 81, 84, 155, 157, 158, 159-60, 182, 187; positive aspects of, 35, 81-82, 182-83; and the church, 78-80; bourgeois character of, 81, 182; negative aspects of, 82-84, 183-86; opposed to fascism, 108; López Mateos promotes, 175; mentioned, 48, 89, 93, 168

Mexican Social Security Institute, 139, 183

Mexican Telephone and Telegraph (AT&T), 118

Mexican Tramways Co., Ltd., 118
Mexican War, 95
Mining industry, 57, 183, 184
Monroe Doctrine, Lombardo criticizes, 22, 95
Morelos, José María, 73, 79
Morones, Luís, heads CROM, 15; secretary of industry, 15; disputes with Lombardo, 26-27
Movimiento de Liberación Nacional (MLN), formed, 178; PPS criticizes, 178-79; appraised, 187, 197
El Movimiento Sindical Mundial, 150
Muncipal freedom, lack of, 76-77

National Anti-Imperialist Front, and Mexico's social classes, 59-60; labor unity prerequisite to formation of, 64, 84, 86, 117, 189; formation of principal strategy of PPS, 72-73, 84, 157-58, 169, 171, 177, 187; prerequisite to transition to socialism, 84-85, 86, 117, 137, 168, 189; PPS tactics for formation of evaluated, 188-98; and Viet Nam, 189; and PCM tactics, 194, 196, 197. *See also* Popular (People's) Democracy
National Committee of Proletarian Defense, and PCM, 37; organized, 118; pact of, 118-19; mentioned, 35
National Federation of Teachers, Lombardo secretary general of, 25
National Peasant Confederation, 126, 128, 135
National Preparatory School, Lombardo attends, 4; and positivism, 5; re-organized, 6; Lombardo teaches in, 12, 17; Lombardo director of, 16; Lombardo criticizes, 31, 69-70
National University of Mexico, Lombardo graduates from, 12; positions held by Lombardo within, 16-17; Lombardo expelled from, 26, 132. *See also* Generation of 1910
Nationalism, young Lombardo's expressions of, 7, 12-13, 19, 21, 24; Marxist conception of, 35-36
Nationalization, of electric energy industry, 47, 144, 179n; solution to problems of Mexican economy, 47, 58, 170, 171, 179-80; López Mateos promotes, 47, 144-45, 175; in Mexican economy, 58, 183, 188; of railroads, 124, 136; of petroleum industry, 125-28, 136, 137-38; PPS proposals for, 160, 170, 171, 179-80; and 1952 elections, 165; and socialism, 190
Nietzsche, Frederich, 34
North Atlantic Treaty Organization (NATO), 42, 116

Obregón, Álvaro, 17
Organización Interamericana de Trabajadores (ORIT), tool of imperialism, 83; organized, 150, 153
Ortíz Rubio, Pascual, 118

Pacto Obrero Industrial, 140-41, 156
Padilla, Ezequiel, 141
Panama Congress, 96
Pan American Federation of Labor, 23
Partido Acción Nacional (PAN), characteristics of, 72; ally of imperialism, 72, 73, 84; and church, 72, 79; contrasted with PPS, 73; opposes Mexican Revolution, 158; and PRI, 193, 195; mentioned, 148, 163. *See also* Elections
Partido Communista Mexicano, Lombardo criticizes, 21, 36-39, 61, 178; and Trotskyites, 39, 178; major source contention of with Lombardo, 65; represents workers, 72, 157; and electoral law, 76; and CTM, 121, 142; and petroleum strike, 126; and popular front, 128; Lombardo never member of, 129; and Liga Socialista Mexicana, 156; and formation of PPS, 157; and unification with PPS, 177-78, 186-87; appraised, 194, 197; membership of, 197. *See also* Elections
Partido de la Revolución Mexicana (PRM), CTM supports formation of, 62; Lombardo addresses congress of, 110; Cárdenas organizes, 128, 155; structure of, 128; Cárdenas' conception of, 135; and 1940 elections, 138; government dominated, 155-56, 163; mentioned, 157
Partido Laborista Mexicano (PLM), political arm of CROM, 15; Lombardo governor of Puebla, alderman, and deputy as member of, 17; Lombardo proposes dissolution of, 26

Index

Partido Nacional Democrático Independiente, 156
Partido Nacional Revolucionario (PNR), and Six-Year Plan, 136, 137; mentioned, 128, 132, 155, 163
Partido Obrero Campesino, Marxist character of, 38; unifies with PPS, 177-78, 187, 196, 197
Partido Popular Socialista (PPS), and CPSU, 39-40; attitude toward government of, 60, 158, 171, 189-91, 192-98; and dictatorship of proletariat, 61; contrasted with PRI and PAN, 73, 162-63, 195; calls for political reforms, 76-77; on Catholic church, 79; on peaceful transition to socialism, 87-88; government opposes formation of, 142, 159; and UGOCM, 145-46; and SNTE, 146-47; and *Avante*, 147-48; political education of members of, 148, 170, 172, 174, 193; Lombardo anticipates formation of, 155; formed, 156-59, 162-63, 186; principles and programs of, 160-61, 170-71, 179-81; structure of, 161-62, 169, 170, 171-72; internal disputes of, 163-64, 166-68; changes name, 170, 186; selection of candidates of, 162, 172-73; membership of, 174, 186, 197; evaluation of strategy and tactics of, 188-98; mentioned, 38, 42, 151. *See also* Elections, Foreign investments, National Anti-Imperialist Front, Popular (People's) Democracy
Partido Revolucionario Institucional (PRI), forces workers to participate in, 63; function of, 72-73; electoral practices of, 75-76, 186; and Universidad Obrera, 148; deficiencies of, 157; attitude of PPS toward, 158, 189-91, 192-98; opposes formation of PPS, 159; dominated by government, 163; motives for reforms by, 190; factions within, 190-91, 193. *See also* Elections, Partido Popular Socialista
Peace, imperialism threatens, 93-94, 116; Soviet Union defends, 100, 115-16; possibilities for, 101, 116; struggle for, 121, 157
Perón, Juan, 150
Petroleum industry, under foreign control, 44-45; under national ownership, 57; nationalization of, 125-28, 136, 137-38
Philosophy of life, 34-35
Platt Amendment, 95-96
El Popular, 131, 141, 147, 153
Popular (People's) Democracy, formation of, 64, 86-88, 94, 169; basis for constructing socialism, 64-65, 84-85, 186, 187; definitions of, 77, 86, 168, 187; in eastern Europe, 102-3; PPS sets as goal, 167, 168, 170, 171, 186; mentioned, 161
Population, growth of, 67, 82, 183
Positivism, content of, 4-5; and Díaz regime, 5; influences Lombardo, 6, 14. *See also* Generation of 1910
Pragmatism, 35
Purified CROM, Lombardo organizes, 27; accepts Marxism as guide, 131; mentioned, 38

Ramírez y Ramírez, Enrique, Lombardo criticizes, 61; founding member of PPS, 159; disputes with Lombardo, 166, 167, 168
Rivera, Diego, 159, 163
Rodríguez, Abelardo, 136
Roosevelt, Franklin D., 95
Rosenberg, Alfred, 34
Royal Dutch Shell Co., 125
Rubio Felix, Lázaro, 145, 159
Ruíz Cortines, Adolfo, land policies of, 50; distributes lands, 146; and 1952 elections, 165, 195

Salgado Medrano, Joaquín, 145, 174n
Scheler, Max, 34
Schopenhauer, Arthur, 33
Second International, 24, 182
Sicily, 107
Siempre!, 147, 153
Siguenza y Góngora, Carlos de, 36
Simmel, Georg, 34
Sindicato de Trabajadores Ferrocarrileros, 1959 strike of, 38, 63-64, 144, 175; withdraws from CTM, 142; joins AOCM, 142; military intervenes in, 143, 144, 175
Sindicato Nacional de Trabajadores de la Educación (SNTE), tactics of criticized, 38, 63-64, 144, 175-76; reunified, 147, 153; attends international conference, 151

Siquieros David Alfaro 144
Sixth Inter-American Conference, Lombardo delegate to, 24
Six-Year Plan, 136, 137
Social classes, definition of, 59; in Mexico, 59-60. *See also* National Anti-Imperialist Front
Social dissolution, law of, 62, 143, 144
Socialism, Lombardo's faith in advent of, 88; as means to human fulfillment, 88-92, 104, 182, 187; construction of, 102-3, 104, 169, 187; provides bases for peace, 116; CTM proclaims as goal, 119-20; PPS proclaims as goal, 167, 168, 170, 171; need for in Mexico, 188-89. *See also* Marxism, Popular (People's) Democracy
Southeast Asia Treaty Organization (SEATO), 116
South Viet Nam, 189
Spanish Civil War, 129
Spengler, Oswald, 34
Stalin, Joseph, 100-1
Standard Fruit Co., 124
Standard Oil Co., 118, 125. *See also* Petroleum industry
State capitalism, progressive character of, 58, 182, 183, 188-89, 190; and PPS programs, 161, 170
Sugar industry, 51-52

Teziutlán, Puebla, 3, 4
Transportation and communications, 54
Trotsky, Leon, 128-29
Truman Plan, 42

Unbalanced development, problem of defined, 46, 53, 188; solution to, 47, 58; state counteracts, 188-89; mentioned, 82, 141, 161, 185
Unión General de Obreros y Campesinos de México (UGOCM), organized, 143; composition of, 145; and land reform, 145-46, 153, 192; mentioned, 151, 185, 193, 196
Unión Nacional Sinarquista, function of, 72; and 1946 elections, 141; and Mexican Revolution, 158
Union of Soviet Socialist Republics, appraisal of, 98-100, 191; example for Mexico, 100; and eastern Europe, 101-3; and non-aggression pact, 109-10, 140; mentioned, 68, 89, 148, 156. *See also* Communist party of the Soviet Union, World War II, Fascism, Peace
United States, imperialism of criticized, 22-23, 42-58, 83-84, 93-98, 113-15, 158, 169, 181, 183-84, 188-89; democracy of, 75, 95; and Latin America, 95-96, 114-15; and education, 68-69, 71, 185-86. *See also* Imperialism, Cuban Revolution
El Universal, employs Lombardo, 4; mentioned, 127
Universidad Obrera, defends Mexico's cultural heritage, 36; financial resources of, 40; function and organization of, 132; expansion of, 148; curriculum of, 148-49; mentioned, 28, 154, 157, 193
Universidad Obrera, 131
Universidad Popular, Lombardo speaks before, 8; founded, 11; Lombardo secretary of, 11-12

Vallejo, Demetrio, 144
Vasconcelos, José, 5, 11, 19n
Vejár Vásquez, Octavio, 156
Velázquez, Fidel, 138, 139, 142, 150
Vidriera de Monterrey, S.A., 123
Villaseñor, Victor Manuel, 61, 99, 156, 163

Warsaw Peace Conference, 89-90
Wilson, Woodrow, 9
Women, rights of, 65
World Federation of Trade Unions, CTM withdraws from, 142; AOCM affiliates with, 142; UGOCM joins, 143; SNTE affiliated with, 147; organization and history of, 149-50; rejects Lombardo's resignation, 151; mentioned, 103, 158
World War II, Lombardo on unity of Christians and socialists during, 78; interpretations of, 109-13, 140; allied unity during, 113-15, 140; mentioned, 62, 74, 102

Yocupicio, Ramón, 134
Youth, problems of, 66-67, 186
Yugoslavia, 102

Zapata, Emiliano, 36, 73

www.ingramcontent.com/pod-product-compliance
Lightning Source LLC
Chambersburg PA
CBHW021403290426
44108CB00010B/360